The publisher gratefully acknowledges the
generous contribution to this book provided by
the Barbro Osher Pro Suecia Foundation.

On Holiday

1. *Changing Fortunes: Biodiversity and Peasant Livelihood in the Peruvian Andes,* by Karl S. Zimmerer

2. *Making the Invisible Visible: A Multicultural Planning History,* edited by Leonie Sandercock

3. *Imperial San Francisco: Urban Power, Earthly Ruin,* by Gray Brechin

4. *Imposing Wilderness: Struggles over Livelihood and Nature Preservation in Africa,* by Roderick P. Neumann

5. *Displeasing Prospects: Gender Development and Environmental Intervention,* by Richard A. Schroeder

6. *On Holiday: A History of Vacationing,* by Orvar Löfgren

On Holiday

A History of Vacationing

ORVAR LÖFGREN

UNIVERSITY OF CALIFORNIA PRESS
Berkeley   Los Angeles   London

University of California Press
Berkeley and Los Angeles, California

University of California Press, Ltd.
London, England

© 1999 by the Regents of the University of California

Library of Congress Cataloging-in-Publication Data

Löfgren, Orvar.
 On holiday : a history of vacationing / Orvar Löfgren.
    p.   cm. — (California studies in critical human geography ; 6)
 Includes bibliographical references.
 ISBN 0-520-21767-5 (alk. paper)
   1. Travel.   2. Holidays.   I. Title.   II. Series.
 G156.L56   1999
 910.4—dc21   99-31304

Manufactured in the United States of America

10 9 8 7 6 5 4 3 2 1

For Anne-Marie

Contents

Illustrations

Acknowledgments

This book has been many years in the making. A number of friends and colleagues on both sides of the Atlantic have read and commented on different versions or parts of the text: in Sweden, Billy Ehn, Jonas Frykman, Ulf Hannerz, Anders Linde-Laursen, Tom O'Dell, Katarina Saltzman, and Birgitta Svensson; and in America, James Clifford, Shelly Errington, John Gillis, Richard Wilk, and Allan Pred (who also got this book project started). Thanks to all of you! A thanks also to Alan Crozier who tidied up my English, Lindsay Kefauver and Eva Swahn who helped me with the illustrations.

Most of the writing took up my two periods as visiting researcher at University of California, Santa Cruz, where I enjoyed the atmosphere of a fantastic campus and the warm hospitality of the Anthropology Department. A special thanks also to Cowell College who let me have the best rental in town: the provost's house, overlooking the Monterey Bay and placed between the university pool and the library—the perfect location for writing a book on vacations.

My research has been part of the interdisciplinary project "National and transnational cultural processes" financed by the Swedish Research Council for the Humanities and the Social Sciences.

Introduction

In the winter, summer becomes inescapably visible. Walking through a vacationland in January feels rather like an archaeological expedition through the remains of an alien culture. I am the only inhabitant of this wintry landscape out at the coast, moving freely between the abandoned houses, crossing lawns, and glancing through windows.

The barren bushes and threadbare winter grass mercilessly expose frost-bitten leftovers from summer: lost toys, tennis balls, a Martini bottle cap, faded confetti from end-of-season parties. Looking through veranda windows, I can see the artifacts from a life of leisure, now in patient hibernation: barbecue grills, croquet mallets, sandals, and straw hats. Along the bathroom windowsill are faded plastic containers with

1

all kinds of strange ointments, sun blockers, insect repellants, *après-soleil* lotions. In the bleak winter light this abandoned vacation culture seems very exotic. A strange tribe of ultrahedonists has been living here, leaving only traces of a life for pleasure.

I am on the west coast of Sweden but could just as well be exploring the ghost towns of vacationlands on the other side of the Atlantic, in Maine or North Carolina. These are silent landscapes stripped of their inhabitants. Many in the local population have been priced out, some make a living as caretakers and service personnel for the short but intensive season and the long stretch of the off-season. This forlornness makes the materiality of holiday life stand out very clearly: all the props and stuff silently waiting for their fun-loving owners to return.

In other ways, however, this landscape is not abandoned at all but densely populated by daydreams, images, and fantasies—mindscapes of staggering proportions. Back home in the cities people are busy remembering past summers, scheming, and dreaming about upcoming ones. The travel sections of the daily papers burst with fantasies about your next vacation, promising everything from a magical vacation package, invitations to the "fine art of overindulgence," "truly genuine experiences," perfect adventures, holidays you'll never forget, getaways, and escape routes.

Simultaneously moving in a physical terrain and in fantasylands or mediaworlds, we create vacationscapes. Personal memories mix with collective images. The view down at the beach, the little cottage by the meadow, the sunset over the cliffs, these are sceneries constantly framed, packaged, and promoted, shaped by at least two centuries of tourist history. Ruins and relics from earlier periods of vacationing are strikingly evident, even in the town where I am writing these words. Santa Cruz reads like an archaeology of California vacationing. In 1866 people gathered down at the shore to watch that new breed called tourists disembark from the steamer from San Francisco. They were visitors to what was now called the Naples of the Pacific coast. Other attempts to market this growing seaside resort likened it to the isles of Greece, where "Sappho loved and sang." A swimming tank had been built close to the beach and for a couple of dollars tourists could also get swimming lessons in the surf or in the river that empties into the bay.

The railways over the mountains and along the coast provided the necessary step for further development. In 1888 a traveler described the ride over the mountains as "an airline through the woods to the ocean." People from San Francisco and the inland started to build seaside cottages for summer vacations. Already in the 1870s there was a "most English-looking cluster of cottages" on the beach of nearby Capitola. Today most summer cottages have been engulfed by the urban sprawl. Tourists were attracted not only by the beach but by the redwood forests, advertised as "the Switzerland of America" (great camping!). Around the turn of the century there were a hundred thousand visitors in town each summer.

Down at the beach stands the boardwalk, the last one left along the coast, opened in 1907, with both a casino and "the Most Brilliant Natatorial Exhibition to be Found on this Continent." This giant indoor swimming pool had a sun-room balcony with potted palms and hundreds of dressing rooms and plaster statues of gods, goddesses, and water babies of the sea. Today the casino houses a deafening array of arcade games and laser shoot-outs, the old natatorium has been converted into a minigolf course. Just across the road the vast parking lot marks the location of the once so fashionable seaside hotel, Casa del Rey, built in Spanish style and opened in 1911 with two hundred beach cottages attached to it. Then the new slogan was Visit the Riviera of America. The Casa was turned into a retirement home in the 1950s and was torn down after the earthquake in 1989. Today the beach cottages are the city's problem area, which tourists are told to avoid.

Parallel with the boardwalk run the old railway tracks, which back in 1931 saw the first Suntan Special arrive from San Francisco, signaling that California beaches had entered the new era of sun worship. At the site of the old Sea Beach Hotel lies the Dream Inn, built in 1963, a classic example of the modernist California resort hotel. At this stage California dreaming was an export commodity and the surfing pioneers, celebrated in the little surf museum close by, were becoming a world movement, with a little help from the Beach Boys.

The tourist history of Santa Cruz illustrates a constant linking of the local and the transnational, a steady in- and outflow, not only of tourists, but of marketing strategies, images, icons, fantasies, and tourist

Figure 1. Santa Cruz beach between the boardwalk and the sea in the 1920s. (Photo Special Collections Library, University of California, Santa Cruz)

technologies. But the town also reminds me of the ways in which tourists differ. Up at the old mall visitors stroll in search of galleries and bookstores, cappuccino or sushi, down at the boardwalk there are Buds and burgers. By the lighthouse the surfers hang out, while the hikers and mountain bikers roam the Santa Cruz mountains. Santa Cruz thus contains many vacationscapes, kept separate not so much by physical as by cultural space: the tastes and interests, the mindframes and selective visions of its visitors.

Vacationlands may appear like territories of freedom, freedom from work, worries, rules, and regulations. But behind this carefree facade there are many unwritten rules. The skills of vacationing have a long history, and into each new vacationscape we bring expectations and anticipations as well as stable routines and habits.

LEARNING TO BE A TOURIST

"What is a tourist?" asked the Swedish author Carl Jonas Love Almqvist in a series of newspaper articles from Paris back in 1840. In those days "tourist" was still a novel concept, imported from Britain and surrounded with a good deal of curiosity. What is a tourist, how do you become a tourist? A new mode of consumption was emerging, based on the idea of leaving home and work in search of new experiences, pleasures, and leisure.

A hundred and fifty years later tourism occupies a large and rapidly growing part of people's consumption in the northern hemisphere. We invest a lot of money, time, and emotional energy in vacationing but may find it hard to think of these activities as producing the world's largest industrial complex. What started as a quest to get away from it all, often as a form of anti-consumption, to breathe fresh air, relax, do nothing, gradually became institutionalized into sites of production, providing hotel beds, breathtaking sights, transport systems, snacks, and souvenirs. Maybe it is the lightweight airiness of a few days at a beach or a hike in the wilderness that makes us forget the massive infrastructures needed to provide such moments on a large scale. During the last few decades the growth rate has been staggering. In the mid 1990s around 7 percent of the total workforce, some 230 million persons, were employed in tourism, with over 600 million arrivals per year, and a spending of $3.4 trillion dollars. For a long time this growth was concentrated in the Western world and the northern hemisphere, but toward the end of the twentieth century new mass destinations and new groups of tourists emerged all over the globe. After the Americans and the Germans, the Japanese are the biggest spenders on the market, and in countries like India, the fast-growing middle class forms an expanding market of millions for international tourism. For the year 2020, tourist organizations predict that 1.6 billion of the world's 7.8 billion people will make a trip abroad.[1] The rapid growth rate produces not only new vacation packages but also new, albeit unevenly distributed, wealth, as well as new environmental and social problems.

Since the late eighteenth century the tourist industry has spearheaded new forms of production and consumption. It has developed the production sites of hedonism—a great weekend, an unforgettable event, a week of family fun, an exciting adventure—commodities carrying a heavy symbolic load.

The label "the tourist industry" bundles together very different kinds of actors: a Bombay bus owner taking locals on weekend excursions, a municipal licensed guide offering walks through Marrakech, a global resort chain always on the lookout for new beach-front property, a deck chair rental on Majorca, an international airline company, a Thai bar owner providing drinks and prostitution in Pattaya, a publisher specializing in guidebooks, Somalian peddlers trying to make a living on Italian beaches, a helicopter pilot selling sightseeing flights in Hawaii, investors moving capital from destination to destination, armies of migrant laborers doing anything from hotel laundry to washing dishes.

Research on tourism has become quite an industry, a densely populated field of interdisciplinary studies. It has also developed into a specialty, which has not always been a good thing. Specialized tourist researchers often feel a need to legitimate their seemingly frivolous topic by pointing out its economic and social importance, but surely tourism is too important a topic to confine within the boundaries of "tourism research." Over the years the most interesting work has come from scholars who explore this field in order to get a more general understanding of the workings of the modern world.[2]

This book looks at some of the ways in which vacationing has evolved as such an important part of modern life, exploring how tourists have pioneered new ways of seeing the landscape, of claiming space and taking place, searching for new experiences and understandings. I view vacationing as a cultural laboratory where people have been able to experiment with new aspects of their identities, their social relations, or their interaction with nature and also to use the important cultural skills of daydreaming and mindtraveling. Here is an arena in which fantasy has become an important social practice.[3]

Tourist dreams colonize all those other fifty weeks, when we are not on vacation. Since we construct vacations in terms of otherness, of getting away from it all, they make some facets of our everyday lives and tensions more visible. Vacations remain one of the few manageable utopias in our lives. As utopian ideas they attract a great deal of cultural energy but also frustrations and disappointments.

My book attempts an archaeology of the present. It explores two centuries in the making of modern tourist experiences and sensibilities. There are many ways of writing the history of tourism, and some of these narratives risk falling into evolutionary or devolutionary traps, like "from the Grand Tour to Europe on $5 a day," and their straight narratives may also crowd out or marginalize certain tourist experiences. I want to use the historical perspective as an analytical tool to problematize the present, comparing very different eras and arenas of vacationing. How have we acquired the skills of taking in a sight, having a picnic on the beach, or producing a holiday album? In learning to be tourists we haul along a lot of baggage from earlier periods, often in rather unreflective ways.

This is why it is often rewarding to look at some of the settings where new forms of tourism emerge: the first Riviera hotel to open for the summer season, the early honeymoon site of Niagara Falls, or the fresh experience of auto camping. In the formation of a new phenomenon, there is often an uncertainty, an openness that routine soon closes off, making the experience obvious and trivial. What is a resort? or great scenery? or an afternoon at the beach?

The tensions between past and present play an important role in the tourist industry, which is based on a strange mix of stubborn traditionalism and a constant search for novelties: new sights and new experiences. Much of the marketing of a vacation resort or the organization of a tour program depends on cultural forms already developed in the eighteenth and nineteenth centuries. The industry constantly reinvents itself, there is a strange kind of stable changeability or persistent fickleness in which new destinations, attractions, and holiday programs emerge and old ones grow stale. Novel concepts and trends like post-tourism, "event management," eco-tourism, or heritage industries may in a longer historical perspective turn out to be oscillations within a rather stable structure. Many views expressed in the discussions of postmodern tourism are strikingly ahistorical.

Another tension in the world of vacations is central to the book: it has to do with the relations between the local, the national, and the transnational. Tourism often appears to be the ultimate form of globalization, an industry so standardized that any resort weekend basically would look the same elsewhere, as long as there are some palm trees and a stretch of sandy beach available. Tourism has always been a transnational mode of production. Even in the attempts to develop or market tourism with a local profile of uniqueness, tourist boards and tour operators borrow freely across national borders as, for example, in the case of Santa Cruz. This mode makes the history of tourism a rewarding field for studying the long-term processes of the localization of the global. The tourist industry illustrates the ways in which cultural differentiation results from a standardized marketing of appetizing, exotic otherness.

It is important, however, to see that standardized marketing does not have to standardize tourists. Studies of the staging of tourist experiences in mass tourism often reduce or overlook the uniqueness of all personal travel experiences: two vacations will never be identical. Many discussions on mass tourism slip into the dangerous genre of the prefabricated experience, the packaging of the package tour, and join two centuries of tired stereotypes that set "the real traveler" against the *turistus vulgaris*.

For these two reasons this book travels widely in time and space, but I am not aiming at a global reach. I limit myself mainly to a comparison of the making of some European and North American vacation worlds, although as I will show in the later part of the book many of the ideals and routines produced in these settings are today truly global. In the tourist fashion, I will follow certain cultural phenomena as they are transplanted and developed in various spatial, temporal, and social settings, from the French Riviera to Yosemite. Most of my own research (like most of my tourist life) has been focused on Scandinavian and Mediterranean vacationing, which means that material from other places draws heavily on the rich literature of tourism.[4]

There is one more reason for this comparative approach. The frequent talk about Mr. and Ms. Tourist underplays the very different modes of becoming and being a tourist. Tourist research sometimes bundles together the highly varied experiences made by tourists into "the Tourist Experience." Far too often it gives vacationers the role of easy prey, unwitting objects of manipulation: herded into charter buses and transported from sight to sight. Or the research gives a rather one-dimensional version of tourist life: focusing on the making of "the tourist gaze." Tourists become all eyes, no bodies (and sometimes no brains).[5] My focus is on the broader scope of vacationing, with an emphasis on the everyday practices and routines of tourist life: spending a day at the beach, watching the sunset, hiking in the wilderness, or taking the family for a vacation by car.

The book has three parts. The first two explore a polarity, which the French sociologist Jean-Didier Urbain calls the tension between the Phileas Foggs and the Robinson Crusoes of the tourist world. Most tourist research focuses on the male and middle-class model of Phileas Fogg—the ardent and hurried traveler in search of new sights. There is, Urbain reminds us, another important tradition, whose literary model would rather be the Robinsonian desire "to get away from it all"—to find an unspoiled corner of the world, to relax and build up an alternative life.[6] Yet the lives of traveling Foggs and Robinsons illustrate another slant on the tourist experience. To explore the dimensions of class in narratives of tourism over the centuries, I follow the ways in which the talkative and often distinction-ridden middle classes have set the norms of vacationing, defining others as outsiders, marginalizing others' experiences.

The first section, "Landscapes and Mindscapes," deals with the microphysics of traveling and sightseeing, learning to enjoy a sight, setting body and mind in motion, producing vacation memories. It explores some basic aspects of tourist experiences, mainly in the Phileas Fogg tradition.

The second section, "Getaways," deals with the making of the Robinsonian quest of looking for elsewherelands, first in the development of "cottage cultures" of summering in Scandinavia and North America, and second by following the ways in which the Grand Tour to southern Europe developed into the mass tourism of package tours to the Mediterranean sun and beaches, which later would become the model for the global quest for a tourist paradise of eternal sunshine, palm trees, and white sands.

The third section, "Between the Local and the Global," treats some of the ways in which tourism is both standardized and constantly transformed in the transnational flows of ideas, props, and travelers. Its first two chapters look at the making of the global beach and the resort experience, while the last chapter starts by dealing with the most favorite pastimes of tourists—observing all those other tourists—and ends by discussing the ways in which tourism has shaped the modern world, from the eighteenth-century pioneers to the cruise ship's passengers at the end of the twentieth.

part 1

Landscapes and Mindscapes

Looking for Sights

PEAK EXPERIENCES

Must lie in the sun and feel the rays on my skin

Must lie under the shade of the palm tree

Must stretch the sail and set out before the wind dies

Must show the kids the flowers on the hillside

Must taste the liqueur flavored with camomile

Must dive deep

Must explore the world beneath my feet

Must make love

Must, before the day turns into evening

Must enjoy both life and tranquillity

This almost paralyzing list of imperatives for carefree enjoyment was the start of a winter 1997 campaign for a new chain of Mediterranean summer resorts called Blue Village. Who could resist it? As a top-ten list of tourist "musts" it pulls together the results of a long learning process on what vacationing is supposed to be about. It also sets the stage for a discussion of what constitutes the basics of tourist experiences. Behind the standard question, what did you experience on your vacation? lies the notion of tourists and vacationers in constant search of sights and attractions, impressions, events, or adventure.

Back from one trip or planning the next, you only have to leaf through the bulging advertisement section in the *New York Times* travel section to see how central this focus on experience is in the marketing world. Here tour operators and resorts promise to enrich our vacations, teach us to relax in all possible ways, with slogans like Priceless Memories Have Never Been More Affordable.[1] Nowadays tour operators train their staff in "expectation management," "experience monitoring," and "satisfaction evaluations" or, in operations like *Dream Vacations,* stand ready to help you "choose the vacation experience that matches your vacation expectations."[2] There is also a burgeoning market for self-help books like *Travel That Can Change Your Life: How to Create a Transformative Experience* in which you wade through hints for creating a richer travel experience or a good vacation mindset.[3] After plowing through such a text you're not sure if you ever want to travel again.

Do we live in an age obsessed by having great experiences? An age in which places like Freemont Street in Las Vegas are malled in and redesigned as "the Freemont Street Experience," following the popular trend of tourist architecture as event? Some observers are rather too quick to answer Yes. One of them is the German sociologist Gerhald Schulze, who launched the concept of an *Erlebnisgesellschaft*—a society obsessed by the need to have rich and numerous experiences. His argument is that since the 1980s we face a rapidly rising demand and commodification of the eventful. We continually ask one another: how was it, how did it feel?[4]

Schulze analyzes an expanding market, where experiences become commodities but also wear out, producing a constant demand for escalation toward a more eventful life. Along with many others observers of

Figure 2. Vacations as the prime time of family togetherness form one of the most common themes in travel advertisements. This ad comes from the 1996 Blue Village campaign. (Photo Scott Gog, Fritidsresor)

contemporary society he sees an aesthetization of everyday life and a focus on the staging of events. As in the advertisement for Blue Village, one strategy of intensification is to invoke all the senses.[5]

Much of Schulze's debate sounds strikingly familiar and sometimes falls into the old genre of a critique of civilization: "today we are living in a commoditized and shallower culture, but back in the old days . . . " It is akin to remarks describing people of today as "cultivating experience," in contrast to earlier generations who "simply had it."

Schulze makes some good points in showing us how experiences are framed and marketed, but I reject the notion that we now are living in an *Erlebnisgesellschaft*, fundamentally different from earlier periods. His analysis seems to me surprisingly ahistorical. If we study the making and remaking of tourist experiences during the last two centuries, a much more complex picture emerges. Tourism constitutes one of the most important sites in which individuals have explored and cultivated sensual experiences over the last few centuries. Here we find a constant debate and reflection on the nature of good or true experiences, a rich or elevating event, as well as a framing and ritualization of the eventful. The participants tirelessly describe, measure, compare, rank, or criticize the forms and contents, the colors, flavors, and feel of experiences.

In the following I explore some of the ways in which tourist experiences have been produced in different periods and cultural settings. Searching for a starting point I choose to present the reflections by two northbound travelers in eighteenth-century Sweden.

VIEWFINDERS

In early May of 1732 the twenty-five-year-old botanist Carl Linnaeus rides out from the university town of Uppsala on a journey to Lapland. Countless observations fill his travel journal right from the first day. He comments on the changing soil conditions, registers the vegetation in ditches and meadows. He describes song birds, the proportions of fir trees, and the behavior of young geese, and notes peculiar-looking rocks.[6] It is not a text without poetic dimensions, but it is a totally different prose from the one used by the twenty-nine-year-old Carl Jonas Linnerhielm in his account of a voyage through the same landscape half a century later. Linnerhielm is not out to collect minerals or flowers; he collects views and moods. His description of the landscape includes a constant ranking of aesthetic values. The first manor house he passes "is a mean and flat location," but the next is "beautifully situated, with an air of grandeur." Here Linnerhielm finds a rather perfect view, composed of rolling meadows with shady trees and a winding stream, all very suitably framed by sloping forests.[7]

Both travelers describe resting by a stream that first day of their journey. Linnaeus immediately starts pondering about the ways in which the current shapes the elevation of the sandbanks. Linnerhielm finds "a babbling brook . . . so clear that the finest grain of sand was visible" and starts to play: "By adding a few small stones I increased the slow speed of this stream, without diminishing its clarity, which gave my soul the most pleasurable images and rewarding afterthoughts."[8] Linnaeus and Linnerhielm are traveling through the same landscape, in 1732 and 1787. They both belong to the age of the collector, but their frames of reference are quite different. Linnerhielm puts it very directly in the foreword to his first volume of travel writings: "I travel to see, not to study." What constitutes this new kind of seeing?

His first voyage in 1787 and many subsequent ones resulted in three travel books, printed between 1797 and 1816 with his own illustrations. He has been called the first proper tourist in Sweden, a landed gentleman traveling for pleasure and nothing else. The two travelers not only represent the roles of the scientist versus the tourist, they understand the landscape very differently.

Linnerhielm is a member of what is still a rather exclusive European brotherhood that later became a mass movement. Many of his spiritual brethren are found in England. One of them is the clergyman James Plumptre from Cambridge, who starts out on a journey through the Lake District in the summer of 1799. He begins the story of his travels by listing what he calls his traveling "knick-knacks," which included drawing pads, notebooks, a small watercolor set, a telescope, a barometer, maps, the pocket edition of William Cowper's poems, abridged versions of various tour books, and also a Claude-glass. This fashionable item was a small convex mirror that miniaturized the reflected landscape and gave it a darker, more artistic tint: it was an instrument for focusing, framing, and composing, named after the landscape painter Claude Lorraine, famous for his special light effects.[9] By using lenses of different tints, the traveler changed a single landscape: moonlight, dawn, winter. Like Linnerhielm, Plumptre was in search of picturesque views, which could be fixed through the lenses of the Claude-glass, sketched in watercolors, or described in the travel diary.

Linnaeus's saddlebags also contain traveling knickknacks: a looking glass, a list of the region's plants, a bunch of papers for pressing flowers and making sketches, a microscope, clean shirts, a comb, and a wig, but there is no room for a Claude-glass—at that time it had not yet left the artist's studio. Instead he carries a measuring rod. Linnaeus is moving through another kind of aesthetic, moral, and political terrain. His ambition to collect useful information, to gather facts, parallels that of many other of his contemporary travelers of the late seventeenth and early eighteenth centuries. In many ways his journey fits into an earlier tradition of traveling for a practical purpose, for commerce or fact finding. The trader's eye looked for information on local economy and society. Even nonscholars often journeyed with a scholarly frame of mind: always on the lookout for useful knowledge. Maximilian Mission's guidebook, *A New Voyage to Italy* from 1695, for example, suggested that the traveler should carry with him a fifty-fathom cord knotted every foot for determining the heights of towers.[10]

The Linnaean tradition continued in the specific genre of scientific explorations, but it was travelers like Linnerhielm and Plumptre who laid the foundations for modern tourism. The perspectives represented by Linnaeus and Linnerhielm could also coexist among the early tourists. In his restless development of American politics, industry, and aesthetics Thomas Jefferson also found time to discuss landscape and tourism. In his *Notes on the State of Virginia* from the 1770s he describes the Natural Bridge, a good example of what travelers in those time liked to call "Nature's oddities." He starts out with a scientific description of this cliff formation straddling a stream, in the style he had learned from Linnaeus, but all of a sudden the language changes into a style that Linnerhielm would have liked.[11] "It is impossible for the emotions arising from the sublime to be felt beyond what they are here. So beautiful an arch, so elevated, so light, and springing as it were up to heaven! the rapture of the spectator is really indescribable!"[12]

COLLECTING SCENERIES

Linnerhielm's baggage does not include a measuring rod or a knotted rope, but he carries a well defined mental measuring tape. Like Linnaeus, he is out to weigh, evaluate, and describe, but the object is sceneries and situations. Landscapes are classified as boring, ugly, too regimented, appealing, enchanting, or perfect. Already in early tourism we meet the paradox: the need to communicate the experience of a personal and unique confrontation with the landscape, in words or watercolors, creates a comparative framework. The experience of other travelers invades your own. Is this as rich or strong an experience as those others claim?

The eighteenth-century pioneers of modern tourism developed the kind of virtual reality called the picturesque: a certain way of selecting, framing, and representing views. It taught tourists not only where to look but also how to sense the landscape, experience it, and it is still part of our travel kit although the term has lost its more precise eighteenth-century meaning. Today the term may refer to a rugged landscape, a quaint village, or an old quarter of the town.

In the making of the tourist quest for the picturesque in the late eighteenth century, art played a key role in teaching the pioneers where to look and how to look in the landscape.[13] And there was a desire to teach nature to imitate art. The "paintability" of the landscape came into focus, drawing on the new developments in landscape painting during the sixteenth and eighteenth centuries, but the making of the picturesque was also shaped by an ongoing dialogue between many arts: aesthetics, literature, music, and—not least—gardening.

The first step in the transformation of this concept of the picturesque from an aesthetic theory into tourist practice emerged among the pioneer generations of the Grand Tour to the classical sights of southern Europe. Aristocrats from the north learned to view the landscape in a different frame of mind as they passed the Alps, and they also brought home paintings of masters such as Claude Lorraine and Salvator Rosa as well as travel books in the newfangled genre of *voyages pittoresques*, with plenty of etchings, as souvenirs. The interest in southern travel and the consumption of landscape painting à la mode created a veritable export industry among Italian landscape painters. For the northern buyers these sceneries introduced a new way of seeing and judging the landscapes at home. Although this process was most marked among the English gentry, we can follow it all over northern Europe and America. For many the model landscape of the picturesque was found in the famous tourist setting of Tivoli outside Rome. A Swedish visitor writes home in 1787 that here you can learn about the picturesque: "Never before have I grasped this term better than here," he declares and continues by pointing out that a good painter is never satisfied with what nature has to offer in one and same scenery. No, he adds more objects: "a ruin, a castle, a hill, a valley, a forest, a plain, a stream, etc.; in order to make the painting much more interesting and variable through such a composition."[14] If nature itself can bring forward such a richness, it comes close to being an artful composition and thus it can be called picturesque, he concludes. The landscapes around Tivoli had such a perfect mix of paintable qualities that you didn't have to rearrange them in your mind, they could just be painted as they stood.

The craving for the picturesque was found all over Europe, albeit with national variations, but it was in England that its combination with travel was institutionalized. A central role was played by the schoolmaster William Gilpin, whose travel guides in the Lake District, published from 1782 onwards, instructed the traveler where and how to look for the picturesque and how to capture it in sketches with the aid of a Claude-glass. Already by 1807 a British observer stated that summer traveling with the object of studying the picturesque now was looked on as essential.[15]

Learning the picturesque thus meant being able to locate landscapes with special qualities. It was the interplay of certain elements, shadow and light, foliage, irregular and varied landscape features that made a truly picturesque view. The picturesque motif often carried an air of nostalgia, epitomized in the idyllic rural life. Signs of decay, an old cottage, a ruin, a tombstone further stressed this atmosphere. Melancholy laments over the passing of time, as well as the insignificance of human beings became important parts of the picturesque sensibility.

The task of the tourist was to track down these paintable landscapes and lift them out of the duller surroundings, fixing them as pictures, then represent them in sketches, watercolors, and words. A traveler in the Lake District in 1779 describes his successful capture of a truly picturesque scene: "On the Right, from behind a piece of Rock which projected, breasted forth a Torrent of Water which I caught in my Glass (through a tree romantically fix'd in the Bare Rock & twisted) shining like diamonds, a Picture the finest my eyes ever beheld."[16] There was an element of hunting and gathering in this pursuit. Using the technique of framing, you could impose some kind of order on the unknown and untamed landscapes that confronted you. The wild was still seen as chaotic.[17]

The making of the picturesque has often been seen as the first step in developing "the tourist's gaze," but such an argument misses the fact that the picturesque above all was about sensibility: a search for atmosphere and sceneries that opened your senses and sent your thoughts flying. It is striking how rapidly this language of aesthetics and emotions spread over the Western world. Linnerhielm travels within a constant frame of the picturesque. He is an avid reader of English sentimental journeys, French *voyages pittoresques,* and German explorations of pastoral idylls. He makes constant references to the two artists he worships, carrying their sceneries as a measuring rod—Salomon Gessner, the Swiss poet and artist, author of the bestseller *Idylls* from 1756, and Claude Lorraine: "I wonder what Claude would have thought of this landscape," or "This is scenery worthy of Gessner."

THE THEME PARK

The cosmopolitan nature of the new elite tourism meant that people could become part of an international community of travelers without ever leaving their home region. Another important element of pioneer tourism helped these domestic travelers: the romantic English garden. The new model of the perfect landscape not only circulated in etchings and texts but materialized all over Europe during the eighteenth century. This "modern garden," as the British pioneers often called it, was a reaction against the earlier regimented aesthetics of the French baroque garden, with its symmetry and disciplined nature. Throughout the Western world new parks were now being laid out in the English style, in a deliberate attempt to produce nature at its best. Now landscape architects abhorred "all that is regular," yet at the same time they spoke of the importance of touching up or concealing unsuitable aspects of nature. The landscape was to acquire a set of suitable accessories and serve as a training ground for pioneer tourists. Here they learned to experience nature in novel ways and to sharpen their sensibilities.

In his journey north Linnerhielm stops at the newly constructed English garden at the manor of Forsmark. He walks around full of praise for its delights, its many surprises and moods, thrown between the wild and the idyllic. He saunters along winding paths and little brooks. Behind every corner there are fresh surprises: a shady arbor, a bridge, a sculpture, or a little hall of mirrors, a Greek temple. For Linnerhielm the walk through the park is a serious business—this is a cultic site of the emotions. One of his contemporaries describes the same park as "a wilderness, not sweet and beautiful, but strong and beautiful."[18]

The present-day visitor to Forsmark, armed with Linnerhielm's description, is unlikely to share this enthusiasm. The park has remained much the same, but everything seems so small and paltry, and above all tame. Walking through the same landscape as Linnerhielm, we lack the cultural conditioning that made this stroll so powerful to eighteenth-century visitors. They experienced rapid shifts between the idyllic and the wild and were able to project moods and visions with the help of hints and fragments and read the many hidden subtexts. Tiny landscape details had far-reaching literary, historical, and aesthetic connotations, stimulating the mind and creating a massive symbolic space out of this little park, in which Linnerhielm found "everything prepared to surprise." As modern visitors we lack these cultural lenses. We walk the same grounds but move in a different mindscape.

Figure 3. The English garden at Forsmark in the days of Linnerhielm's travels. (Drawing by Elias Martin)

Close to Forsmark Linnerhielm visits another manorial garden, which still retained the old-fashioned French style, and reflects that his idol Claude Lorraine never would have drawn any inspiration from these "stiff and geometrical plantations."[19] But the "naturalness" of the English garden was a highly staged naturalness. It was an attempt to elaborate "nature," and the irony is that many English gardeners derived their early inspirations from landscape painting, not least Lorraine's sceneries.[20]

The new parks rapidly became a popular destination for pleasure trippers. The way they were used tells us about the new sensibilities and technologies of sightseeing. In the English garden visitors learned to position themselves in order to take in a view and identify a picturesque sight. Here they cultivated the art of outdoor daydreaming, linking landscapes of fantasy and contemplation with the terrain through which they walked. The careful staging of the stroll would carry visitors from scenery to scenery and into new moods: from melancholy and nostalgia to drama and excitement. A dreaming stroller could sit down on a bench under the shady trees and let her thoughts wander elsewhere: inside toward the self, back in history with the aid of the classical monuments, away from society and everyday life to the land of utopia.

Linnerhielm's Danish contemporary Christian Molbech enacts this process during his visit to a Danish pleasure garden, built in the 1790s. With Linnerhielmian enthusiasm he describes the walk from surprise to surprise. He crosses a small bridge and wanders along a mysterious and shadowed path and suddenly encounters "the Norwegian chalet." Here in this solitary setting it is possible to let the mind fly, he notes, and he is "transported to the Norwegian mountains, where buildings like these belong."

After enjoying the stillness by the Norwegian chalet he hastens along through "this world of fantasy." Passing a meadow he enters a shady and solitary grove where the thatched dwelling of the hermit is situated. On the table inside the hut there is an hourglass with two skulls, and above the door an inscription: "Death is certain, but the hour of Death uncertain!"[21]

The cottage or hermit's cave was a standard element in the English garden. At Forsmark the park's wildest part vividly impresses Linnerhielm. Where the path turns by a rock he finds a grotto and "in its shadows a hermit, sitting with a book in his hand. He is dressed in a deep purple cloak and has a gentle but serious expression" (the figure was made of wax and was later eaten by rats).

More ambitious garden projects tried to supply real hermits. In 1791 a Swedish newspaper mused over the attempt of a British gentleman to recruit a live hermit. Applicants were required to endure seven years in total silence in the hermitage of the garden, to wear sandals and simple dress, not to cut their hair or nails, to drink water from the babbling brook, and to sit with a Bible, some optical elements, and an hourglass in view of visitors. The remuneration for these seven years would be 700 guineas, but alas the chosen applicant endured only three weeks.[22]

The standardization of sceneries, surprises, and follies was made possible by study tours to England and above all by the international circulation of garden plans and instructions. Toward the end of the eighteenth century there were a number of popular handbooks on the landscaping of romantic gardens. Amateurs and professionals could find blueprints and do-it-yourself hints, which described the production of follies and surprises, as well as models of suitable hermit cottages. One result of this standardization was that tourists could feel at home in any English garden, be it located in Germany, Denmark, Scotland, or North America. Park after park sprang up, fitted out with the same, fairly fixed assortment of sceneries and props. The entrance ticket was the cultural capital of classical learning needed to interpret the many symbolic hints.

The formula of the romantic park turned out to have great staying power. It became the blueprint not only for urban parks of the nineteenth century but also for a coming world of tourist theme parks, from open-air museums to Disneyworlds and adventure lands all over the globe; a new surprise behind every corner of the winding paths, a little flag marking a scenic photo spot. In the same way the language of the picturesque is still with us, in travel catalogs, picture postcards, and guidebooks.

The rapid spread of the new sensibilities in the form of the picturesque created a highly cosmopolitan, albeit still thin, layer of tourist pioneers in Europe and North America. To understand this rapid internationalization of tourist practices and standards, we have to look at the social situation of these pioneers. Many were rural gentry, clergy, and teachers. They shared a background of higher education but also a position of relative isolation. Out there in their parishes and manors they longed for the kind of intellectual communion many of them had encountered during their early university years. Like Linnerhielm they were alone with their libraries and most of them could not afford to travel on the grand, international scale of the higher aristocracy. They perfected the art of intellectual daydreaming, investing in new books on travel and gardening, and were in constant mental (and sometimes in written) communication with their colleagues or mentors out there in the world.

Their aspirations to describe, represent, evaluate, and compare also produce an urge to communicate: to show off, to write, to force others into comparison. Competition requires social exchanges—you cannot remain silent. Early tourism thus is very much about establishing norms and genres of representation. Pioneers such as Linnerhielm and Plumptre grapple with the terms of these new modes of experience. There is much open reflection on how to select, judge, and represent.

The tourist pioneers were eager to draw the line between themselves and the unsophisticated and uneducated others, whom they saw as lacking aesthetic competence. In his description of the natural bridge, Jefferson complains that local people have no eyes for monuments like these and thus echoes the complaints of his contemporaries. The common folk in Europe and North America just worked the land—they did not seem to be able to take in the landscape. A similar argument appeared in Ralph Emerson's essay on "Nature" in 1836. The farmer may own the fields but cannot lay claim to the view. Only poets and artists can integrate all the parts of the scenery into a true landscape experience.[23] (What the tourist pioneers did not realize was that the farmers and peasants had their own and very different aesthetic views of that same piece of land.)[24]

NEW SENSATIONS

The cult of the picturesque also illustrates another tourism mechanism, the tension between routinization and improvisation, between the predictable and the surprising, which produces a craving for fresh sights and novel experiences.

A side effect of the standardization of the attractions in the romantic garden was boredom. Linnerhielm inspects the grave of the Roman hero Belisarius, one of the attractions at Forsmark, but complains of having just seen the same sepulchral monument in the manorial garden of the next parish. Is this Roman hero buried everywhere? The winding paths are now too foreseeable.

The hunt for the picturesque could thus grow stale. As we have seen, the mentality of the picturesque became a way of evaluating the landscape. Tourists like Plumptre and Linnerhielm continually talk about the picturesque in terms of more or less, which could wear the landscape down: too many beautiful, or pleasing, sceneries. The effect shows up in the travel journals' dutiful records. All those superlatives and exclamation marks turn into routine. In Bishop Percy's notes from his 1775 Scottish tour we can observe this struggle: "the immense Group of stupendous Mountains beyond it to the North, rising up in gigantic scenery beyond one another, form a succession of Picturesque wonderfully great, astonishing & picturesque fine Picturesque beyond all descriptions, & to which no Language can do justice."[25] In exasperation the bishop crossed out the last two "picturesques," making his point forcefully. The cult of Claude slowly turned into the derogatory label of "Claudianism," and in Jane Austen's novels we find ample examples of battles between those who were still infatuated by the picturesque and those who had started to satirize it. The pleasing views came to seem less pleasing to the senses, the pen, and the brush.

Alongside the fervent and tear-filled emotions aroused by the romantic park, we can discern a longing for more powerful and dramatic impressions. In the midst of all the idyllic harmony there grew a need for a heightened sensation, a cult of the sublime—"all that surprises the soul, all that creates a sense of fear," as Diderot defined the concept.[26] During the eighteenth century the idea of the sublime traveled from philosophy and art theory into tourism. In this journey the concept, like the picturesque, went through several transformations, as well as a trivialization.

The novel cult of the sublime, as a yearning for the wild and surprising, emerged in the new motifs chosen by romantic landscape painters.

They scorned pastoral idyll and the calm sea in favor of "nature's great upheavals"—surprises and shocks. This doctrine appeared in an 1828 Swedish handbook on landscape painting, which discusses how various natural phenomena may evoke differing emotions, and how nature should ideally be on a gigantic rather than a gentle scale. A good artist must paint high mountain regions, steep waterfalls, volcanoes, landslides, floods—in short, "nature's oddities," as a way of evoking what the author calls "profound emotional disturbances."[27] Storms should rage both in the landscape and in the beholder's soul. The sublime refers not only to the majestic or magnificent, but also to the terrifying or awesome, the presence of forces stronger than man, be they demonic or godly. Moments of the sublime must grip the onlooker, through the dialectics of the repelling and the fascinating. Landscape gardeners tried to introduce elements of the sublime, a craggy rock, a small cataract in their parks, but such items could not satisfy the new longing for the wild.

THE ULTIMATE WATERFALL

It did not take long for the quest for the sublime to become institutionalized. One of the favorite attractions was the waterfall, which for the tourist pioneers came to represent the perfect mix of "terrible beauty": a wild, but not too wild, nature.

On the road to Lapland in 1732 Linnaeus visited the famous Swedish falls at Älvkarleby. The scenery impressed him, but his attention focused on the geology and flora of the setting, as well as the power of the falls, the effect of the mist, and the possibilities for salmon fishing. Half a century later Linnerhielm arrived there and of course described his visit in quite different terms. The first sight of the falls simply rendered him speechless. He had to return next day for a second look: "Arriving I felt the same elevated pleasure as last time and admired with surprise all this terrible beauty. . . . As I left at last, it was as if my senses had been given freer reins, I felt the sweetest tranquillity."[28] After this experience, waterfalls became the staple of his itineraries along with romantic gardens, ruins, and picturesque sceneries. His next waterfall experience was described as "a pleasant shudder," while another reaction typical of the times was "quivering rapture." The waterfall was fascinating not only because it was accessible; the untamed torrent also became something for new freedom-worshiping romantics to identify with. All over Europe tourists found themselves drawn to waterfalls as a kind of *Gesamtkunstwerk*, which affected all the senses: the roaring sound of the falls, the changing colors, the sensation of the cold mist rising from the falls, the taste of fresh water.

Among eighteenth-century travelers schooled in the tradition of the Grand Tour, the famous waterfalls of Tivoli and Terni were the model of comparison. Looking at a mighty Swedish waterfall, a Swede recently returned from his southern tour judged its qualities in comparison with the cascades of Terni.[29] But were the falls of Terni really wild and sublime enough? If waterfalls offered the truest sublime experience, the mighty Niagara Falls on the border between Canada and the United States were to become the greatest natural wonder in the world: "the most romantic of awful Prospects Imaginable," as an early visitor put it.[30] Already in the late eighteenth century they attracted American as well as European tourist pioneers as an icon of the sublime.

The first extensive descriptions of the falls belong to the scientific Linnaean genre. Linnaeus's disciple Pehr Kalm visited the falls in 1750, and in his long-winded commentary there is no trace of the sublime.[31] With the help of French officers and soldiers from the nearby fort, he travels in a birch canoe and struggles several miles across hilly country. Arriving at the falls, he measures the temperature of the water and then sits down by the edge to record his observations, with pen and ink. Like the traveler recommended to carry a measuring rope, he spends a long time contemplating the exact heights of the falls, how far the roaring sound may travel in different weather conditions, the reach and effect of the spray, hanging like a mighty mist over the landscape. Kalm does confess (unlike Linnaeus observing the falls of Älvkarleby) that the sight makes the hairs on his neck stand on end, but we have to turn to later visitors to find a more emotional description. The next generation was interested in measuring their rapture, rather than the water temperature. For them the falls supplied an intense and personal experience of being in communion with nature, but even the early tourists at Niagara grappled with the problem of translating this experience into the language of sublimity. How could you communicate the overwhelming greatness of this moment? Some pioneers chose the same strategy as Linnerhielm and declared themselves speechless and then hastened to list the superlatives. In these narratives of Niagara we follow the vocabulary of the sublime: breathtaking, awesome, grandiose, gripping, moving, majestic, overwhelming . . . [32]

Another problem had to do with the emergence of a tourist infrastructure at Niagara. As the falls became more accessible, through the Erie Canal, finished in 1825, and later thanks to the railways, and as hotels and sightseeing platforms were erected, the falls lost some of their sublimity. And as access became easier, the element of adventure and danger diminished and thus devalued the experience for some. A Lieutenant Francis Hall coined a maxim that would become a stable element in adventure tourism: "the effect produced upon us by any object of admiration is increased by the difficulties of approaching it."[33]

For some men the advent of women tourists signaled this change—it threatened the masculinity of the Niagara experience as wilderness adventure. It also tied in with changing male ideas about the gendering of emotions. The strong sublime experience was for men, while the meeker picturesque views suited the sensibilities of women.[34] What is, striking, however, is that many of the most passionate descriptions of visits to the falls came from women tourists, and they were often very personal experiences: "My dreams are very wild here. I am not calm here. A great voice seems to be calling on me," one woman stated, and another wrote about "the terrible loveliness" and continued, "I feel half crazy whenever I think of it." Harriet Beecher Stowe "felt as if I could have *gone over* with the waters; it would be so beautiful a death; there would be no fear in it . . . "[35]

For those middle-class women who now had the chance to travel, tourism could be liberating in more than one way. Not only was it a chance to escape from the routines of everyday domestic life, it was also a chance to transgress traditional boundaries. Niagara came to represent a new kind of freedom for them.

Figure 4. The sublimity of the Niagara experience made it a suitable honey-moon destination. The result was thousands of photos like this: the happy cou-ple against a background of torrents of water. (Photo Local History Depart-ment, Public Library, Niagara Falls, N.Y.)

For both men and women the search for the sublime had a strong element of sacralization, but that religious feeling called for silence and serenity, preferably also the chance to be alone or only with chosen fellow travelers. With a growing number of visitors the criticism of mass tourism mounted and de Tocqueville vented a classic opinion: if you want to experience the real Niagara, you have to hurry up—soon it'll be too late.[36]

As Niagara became an icon of the sublime, celebrated in tourist guides, travel books, and poetry and depicted in all kinds of visual media from oil paintings to cheap prints, a new kind of tourist angst developed: what if the sight did not live up to your heightened expectations, based on earlier representation? What if the images were more wonderful than the real thing? The art of "being utterly Niagarized" became increasingly complicated.[37] How could you place yourself at a vantage point where hotels, zealous guides, or other tourists did not disturb the view or the tranquillity; what time of day, what kind of weather conditions were the best?

Among the new tourist groups were the honeymooners. The first "cooing couples" were mentioned in the late 1830s, when honeymoon travel was still a newfangled idea. The development of Niagara as a favorite honeymoon destination was probably linked to the original quest for the sublime, a place for passion and romance, but also to the rapid transformation of the scene into fashionable social life and entertainment. The year 1838 saw not only the first mention of honeymooners but also the advent of the first billiard rooms.[38]

For many who came here on their first vacation, Niagara became a training ground. How do you approach a great landscape attraction, how do you spend your holiday in leisurely ways, get your photograph taken, select souvenirs, go on guided tours, socialize with other tourists from very different regions and stations of life? How do you handle the newfangled idea of a honeymoon? Guidebooks gave hints on how to construct a tourist program, how to select and combine, and how to behave yourself in this new situation.

The old tourist elite viewed the new groups with disdain, and the classic battle against "vulgar tourism" escalated. Niagara was described

as the demise of the sublime into the ridiculous, the wild into the domesticated and tame. In the battle of cultural distinctions between different kinds of tourists it took on a new aura: that of the tacky, overexploited tourist trap. The growth of an ironic genre lamenting the
vulgarization of Niagara was thus one of the effects of the broadened
popular appeal.

For some, Niagara offered an amusing place to visit and a chance to
view a fantastic scenery, thanks to the blessings of civilization and technology; for others it became a place to avoid. Those in search of sublime
communion with the wild had to find more primordial wildernesses.

MOUNTAIN FEVER

The interest in waterfalls constituted the first step out into the wild, but
the demand for greater emotional storms led people above all toward the
mountains, the sort of scenery that earlier generations of nature lovers in
the eighteenth century had spoken of with distaste. When Carl Linnaeus
first saw the Lapland mountainscapes in 1732, his reaction was vehement.
He wondered if he was in Asia or Africa; everything was unfamiliar and
chaotic, and he could see nothing but "bare mountains on bare mountains, no forests, no houses, no fences, no roads, no singing birds, no sun
setting."[39] This was a repulsive wildness. We find a similar reaction from
Samuel Johnson in his travel account, *A Journey to the Western Isles of Scotland* from 1775. He saw the mountains as hopeless sterility: "dismissed by
nature from her care and disinherited of her favours."[40]

Both in Sweden and Britain such verdicts soon came under challenge.
The new generation of romantic British poets viewed the mountains as a
scenery filled with all the blessings of the sublime. Here, in the terrible
and majestic wilderness, you try to make contact with a divine force.
Gilpin's handbook also established criteria for ranking the beauty of
mountain sceneries.[41]

As in the case of the waterfalls, we find a search for the most sublime
mountain sceneries. General agreement emerged relatively soon. If the
picturesque ideal's first model was the pastoral landscapes of Italy and

the south, the most sublime mountain sceneries were those of the Lake District and Scotland. But Switzerland's peaks shortly took precedence.

The longing for the freedom of the wilderness found its prime expression in what was called the thirst for the Alps. Jean-Jacques Rousseau expressed his longing for mountain streams and "threatening abysses at my side!"[42] This pure, magnificent landscape gave rise to elevated thoughts. A Norwegian traveler wrote of Switzerland in 1790 that the country's patriotic constitution and magnificent scenery combined to beautify the place.[43] The cult of the Alps was a combination of aesthetics and politics. Travelers yearning for freedom found an ideological model in Switzerland, with its heroic and democratic history.[44]

Huge spaces, clear air, intoxicating solitude, and a sense of freedom made the mountain expanses into a romantic and revolutionary utopia. Even an idyllist like Linnerhielm in his later years began to acquire a taste for "the awesome majesty of the mountains," and for him as for many others the adjective Swiss acquired immense prestige. As eighteenth-century Swedes had searched for Italian features in their own landscape, now one spoke of "a Swiss view" when confronted with a pleasing Nordic prospect. In the United States many places, from the Catskills in the East to the Santa Cruz mountains in the West, competed for the tourist label "the Switzerland of the USA," and we find similar rhetorics about mountains as the terrain of freedom here.[45]

The quest for mountains meant a redrawing of the tourist map in both Europe and North America. Switzerland developed a booming tourist industry, soon followed by another marginal country: Norway. The European alpine thirst transformed Norway's mountain regions into Scandinavia's first international tourist attraction—for the British in search of the wild these mountain regions on the Atlantic coast were more easily accessible than Switzerland. The same mountains that Norwegian visitors still in the 1820s described as "wild and awful" or "a melancholy lifeless and monotonous desert" were described a decade later in enthusiastic terms by one of the first visiting Englishmen. Neither the Swiss Alps nor the Himalayas can compete with the beauty of these Norwegian views, he writes in his travel book from 1833, which was to attract a steady flow of English visitors to Norway.[46]

NATIONALIZING THE SUBLIME

The Norwegian example also illustrates the ways in which the romantic longing for the wild became intertwined with another international quest: that for national identity. Inspired by the British reevaluation, Norwegians started to look to the mountains in their attempts to forge a national culture as an alternative to the forced political union with Sweden since 1814.

As in Switzerland there was a link between landscape aesthetics and politics. The new greatness of this landscape did not, however, derive from its similarity to the Swiss Alps but from the fact that it constituted something truly Norwegian. The mountain peasants who inhabited these regions came to be seen as the true Norwegian folk. This urge to nationalize nature emerged at the end of the eighteenth century but became a strong force during the first half of the next.[47]

In the foreword to Linnerhielm's first travel book from 1797 we already find traces of national pride. He was greatly irritated by the way his mentor Gilpin, in his 1792 book *Observations relative to picturesque beauty,* made it clear that British mountains had a higher aesthetic quality than others: "The mountains of Sweden, Norway and other northern Regions are probably rather masses of hideous rudeness, than Scenes of grandeur and proportion."[48] Another contemporary Swedish nature lover stated the new faith in Swedish scenery in a more blunt way: "A Swede should love Swedish mountains most."[49]

And yet the nationalization of the landscape was not an even process. It is most evident in countries that saw themselves as marginal to the grand narrative of Western civilization—the Scandinavian countries, the United States, and, later, Canada—where the wilderness and the quest for the sublime became a central arena for national culture-building. They invoked an abundance of nature to offset their lack of high culture.

This reevaluation of the landscape was perhaps most striking in the United States. The reasons for this are many. John Sears analyzes the making of "sacred places" in early American tourism and attributes them to both a strong religious tradition and a postrevolutionary nationalism.[50] Others point to the marked inferiority complex of nineteenth-century

Figure 5. The mountains soon developed into the model for active vacations. In this advertisement for Glacier National Park all tourists are on the move. (Minnesota Historical Society Library, St. Paul)

American intellectuals, the constant harping on the lack of culture and history in the new nation: "No monuments, no ruins, no Eton, no Oxford, no Epsom, no Ascot, no antiquity, no legends, no society in the received sense of the word—the grievance runs from Hawthorne to Henry James."[51]

The idea that America was an adolescent nation lacking in culture directed the focus onto the wilderness. When John Ruskin wrote: "I could not even for a couple of months live in a country so miserable not to possess castles," his words struck home for American travelers who deplored the lack of picturesque ruins.[52] But couldn't the rugged mountains and the craggy rocks, the strange and twisted trees of the primeval forests compensate for this? A new language of "organic ruins" developed among American tourists, and in the sublime tradition there was a marked religious element in this new celebration of the American wilderness, the awesome panoramas, and the mighty mountain cathedrals.[53]

Already by the 1820s a mountain tourist industry was developing in the eastern United States. With the help of steamboats and railways the Catskills along the Hudson River and the White Mountains became easily accessible. Authors and painters played a crucial role in producing this romantic scenery. One of them was "America's first wilderness painter," the British-born Thomas Cole, founder of "the Hudson River school" of landscape artists. His hero, like Linnerhielm's, was Claude Lorraine, and he went on painting pilgrimages to Italy, later to transform the European picturesque and sublime into his American panoramas.

Cole helped to make the first fashionable wilderness hotel a success, visiting the new Mountain House when it opened in 1824, and he painted a number of scenic sights in the area. Perhaps the most famous was his "Falls of Kaaterskill" from 1826, but in his search for an Arcadian America he had to leave out the trappings of the tourist industry, which already had invaded this popular sight: a viewing tower, steps, and handrails. Instead he added a lonely Indian warrior, a symbol of wilderness that had already by then become nostalgic, as the natives of the Hudson valley area had more or less been wiped out.[54] The Catskills falls became a well organized "tourist must," which made for cynical comments on the commodification of the landscape by some visitors in the 1850s:

The process of "doing" the sight, for those who have limited time, is very methodical. You leave the hotel and drive in a coach to the bar-room. You refresh! You step out upon the balcony and look into the abyss. The proprietor of the Falls informs you that the lower plunge is about eighty feet high. It appears to you to be about ten.

The proprietor of the bar-room is also the genius of the Falls, and de-rives a trade both with his spirits and with his waters. In fact, if your ro-mantic nerves can steady the truth, the Catskill falls is *turned on* to ac-commodate poets and parties of pleasure.[55]

For twenty-five cents the sluice was opened and the tourist was then de-livered back to the Mountain House in time for the formal dinner.

The institutionalization of sights was greatly helped by the ways in which the wilderness entered the parlors of middle-class homes. En-graved volumes like *Picturesque Views of American Sceneries* from 1820 and *Hudson River Portfolio* from 1826 domesticated the wild and created an appetite for "doing sights," and by the mid-century millions of land-scape reproductions circulated on the American market, in books, maga-zines, and individual prints. There was also a rapid growth in the guide-book trade, which further helped to institutionalize tourist travel.[56]

The luxurious Mountain House became a sight in itself, as tourists started to go on "the fashionable tour," as an American counterpart to the Grand European tour. In the 1820s the circuit took travelers from New York City up along the Hudson River, viewing the Catskills, per-haps stopping at Saratoga Springs, and then to Niagara through the new Erie Canal. The tour combined the new interest in American nature with visits to historic sites, but also an interest in new technological wonders, which this early generation of American tourists had no trouble combin-ing with the romance of the wild.

Such pioneer tourism became an important part of American nation-making, a territorialization of the national. In this process landscape and history merged in a powerful way: early Americans walked the very same ground where we are standing now. (The question was, of course, which Americans: indigenous inhabitants, or early white settlers?)

As the Hudson panoramas and the mountainscapes of the East became too tame, the American tour expanded westwards, in search of "real wilderness." The tourist discovery of the breathtaking Yosemite Valley in the Sierra Nevada during the 1850s is one example of this new focus. In 1866 one of the early visitors described his first sight of the valley:

> The overpowering sense of the sublime, of awful desolation, of transcending marvelousness and unexpectedness, that swept over us, as we reined our horses sharply out of green forest, and stood upon high jutting rock that overlooked this rolling, upheaving sea of granite mountains, holding far down [in] its rough lap this vale of beauty, of meadow and grove and river,—such tide of feeling, such stoppage of ordinary emotions comes at rare intervals in any life. It was the confrontal of God face to face, as in great danger, in solemn, sudden death. It was Niagara, magnified. All that was mortal shrank back, all that was immortal swept to the front and bent down in awe.[57]

Not only is this a model description in the international language of the sublime experience, it is also illustrates the new tone of national pride based on the perceived uniqueness and greatness of the vast American wilderness.

It is no coincidence that the idea of the national park developed in America—the first being Yellowstone in 1872—only to be exported over the world as an element in the international list of the necessary infrastructure of "what a real nation should contain." In the same manner the United States had been on the receiving end in borrowing ideas and blueprints for nationalizing its wilderness. The nineteenth-century American tradition of wilderness painting borrowed not only its sublime focus from Europe but also French and British painting styles.[58] The end result was a specific American articulation of that wilderness, which was to be developed further in the powerful American tradition of wilderness photography, culminating in Ansel Adams's sacral representations of Yosemite. But as Rebecca Solnit shows, photography already played a crucial role in the establishment of this national park. It was not panoramas in oil but the new techniques of landscape photography that swayed bureaucrats in Washington, D.C., selling them on the idea of safeguarding this wilderness already in the 1860s. Landscape photography was still a stunning novelty, a powerful medium of persuasion.[59]

The nationalizing of the sublime, as in the early pilgrimages to the Niagara, the panoramas of the Hudson River, or the mountain cathedrals of Yosemite, had several effects. One is that no onlooker had to ponder about whether France's frequency and quality of picturesque sights compared to those of the United States, or argue about whether the mountains of Yosemite represented "as grand panoramic views of mountain and valley as [tourists] can find in Switzerland."[60] In their unique Americanness these landscapes were not to be compared on an international scale. They were, so to speak, taken out of the tourist competition, but from this it also follows that to understand and take in their greatness, the viewer had to be a true American. Thus the nationalization of the sublime added a new dimension of the sacred: the feeling that in certain landscapes you were in communion with nature and with the spirit of the nation itself.

The tourist cult of the wilderness produced a new national pride in the uniqueness and freshness of the New World. Thomas Cole pointed out that "all nature here is new to Art. No Tivoli's, no Terni's, Mont Blanc's, Plinlimmon's, hackneyed & worn by the daily pencils of hundreds, but virgin forests, lakes & waterfalls."[61]

As we have seen, tourism itself threatened this rhetoric of virginity and freshness, expanding and improving its reach, through steamboats and railways. This new mobility, of course, also produced novel ways of experiencing the landscape.

On the Move

Scenery Unlimited!

Only the Vista-Dome California Zephyr gives you so much to see, so much to do!

You look up, look down, look all around as you enjoy day-long views of the colorful Colorado Rockies and California's famous Feather River Canyon through the High Sierra.

This advertisement from the early 1950s belongs to the great sightseeing era of the railways, as they were battling increased competition from bus and air travel. While Pan Am flew its Strato-Clippers across the Atlantic, the California Zephyr had five Vista-Domes in each train. There was also the Strata-Dome, another double-decker railcar with panorama windows

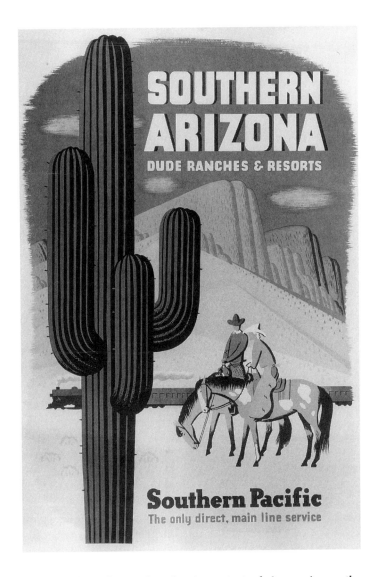

Figure 6. The railways played an important role in opening up the West for tourism and developing the idea of the package tour. And as palm trees signified southern California, the cactus became the icon of the Southwest. (Poster for Southern Pacific, California State Railroad Museum Library, Sacramento)

and seats that revolved, equipped with instruments such as a speedometer, to tell you how fast you were going, as well as an altimeter to inform you of how high above sea level you were riding.[1]

The Greyhound alternative was the "Scenicruiser" double-decker. A typical 1958 advertisement depicts a couple inside this new bus enjoying "the vibrationless Air Suspension Ride" as they watch a snowclad mountain gliding past the panorama window.

Advertisements like these have a timeless quality. The railway developed an early marketing of sightseeing, but the art of scenicruising, as sightseeing in motion, was not alien to eighteenth-century tourist pioneers. The tours of the Lake District included boat trips, and the helpful Gilpin supplied tips in his 1782 book on how to experience the landscape along the River Wye, plied by a flotilla of specially designed boats with tables for sketching and writing. Patricia Jasen points out the degree to which Gilpin's river guide was cinematic.[2] He talked about the side screens and the front screen of the boat slowly floating down the river while picturesque scenes presented themselves.

With the development of steam, water cruises became a novel way of taking in the landscape, *gliding* past it. In North America rides along rivers like the Hudson or the St. Lawrence became immensely popular. The steamboat supplied a new framing of the moving landscape, which travelers could now observe through the glass windows or from the deck chair, but the increased speed also forced them to learn new ways of focusing in order to be able to take in a panorama. This certainly did not come naturally. Linnerhielm, for one, did not feel himself capable of the panoramic gaze. Climbing up a hill he looked out over several parishes but found that it really was too much:

> I am forced to admit that my brief glance did not totally enchant me. It was too rich to take in during a brief moment, too extensive to please. It was a whole landscape, not a view.[3]

The panoramic view grew out of the staging of the sublime, in which the dramatic qualities of *vastness* became a central criterion. The wide open spaces, like the mountain sceneries, became sought after.

Philippe de Loutherbourg, a French theatrical set designer and land-scape painter with a flair for dramatic sceneries working in London, de-veloped the Eidophusikon in 1782. It was a miniature theater with sound and lightning effects for illustrating the mightiness of nature. Here you could, for example, witness a raging storm with the illusion of move-ment.[4] Five years later the first panorama, in the form of a wide-screen landscape encircling the spectators, was presented in London, an inno-vation that would prove to be a great entertainment success during the following century. Different versions such as dioramas and cycloramas were developed, and in 1822 the first moving grand panorama was pre-sented in Paris.[5] Through a dark entrance you moved into a circular hall with benches facing what looked like a window. Here a view of Mount Etna at night was revealed, and little by little you could observe the day breaking, transforming the landscape. As night fell again there came a sudden and dramatic volcanic eruption. Amidst rumbling sounds the mountain spat out lava![6] What made the early panoramas so sensational was the strong feeling of movement, through the clever use of light and sound effects and changing tableaus.

The panoramas presented the urban public, especially those who never had the chance to travel widely, with a chance of viewing some of the world's most awe-inspiring sceneries. They brought the wilderness into the city, like the three-mile-long moving panorama of Niagara, con-sisting of a hundred different views, which toured the United States dur-ing the 1850s. The famous German geographer Alexander Humboldt stressed the didactic importance of the panorama in this era. The feeling of being transported elsewhere was made possible because the spectator was enclosed "within a magic circle, and wholly removed from all dis-turbing influences of reality."[7]

The technology of panoramas became more and more sophisticated in producing what we nowadays would call "the virtual reality effect," and by the end of the century it fittingly became a mixed medium, using the novel techniques of the cinema. And the interest in panoramas reor-ganized tourist topography. To search out a panoramic view in nature you had to aim for elevated positions and open vistas. A special result of this was the nineteenth-century craze for sightseeing towers. A local mapping of these new structures in a popular Swedish tourist region to-ward the end of the nineteenth century gives an impression of booming oil fields—wooden tower structures everywhere.[8] All over the sightsee-ing world were new paths, leading to panoramic viewpoints on cliffs and hilltops. The quest for breathtaking sceneries brought new elements of focus and framing to sightseeing. The arduous climb became a means to an end: you were in transit, getting ready to take in the panorama, which lay waiting up there as a reward. Then you would find out whether the scenic moment was worth the climb.

The elevated position had several effects. First of all it could amplify the sublime feeling of the mightiness of Nature and the insignificance of human beings. Looking down on the Hudson valley from the Mountain House in the Catskills, one observer remarked in 1846:

> Crawling far below, man is but an atom, hardly visible . . . a fashionable lady's hat and feathers dwindles in the distance to the size of a mush-room.[9]

There was also a feeling of control, with the world at your feet, combined with the dizziness of the height. The landscape had the power to take your breath away, but at the same time there was a feeling of empower-ment. The panoramic gaze was part of a new technique of vision, which underlined the observer's detachment from the landscape: looking in, from an outside position. A sweeping glance set the landscape in motion in front of you, at a pace you controlled.

On board steamboats and trains travelers learned to handle movement and landscape in new ways. The accelerating speed at which the land-scape passed called for new modes of perception. Early handbooks on railway travel pointed out that you could avoid dizziness or sudden in-dispositions by avoiding traveling backwards and by not looking out of the window. If you did look out, you should make sure to fix your gaze on distant objects, like the sky or the horizon. You should also refrain from reading in order not to damage your eyes and nervous system. And it was advisable to close your eyes on entering a tunnel, in order not to expose the optic nerves to strong contrasts between light and dark.

Figure 7. The quest for panoramas led to the building of sightseeing towers all over the tourist world. Here the Sunday excursionists pose before one of the many towers built in the tourist province of Dalecarlia in Sweden. The man who built this tower also started the first local ethnographic museum in 1897 and scanned nature as well as farmhouse attics in search of attractive objects. (Photo Anders Jones, Leksands Lokalhistoriska Arkiv)

Two Swedish women who traveled on "a steam wagon" in Germany in 1846 had very different reactions. One of them complained because the train wasn't fast enough. She had heard rumors that you wouldn't even be able to see the landscape. Her companion, on the other hand, became dizzy and nauseated as the scenery danced by and stated: "It'll be a long time before I get used to this novel way of traveling, and I dread to repeat the experiment."[10] Different reactions also characterize the testimonies of three train-riding authors. August Strindberg had complaints much like his second compatriot's. The train's vibrations "shook my brains so thoroughly that I lost the ability to keep my thoughts in line."[11]

In the United States Ralph Waldo Emerson observed in 1834: "The very permanence of matter seems compromised and trees, fields, hills, hitherto esteemed symbols of stability, do absolutely dance by you." But only some years later the novelty effect had disappeared for him: "The towns through which I pass between Philadelphia and New York make no distinct impressions. They are like pictures on a wall."[12]

The Dane Hans Christian Andersen was much more enthusiastic. His first rail travel in 1840 was a fairytale experience:

> Ah, the greatness of this innovation! You feel powerful as an ancient magician! We put our magic horse in front of the cars and space disappears; we fly like clouds in a storm, as the migratory birds; our wild horse neighs and snorts, the steam mounts from its nostrils.[13]

The making of the railway panorama included not only a distancing effect but also the use of cinemalike metaphors to describe this experience.[14] All over the world railway companies themselves started to play on the theme of scenicruising by developing the tradition of scenic posters, which is still with us. Panoramas of distant landscapes crowded the train stations, and later on many companies used landscape photos as a preferred form of decoration in their railway cars, thus underlining this link between the rails and the scenic. Wherever you looked, out of the window, inside the car, or on the platform, there were wonderful landscapes meeting your eye.

Many shared Andersen's sensation of space and time being reorganized in drastic ways. Wolfgang Schivelbusch analyzes this aspect in his classic study of pioneer rail travel. First of all it was the feeling of traveling *outside* the landscape. As the velocity dissolved the foreground, the landscape became more distant, and in some ways more unreal. The homogeneous and straight movement of the railway made it seem pure movement, cut loose from the landscape it traveled through.[15] In this way railway travel could also fade into mere transport, a necessary but tedious interlude in transit between the interesting tourist sites.

The restlessness produced a new kind of boredom. As travel shifted into an exact amount of time between two locations, you started to glance at your watch. The standardized journey created a new economy of time, but also a monotony with the thump of the rail joints or the even breath of the steam engine at sea. A traveler en route for Stockholm in 1842 complained of growing dull and apathetic. "Man turns into a machine—this is what you learn by travel on board a steamship."[16]

As travelers tired of looking out the windows, they dismissed the early warnings against reading on trains. Train-riding was now meant for reading, as an antidote to the boredom of travel. In discussing what in England came to be called railway literature, booksellers and critics linked easy reading and easy travel. People sped through this new popular literature, which was marketed at railway stations with the same speed as the landscape passed. A shallow and stressful mode of reading was the result, the critics argued.[17]

Shallowness was also a metaphor used by critics to describe sightseeing from the train. The speed flattened the landscape, made it two-dimensional. The fact that so many tourists chose to be moved passively through (and by) the landscape developed a new urge for movement, a rediscovery of walking.

LEARNING TO WALK

If you look for ways of moving your feet under the heading "walk" you will find that the *Bloomsbury Thesaurus* turns almost lyrical:

> march, stride, tramp, lope, tread, trip, amble, jog, stroll, saunter, shuffle, waddle, dance, leap, toddle, patter, potter, strut, stagger, mince, stalk,

run, gallop, hare, fly, dash, dart, roll, cruise, freewheel, coast, trundle, taxi, chug, stream, travel, roam, wander, drift, stray, shift, dodge, duck, weave, tack, manoeuvre . . .

Most of these modes of walking are not interchangeable. They have or have had their specific time and place, and they have often developed in contrast to each other. They tend to have a history of both gendering and class.[18] In different contexts we can observe how various forms of movement replace or combine and shade into one another. Tourism has been one important arena for experiments with different peripatetic styles. Not only did certain ways of walking belong to the tourist mode of movement, tourists also learned to walk differently in changing situations and settings. If the urban *flâneur* was the (very male) culture hero of the late nineteenth century, the early part of the century saw a romantic cult of rural walking.

One of the crucial questions in the distinction-ridden world of Jane Austen's heroines is: do you have access to a carriage or not? But as Ann D. Wallace points out, they challenge this social need for respectable transport. Jane Austen's heroines start to walk, not because they are forced to, but because they enjoy it.[19]

Wallace analyzes the early history of the literary and tourist cult of walking in Britain, an interest she links to changes in transport technologies, in landscape use, and in aesthetics. In eighteenth-century Britain, as in Sweden, walking was not for the propertied classes. It was a means of locomotion for the poor, the roving itinerants, and the working class. It had all sorts of bad connotations. Wallace sees the improvement of the British road system in the late eighteenth century as important in redefining the nature of walking. Traveling became both faster and more reliable, adding the idea of timetables to the tourist's experience. The development of steamboats and later railways accelerated this change. When the choice of several modes of transport became available, walking took on a new aura. It became a sensual way of moving through the landscape, a way of uniting body and mind, of getting closer both to nature and to rural culture, a way of finding yourself. Now comes the critique of those tourists who are just hurrying from sight to sight, without realizing that it is the actual travel, the movement, that is the great and important experience. The German guidebook producer Karl Baedeker liked to use the phrase *sich (etwas) erwandern*—to get something out of walking—to describe the enriched sense of experience walking gave the traveler.[20]

The wind in your face, the feel of the ground you tread, the exhilaration of working your way forward and the incipient tiredness of your limbs—all these sensations produce the true traveler rather than the tourist. In this early cult of walking, from the end of the eighteenth century onwards, the walker was a modern and open person, not just a parcel that allowed itself to be transported between tourist sights. Mr. Plumptre was one of these pioneers. Not only did he emphasize that his travel journal was of a "pedestrian tour," but he also carried a pedometer in his pocket to record the many miles walked.[21]

The interest in walking was also related to the new forms of landscape patriotism in the early nineteenth century. Roving the countryside, you came in contact with the real folk—you could "walk yourself Swedish," as the author Carl Jonas Love Almqvist put it.[22] Walking in many ways became a mode of transport for intellectuals and artists. Another great propagandist for walking, Henry David Thoreau, stressed how it could set the mind free, open up space for serious thinking and reflection.[23]

Roving the countryside was to develop into a mass movement, albeit with striking national differences. An 1820 guidebook on continental travel noted that walking had become "a mode so commonly adopted that the foot passenger is as well received, even at the best inns, as if he came in a splendid equipage."[24] This mass movement demanded new infrastructures, as, for example, in the institutionalization of the weekend walk in the forest, which owed a great deal to the dynamic tourist entrepreneur Claude François Denecourt, a veteran of Napoleon's army.[25] During the 1830s Denecourt transformed the king's forests around Fontainebleau outside Paris into a popular destination. He was inspired by the romantic cult of the woods, but his ambition was to make this wilderness user-friendly. Thus he developed the nature walk.

With the help of a can of blue paint he produced a system of arrows, domesticating the forest that had previously been seen as impenetrable and inhospitable for the urban visitor. In 1837 he could offer visitors a number of *promenades solitaires.* The blue arrows led you along rambling paths, which were equipped at suitable distances with attractive sights, a beautiful view, a cave, a historic oak tree, or just an interesting rock. This was something far more adventurous than the park promenades, and thanks to the newly established railway between Paris and Lyons, a rapidly growing number of Parisians made the expedition to Fontainebleau, in order to walk eight to ten miles. Some of the pioneers were landscape painters, whom Denecourt provided with brochures on paintable views. As the number of tourists grew he had to produce more walks with blue arrows and more pamphlets with information on the walks, so that the visitors could experience the kind of solitude they expected of the forest.

Denecourt developed the kind of outdoor terrain that later came to be called rambling areas, a suitably wild forest, which could be explored with the help of a pocket guide. He managed to strike the balance between order and adventure for a Sunday outing—alone in the forest but not lost in the wild. A new art of walking had developed, and the forest ramble became an important urban pastime all over northern Europe. In Scandinavian settings it came to symbolize *the* harmless leisure activity. In personal advertisements of the twentieth century it became perhaps the most popular item of self-description together with "quiet evenings at home." An interest in "forest walks" signaled a normal, healthy, mainstream personality.

The countryside walk emerged as a pastime of urbanites and its choreography was further shaped by the arrival of the automobile. Personally, I am reminded of this every time the family goes through the weekend ritual of speeding the car through the urban spaces of transit out to the woods. Once we stop the car and open the car door our whole bodily disposition changes. We stretch our limbs, relax, and take in a deep breath of what we hope is fresh air, open up all our senses to the landscape that surrounds us. No longer are we passing through the landscape, we are *in* it. There is also a pleasing feel of a moral victory. We could be at the mall, but here we are like a real family, going for a real walk.

For some, the very existence of blue arrows or well ordered picnic areas made the country walk too tame an experience. New kinds of wilderness had to be explored.

IN SEARCH OF ADVENTURE

> I really love to be, like, out in the wild habitat,
> where you're totally away from mainstream soci-
> ety. It's just so simple and like real. Climbing is,
> how to call it, it's so natural. . . . I think life is too
> crazy sometimes, and it brings you back to your
> elemental life.
>
> *(nineteen-year-old Californian, female, rock climber)*

> I love the outdoors. Hiking in the mountains is
> probably the richest experience you can have.
> There you live the simple life, appreciate banal
> things like dry clothes and a good campsite. To
> sit on a mountain top and look out over the land-
> scape—that's life. Then I never think about
> stocks.
>
> *(middle-aged Swedish male, stockbroker)*

When Wolfgang Goethe was summoned in 1775 to teach the young Duke Carl August at the court in Weimar, he took his pupil on forest rambles. Together they camped by a fire and felt themselves temporarily free of the demands of society and civilization.[26] This Rousseauian experience of roughing it gave them a more total experience of being in nature, or rather being *one* with nature. Hiking and camping were to develop into dominant forms of tourist movement.

The pioneers of hiking were the mountaineers. The British, in their explorations of the Alps and the Norwegian mountains, led the development and formed the first Alpine club in 1857, followed by the Swiss and the Norwegians and then the French, the Americans, and the Swedes.[27] These Alpine clubs played a vital role in shaping both wilderness hikes and attitudes toward outdoor recreation, although they came to work in very different manners.

The case of Sweden illustrates this process. Many of the Swedish pioneers developed their taste for mountaineering in Norway but then started to look for "Sweden's Switzerland" in the mountains of northern

Sweden, which were becoming more accessible as the railways moved north. It is no coincidence that the Swedish Touring Club began in 1885, three years after the first rail connection between the capital and one of those northern mountain regions, and that most of the founders were male academics, united by their interest in hiking.

What they sought in the mountains was not only magnificent wilderness but also solitude and challenges. "Guide your course, like the eagle, towards the mountains: here can be found solitary, silent places where you can encounter yourself in peace," as one of the club founders put it.[28]

Mountain climbing, with its mixture of the romance of the wilds and the bourgeois morality of achievement and asceticism, seemed to them a superior way of experiencing nature. The mountains offered the chance of struggling against both internal and external nature. There was an elitist tendency in this outdoor fraternity. Soon the Norwegian tourist mountains seemed tame, dull. In the yearbook of the Swedish Touring Club for 1889 we read:

> Galdhöpiggen, the highest mountain in Norway and northern Europe, was hardly known to anyone in the 1850s. . . .
>
> Now, however, scarcely a beautiful summer day passes without the mountain being climbed by hordes of tourists, among them many women. Galdhöpiggen is at present regarded almost with scorn by any self-respecting mountaineer. It does not offer enough difficulties to overcome. It is too easy a conquest. It is demoralizing to struggle against such an opponent.[29]

Another Swedish mountain enthusiast later wrote of the tough ascent of the Kebnekaise peaks that the exertion to overcome them makes the goal twice as valuable (thus echoing the credo of Lieutenant Hall from Niagara): "a mountain that gives itself of its own free will is like a woman who shows no resistance."[30]

In this very masculine and international world of mountaineers, the wilderness is often gendered and represented through female (and rather Freudian) metaphors. Here is John Muir in Yosemite looking up at the sheer face of Half Dome:

Figure 8. Prospectus for walking tours, circa 1915. (Minnesota Historical Society, St. Paul)

I have gazed on Tissiack a thousand times—in days of solemn storms, and when her form shone divine with the jewels of winter, or was veiled in living clouds; I have heard her voice of winds, or snowy tuneful waters; yet never did her soul reveal itself more impressively than now. I hung about her skirts, lingering timidly, till the glaciers compelled me to push up the canyons.[31]

And here is C. L. Rawlins in the same American West more than a century later:

No one is married to a place who has not gotten a mouthful of food from it, picked or grown or hunted down. It is easy to buy and sell ground when you've never known its taste, singular and certain, never taken the hard brown nipple between your lips, rolled your tiny fists against the mountain breast, warmed to the flow of the earth's own milk, rough and rich.[32]

When women entered the arena, not as metaphors but alongside the hairy-chested mountaineers, the reactions were mixed, to say the least. Did women belong at all in the wilderness? When the geologist Clarence King in 1864 complained about visitors who used "cheap adjectives" to describe the sights at Inspiration Point in Yosemite, he lumped together women and "literary travelers"—those male tourists who had now come to represent an overeffeminate style.[33] Such actions and reactions reflect the use of wilderness as a territory in which to try out new gender roles. It became an arena of alterity, removed from the "artificialness of cities," the worries over money or careers: here life was simple, choices clear-cut, with the stillness and vastness of the mountainscapes providing a new space for meditation and transcendence.

In 1818 the New Hamsphire lawyer Estwick Ewans set out on a long winter tour in the wilderness, in search of, as he put it, "the *pleasure* of suffering, and the *novelty* of danger."[34] Later generations of mountaineers were testing themselves in the same manner, busy redefining the concept of maleness, and hardening themselves against what they saw as the too soft or emotional pose of the Romantic era. Behind the new heroic emphasis on hardship there was, however, a more complex reality, different strategies of making yourself "feel alive." The mountain world turned boys into men, but the experience could also turn men into boys, giving them an opportunity to be something more than just strong and silent. In 1873 a Norwegian complained about his fellow mountaineers, who just hurried along the trail. No, you should take time to sit down and enjoy the scenery, perhaps do a drawing, jump and dance for a while, then lie down in the sun and light a pipe and enjoy life.[35]

Against this background of a new male project, which also installed an uncertainty, a worry about being manly enough, the patronizing of women who wanted to take part in the world of mountaineering has a double edge: wouldn't they be a drag on camping tours and hikes? and wouldn't they devalue the adventure?[36] Another tension in the mountaineering world was the growing impact of mass tourism. In the yearbook of the Swedish Touring Club for 1895, a member of the Touring Club board wrote of the need to "raise the tourist spirit," which required "rejecting the coddled ease of the hotels and heading out into the wilderness." The author maintained that "it is this hearty and healthy enterprise, this love of nature in all its moods and changes, and of the adventurous life of the wilderness, this yearning for 'the blue unknown,' which is the tourist spirit." Another nature lover writes of those "who hear with revulsion the locomotive emitting its shrill whistle in regions where previously the timidest animals in the forest roved around in undisturbed tranquillity, and it is obvious that Necken drops his harp and the dryads take to flight at the first sight of a Baedeker."[37] He is part of an international debate, which has been perhaps most evident in American discussions about the uses and misuses of the wilderness.

WHO BELONGS IN THE OUTDOORS?

Soggy cartons float downstream among the air mattress riders. Tent cities choke the peaceful scene with cars, dust and smoke. Bears are seen only on nightly raids on garbage cans, where they compete with the raccoons for the privilege of dumping over the rubbish in search of food. Drunken or rowdy groups of teenagers, few of whose parents are within fifty miles, regularly terrorize their camping neighbors, keep hundreds awake all night, push cars into rivers and stop traffic on Stoneman

Bridge. Bicycles, motorcycles, cars, stores, gas stations, people, more cars and more people have taken over Yosemite valley.[38]

This ranger's report from the early 1960s has many parallels in the one-and-a-half-century debate about Yosemite as pleasure resort or wilderness. It generated great heat already in the 1860s and is still a recurrent theme in newspaper columns. The history of Yosemite seems like an endless struggle over the types of vacationers and kinds of outdoor recreation that should coexist in the same setting. If we search for an arena where different approaches to and styles of outdoor recreation are tried out and confronted, I think it would be difficult to find a more striking case.

In the 1870s the debate turned on a critique of the wealthy Easterners, who visited the valley as pampered sightseers and demanded every modern convenience, touring the valley by horse and carriage. "Occasionally one sees them devouring their guidebooks and checking off the sights as they whirl by, so that they will be sure not to miss anything or see anything twice." One gentleman even brought his stenographer along to take down his account of the day's sightseeing.[39] John Muir wrote a letter to his friend denouncing the new tourists, but added that most of them floated "slowly about the *bottom* of the valley as harmless scum collecting in hotels and saloon eddies." They did not contaminate the real wilderness.[40]

The debate about lifestyles continued and, seen in another perspective, Yosemite became one of the great training grounds for campers and hikers, who could choose between different levels of outdoor hardships. The early campers were usually quite well-to-do, as camping expeditions still demanded a substantial investment in gear. By the turn of the century organized tent camps opened up a cheaper alternative that became extremely popular, institutionalizing a number of important features of American camping life, not least the campfire evenings and sing-alongs, which were a great success. They were hardly established when the first laments of their demise were heard in the 1930s: one ranger noted that people went "with modern social trends, which do not give much emphasis to self-entertainment in the evening or any other time."[41]

In the same period another observer looked over the valley and saw little more than "long stretches of wide road, innumerable buildings, hotels, automobiles, and parking places. . . . Yosemite was no longer a
shrine but a resort. . . . Even the grizzly bears fed under electric light at
government expense."[42]

The great change in Yosemite, as in most other American tourist areas,
came with the advent of the car, which transformed tourist behavior. It
led to an enormous expansion of camping, and the institution of auto
camping became a central part of American vacations. In 1894 there were
four registered cars in the country, and in 1896 Mr. Barnum proudly had
the horseless carriage Duryea parading down many American Main
Streets among elephants and camels, a great attraction. But by 1915 there
were two and a half million cars in America.[43] They were moving rapidly
from tourist sight to tourist tool.

LIBERATING SPEED

Some sunny Sunday very soon, just drive an Overland up to your
door—tell the family to hurry the packing and get aboard—and be off
with smiles down the nearest road—free, loose, and happy—bound for
green wonderlands.

This 1929 advertisement from the Saturday Evening Post is quoted in the
classic sociological study of Middletown, a study that captures the excitement the car brought to American urban life and leisure. In the Sunday school class the children are asked what kinds of temptations we are
facing that Jesus never faced, and one of the children enthusiastically answers "Speed!" Outside there are ads for a local show of auto-polo: "It's
motor insanity—too fast for the movies."[44]

The making of a car society was, at least in the beginning, very much
related to ideas of freedom, just like the wilderness project, but it was a
different conceptualization of freedom, or as Ford marketed its new 1930
model in Sweden: "It is a car for speed and freedom, a car for independent, level-headed youth." The steam engine had collectivized travel,
now the car offered a new individualism and a freedom to go (almost)

wherever you fancied. The old fantasy of motion could now become an individual experience of the self-moved mover, the *auto-mobile*.[45] By a light pressure on the accelerator, you became the master of speed, feeling each extra mile in the vibrations of the car and the wind in your face. Going for a drive was an adventure—just hitting the road, exploring new settings. Freedom and speed went together, or as an enthusiastic Swedish university professor on vacation put it in 1924:

> It is a wonderful feeling of power and freedom you experience in the strong, whizzing car. You become totally independent, master of time and space, there are no distances to speak of, every place that turns up at the horizon can be reached in a couple of minutes, the world lies open for us, littered with gas stations, and the air resistance just refreshes us, brings the blood to our cheeks, yes, carries us.[46]

There was a new intoxication of speed. "To possess a car is to become possessed of a desire to go far afield," wrote an American observer in 1903.[47] How far can you get in an hour or a day? In 1930 an American sociologist was told by an auto-camp owner in Oregon that most postcards mailed for customers reported the miles driven that day or anticipated for the next, and "very seldom is any mention made of scenery passed through. They did not see it, traveling 40 to 50 miles per hour."[48] A new restlessness materialized, as drivers faced new decisions about when and where to stop. "Be your own gypsy . . . abandon all rules and directions," as one of the new guidebooks put it.[49]

In 1934 another Swedish tourist pointed out that motoring gave rise to new experiences of beauty:

> A modern person traveling in a car on a newly laid concrete road can also be seized by the beauty of the landscape through which he passes. Why, the very speed itself, the swift way of traveling, contains the potential for new and powerful impressions of beauty. You drive through a large forest. It takes less than an hour to get through it. If you had traveled the same road on foot it might have taken two days. But that brief time has in a mysterious way reinforced the impression of the depth and mightiness of this forest. Distance is shortened, yet it grows! Your ideas of the proportions of place grow in clarity, your feeling for this grows in strength. The quick journey constantly opens new perspectives, you

have large, wide views, but in all this variation the sense of distance lies vibrating like an undertone. You fly through space, perhaps also sometimes through time.[50]

The car thus fostered new modes of landscape perceptions and sensualities. The French theorist of speed Paul Virilio has called the automobile "a landscape simulator," and it is striking how speeding through a landscape comes to be described in terms of *non*-movement.[51] From the inside of the car you watch the landscape rolling by, as a pioneer motorist put it in 1912, rather like a back-projection in a movie studio.[52] The parallel development of two new technologies, the automobile and the moving picture, became interlinked in many ways.

As driving speed increased and freeways were built, driving took on new qualities. When John Steinbeck decided to take the vacation of his life and drove across the American continent in 1961, he reflected on the ways in which driving produced an arena for daydreaming, as driving techniques are "buried in a machine-like unconscious."[53] On the road thoughts travel fast and far away, and the soft vibrations of the road help to create a trance-like feeling. Later on the innovation of cruise control produced even more day-dreaming at the speed of 55 miles an hour.

The development of car radios and later cassette decks furthered this special atmosphere, setting music both to the passing scenery and to the daydreaming mood. The fast lane of the freeway thus turned into a space for meditation and roving minds, coupled with new types of visions made possible by General Motors' introduction of the panorama window in 1951.

TIN-CAN TOURISTS

A landscape of transit developed as more and more people hit the road—for a Sunday outing or a summer vacation. Traditional hotels and boardinghouses found themselves in fierce competition with a new kind of stopover: tourist camps and cabins, motor homes and courts. Their names signaled a new world of tempo, casual living, and improvised fun, so different from the stuffy old hotels: Kozy Kabin Kamp, Shady Rest Motel, Wigwam Villages, Swing-Inn-Cabins, Follow the Swallows Tourist Camp, Moonlight Court, Shangrila, Tour-Rest Motel. . . . For the "motor-hoboes," the early auto-campers of the 1920s, this was indeed the golden age:

> We were vagabonds then—anyone who had a car. And I was lucky because I worked damn hard for mine. There was a fellowship on the road, all types of people we'd meet. They were wonderful—from all walks of life. I made some swell friends. We all made our tents, and cooked and relaxed. I felt like a pioneer, we were all neighbors.[54]

Speed totally reorganized the tourist landscape, especially in countries with vast distances like the United States and Sweden. Suddenly new territories were opened to weekend tourism.

In Yosemite 65 percent of the visitors were coming in private cars by 1922, which meant that a much wider range of middle-class visitors could afford to go. They arrived overloaded with camping gear. The carrying capacity of the car opened up totally new standards of camping and gave a flying start to the American industry of outdoor equipment.[55] A California camping veteran complained that, as camping had ceased to be aristocratic and exclusive, "it becomes more and more difficult to find an exclusive place in which to practice it."[56] But this was just the beginning.

The 1930s saw the arrival of the new technology of trailers. *Popular Mechanics* enthusiastically predicted that trailering would become so much in vogue that America would be turned into a nation of nomads, in which half the population would live in rolling homes.[57] It was an optimistic guess, but by 1937 there were already about 100,000 trailers on the road, and trailer camps were established all over the United States.[58]

Auto camping, its fans believed, was an institution that would pull America together. The campground became an icon of democratic society. Here people from different walks of life and from different corners of the nation could meet on equal terms, but the car also produced new patterns of segregation and privatization. In the new motel you drove your car directly to the door of your room or cabin, there was no

Figure 9. Wigwam Village in Kentucky was one of the new auto camps of the 1930s, which played on the theme of romancing the nomadic. (Photo Library of Congress)

communal life in the lobby, as in the old hotels with their elaborate public spaces. For the middle class the car also became a means to search out
new territories, "unspoiled by mass tourism," a mass tourism that was
made possible not only by the car but also by the increased frequency of
paid vacations in the 1920s.[59] "Vacations in 1890?" said one Middle-
towner in 1929, "Why, the word wasn't even in the dictionary!" In pre-
automobile Middletown vacations would for most people be the rare
Sunday outing with horse and carriage or a train excursion to Chicago.[60]
With their own car, many working-class families could start to arrange
short vacation trips, sleeping in the car or in tents. Vacations were not
something you had to save up for or plan long in advance, and in your
private car you didn't have to put up any appearances.

America became *the* camping nation of the world. By international
standards mass driving and auto camping came much later to Europe,
where it had its breakthrough in the fifties and sixties.[61] On both sides of
the Atlantic the automobile made tourism more mobile and more family-
oriented. Auto camping not only united the nation but pulled families
together too, or as a middle-class Middletown woman put it: "I never
feel as close to my family as when we are all together in the car."[62] Fifty
years later a Swedish ethnographer described the process in this way:

> The car is a family pack, a preserving jar for five people's relations with
> one another. The car is an exercise in micronationalism. The family is na-
> tionalized by the thin sheet of steel that forms its boundary, by the
> speed, by the dangerous countries on the other side of the windshield.
> Everything is moving except us. We cannot move away from but just
> along with one another. We are a tiny state with borders, laws, ene-
> mies.[63]

Learning to be a tourist, experiencing exotic places and strange foods
often occurred within the framework of "the family vacation" and the
family car. This mode of traveling became an instruction in how to be a
family. The close living, the common project of vacationing developed
new forms of togetherness as well as tensions, which made the family
stand out much more clearly in the social landscape. A British writer remembers his childhood motoring holidays in France, all the strange food

and the changed habits: "I was nervous about the language, the sleeping arrangements, the hotels. The absorbed tensions of a family holiday played on me. I was not happy, to put the matter simply."[64]

Family camping was supposed to ease up the traditional division of labor between the sexes. With the husband at the wheel, anxious to demonstrate that he had full control of the situation as he drove the family into the unknown, the result was the reverse. The family car could become a claustrophobic space of conflicts. A Norwegian driver remembers his first family vacation:

> Unpack and fix dinner, nag the kids, scold and get mad when they turn nasty after sitting in the car too long or nearly getting run over. In the heaviest traffic the wife fell asleep in the front seat. The driver was nervous and under stress in the traffic and out of balance in his words and expressions. The result could be hours-long silence between the spouses, until one of the children let out a howl when they began to fight in the back of the fine new car.[65]

In the new camping life the man's barbecue apron was supposed to symbolize a new gender flexibility. In 1922 Mac's Auto Camp in Santa Cruz presented itself as the place "where the wife takes her ease and where hubby does the baby's wash." Wishful thinking. Family leisure still meant woman's work. A few years later an immigrant woman interviewed in an auto camp put it like this: "Dot kemping. Dot ain't no holiday for us womans. It's yoost vash and cook yoost like de vay ve do it at home. Yoost de same."[66]

HOW WILD IS WILD?

With the arrival of the car, concepts of campsites and campers became highly complex, especially as motorized camping exploded in the 1960s and 1970s; more so in the United States than anywhere else, where it embraced close to 50 million campers by the 1980s. Now a campground could be anything from a clearing in the forests to the over 500 campground towns all over America, of which the largest had 3,500 rental sites.[67]

This expansion also destabilized the ideas about camping. What is a campsite? A fascinating insight into the problems of defining the wilderness experience is offered by a *United States Forest Service Manual* from the late 1970s, which tries to classify five different types of camping sites in the national parks, using the classic continuum from "primitive to modern."[68]

Each category has a commentary on the recreational experiences associated with it. The most developed modern site, which has easy access by high-speed roads, landscaping with mowed lawns and clipped bushes, and conveniences like electrical hookups, laundry, showers, and flush toilets, is designed to "satisfy the urbanite's need for compensating experiences and relative solitude," but "in a secure situation, where ample provision is made for his personal comfort and he will not be called upon to use underdeveloped skills." From there we move on to settings in which the monitoring of campers is more "inconspicuous." Security is still there but "subtle enough to leave the taste of adventure." By now we are moving toward the two categories "primitive" and "secondary primitive," where the visitor should not sense any regimentation, although the Forest Service is still there behind the trees: "minimum controls are subtle." This brochure may read like a Big-Brother monitoring of camping life, but it should rather be seen as part of the ongoing balancing act between marketing security and adventure in the tourist industry.

In a similar way, the never-ending debates on the uses and misuses of places like Yosemite illustrate Roderick Nash's point that wilderness is not a territory but a state of mind.[69] Increasingly the opposite of wild becomes "mild" or "soft." What constitutes an outdoor adventure? Is "soft primitivism" a derogatory label or a balance to aim for?[70] How much of the experience draws on roughing it? Behind these heated arguments are also the increased confrontations between different leisure ideals and routines as the social spectrum of tourists has broadened. The early hikers and mountaineers came from a very narrow segment of society.

It would be wrong to reduce this debate to a devolutionary lament over the destruction of the naturalness of the primitive. Rather, any domestication of the wild sets up its own countermovement. The battle lines constantly shift within discussions of what would enhance or diminish the greatness of the outdoors: mountaineering or rock-climbing, campfires or picnic areas, fishing or golf, light-weight tents or RVs, trekking ponies or mountain bikes, hang gliders or snowmobiles, kayaking or rafting?

The increased pressure on wilderness areas and national parks, especially in the United States, has led to systems of restricted entry and advance reservations, which in themselves have intensified the debate about who and what belongs in the outdoors. Perhaps the most striking example of this is the growth of whitewater rafting. This tourist mode of transport was virtually nonexistent before the 1960s but rapidly developed into a major form of adventure trip, forcing the authorities to step in:

> The morning sun, already burning an 80° day, tops a cliff cut with fine strata of red rock and broken at its foot by emerald cottonwoods and the startling bronze of a river. I don a khaki uniform shirt, shorts, 97-cent hot pink thongs and, clipboard in hand, walk from the trailer to a boat ramp plunked down in nearly a million acres of uninhabited desert. . . .
>
> Officially, I am here to have my peace disturbed. Floaters must have a permit to run this stretch of river in southern Utah. . . . Cheerfully I sign the permit of the outfitter who specializes in theme river trips—stress-management seminars, outings for crystal fondlers or fingernail technicians from East Jesus, New Jersey, overcoming, at last, their irrational fear of Nature. Today's load is priests troubled by lapsed faith—pale, anxious, overweight fellows in the early stages of heatstroke.[71]

This example of a day's work organizing "today's recreational flotsam down the river" is precisely the situation Joseph L. Sax's book *Mountains Without Handrails: Reflections on the National Parks* from 1980 is fighting. It is a text which is an attempt to reflect on wilderness management, but also an example of the cultural ambiguities and contradictions that such an attempt carries with it.

As the author tries to develop a scheme of monitoring whitewater rafting in the Colorado River of the Grand Canyon, he is invariably drawn into the tricky field of defining what is a rich or shallow wilderness experience. A 1996 advertisement for *Whitewater Voyages* is probably the kind of text he most objects to:

> 20 wonderful runs from mild to wild
>
> Gourmet camp cuisine—Skilled, caring guides
>
> State-of-the-art equipment.[72]

Sax argues that those who just want what he calls a "resort experience," choosing the "mild" package tours with raft crews who take care of everything from the navigation to gourmet cooking and high-tech toilet facilities, should step back and leave the river to those who are more serious rafters. What these resorters will get is just a "pale illusion" of adventure anyway. Package wilderness tours serve, for him, "to dull the very qualities of personal engagement that give the river experience authenticity."[73] The serious rafters need to have freedom of movement and pace and not be rushed on by other groups behind them, in order for them to "experience the canyon intensely."

Behind his argument we again find the classic tension between adventure and security, here nailed down into details about being able to cook your own meals and fight your own snakes, but also getting bogged down in questions about whether outboard motors are all right or only oars should be allowed, what kinds of guides you should be able to bring along, how much help they should give.

Texts like these wrestle with the more general problem of what constitutes a good tourist experience. What much of this debate misses is the risk of projecting your own cultural standards onto those of others. The Park Services or firms marketing adventure tours or the Sierra Club may monitor the wilderness experience in great detail, but it is a hard act to control or routinize. In moving out in the landscape, on foot, by bike, train, or car, you set off a complex reaction. Experiences are never just "collecting sights" or "passing through attractions." The wilderness project cannot be staged or managed, because the very conceptualization of the wild remains extremely personal and subjective. "Out there" you might make discoveries that nobody has anticipated, least of all yourself.

Wilderness hikes and motorized camping may seem diametrically opposite ideas about tourist life. "To the auto camper distance lends enchantment; to the true wilderness lover, wilderness creates the mystic influence," wrote a commentator in *American Forest* in 1926.[74] Both categories, however, developed out of a linking of freedom and movement, the freedom of entering the wide open spaces. The organization and practice of this freedom are, on the other hand, quite different. The wilderness offers many different "freedoms from" and "freedoms to." For some it is the freedom from other tourists or the trappings of urban civilization, for others it is the freedom to go as you please, or as a Swedish trailer pioneer put it in 1949: "Next week we will stay in a different place, meet new people, see new waters, new landscapes—but still from the same window. We are nomads, but we are still settled. We are totally independent."[75]

In the move of returning to nature, a strong modernist credo of propelling yourself, the car, or the whole family into the future was also evident. Camping started as a military technology, but its modern form as a vacation art developed mainly in the United States. It was exported through many different channels over the globe. In Britain it was introduced by the one-man institution T. H. Holding, who had experienced the delights of American camping out West in 1853. Touring England to lecture on the subject of "Muscular Christianity," he preached the gospel of living under canvas, as well as canoeing, which he had learned in Canada, and wrote the British outdoor bible *The Camper's Handbook* in 1908.[76] In the twentieth century camping and hiking became global pastimes, two important additions to the list of tourist forms of locomotion.

MOVING BODIES, ROVING MINDS

The history of tourism slips easily into the grand narrative of improved mobility and quicker transport, but new infrastructures like railways and roads did not simply create new tourist demands, they were also the result of them. Their reciprocal effects are striking, for example, in the very uneven development of motorized tourism in the Western world.

When coastal New England states made considerable road investments at the end of the nineteenth century to attract tourists, these were expected to arrive on bikes, but the American bicycle craze was short-lived. The new roads were taken over by the "motor-hoboes." In Europe the bicycle tour remained a very popular vacation form into the 1950s, for all those who could not afford a car. (In 1930 one Swede in six owned a bicycle, but only one in sixty a car.) A whole infrastructure of hostels, scenic routes, and guidebooks developed around this tourist movement.

The great boom in Swedish car ownership during the 1950s and 1960s, on the other hand, was not based so much on commuting to work as on a desire for leisure travel. Most people still lived close to work or could use a well-developed system of public transportation. It was the idea of a family car for outings and vacations that was seen as the great attraction.

Any new technology of movement reorganizes earlier ones, as we have seen. Steam created a longing for walking, the collectivity of the train journey made the automobile into symbol of the return of individual adventure and exploration, a much more sensual technology in which the speed was felt as the wind against the face and the vibrations of the surface. Later on the smooth pace of the freeways opened up a new mode of stillness, meditation, and daydreaming. Some forms of transport are trivialized into transit experiences: you can't wait to get out of the plane or the car to start traveling. Speed may produce an exhilarating feeling of adventure but can also in the long run create a longing for slowness. Old transport technologies are rejuvenated as the new ones turn into routine or monotony. Increased travel comfort can also be experienced as pampering or sheltering.

Exploring these different modes, from strolling, walking, rambling, hiking, and trekking to floating, driving, or speeding through the landscape, it is obvious that we need to discuss the ways in which movement, nonmovement, and experience go together. The cult of the sublime and the panorama made an important connection between motion and emotion. The strong feelings even set your body working, sending a shiver down the spine or making your limbs tremble. The raging storm of the first Eidophusikon or the back-projection illusion of the train and

Figure 10. The car symbolized individual freedom, but the new tourist trails were heavily dependent on state and federal investments in road
improvements. (The Adirondack Museum Library, Blue Lake, N.Y.)

the car explore these connections of moving through a landscape and being moved by the experience. Speed could be experienced as tingling restlessness.

The tourist desire for movement could also invest immovable structures, sightseeing towers, hotel porches, motels with a nomadic aura. "Every journey should be uplifting. Even after you've landed" was the 1997 motto of Hyatt, assuring their visitors that "new horizons" were all over their hotels and resorts:

> Unique restaurants in the sky where you can dine with sparkling cities at your feet. Meeting rooms that free your imagination by opening to grand panoramas. And lobbies that greet you with spectacular architecture and dramatic vistas.[77]

Such an advertisement reads rather like the history of sightseeing but also poses the question of the next chapter: how do moving bodies and roving minds interplay in different situations? How do tourist technologies of movement and representation influence the flight of the mind in different historical and cultural settings? Cyril Connolly put it this way:

> How much of a holiday is spent lying gasping on one's back, in planes, trains, cabins, beaches, and hotel bedrooms, the guidebook held aloft like an awning? We really travel twice—as a physical object resembling a mummy or small wardrobe trunk which is shuttled about at considerable expense; and as a mind married to a *Guide Bleu*, always reading about the last place or the next one.[78]

Telling Stories

We were waiting for our baggage, forming the kind of uneasy collectivity that marks any charter flight. As soon as the conveyor belt spat out our bags, we would disperse to the various hotels along the coasts of Cyprus, but now we glanced surreptitiously at the other families. When the conveyor belt started with a sudden pull, I heard a man next to me talking loudly to himself. Turning around I saw him eagerly filming the suitcases as they appeared on the belt, making a running commentary on the scene into the camcorder's microphone. It seemed a strange choice of subject. It was not until I saw him a week later as we gathered at the airport for the return flight that I understood what he was doing. Here he was again, directing the family as they disembarked from the bus. He was, of course, producing a vacation video complete with opening scene and happy ending, as well as a running commentary.

Two centuries separate this Cyprus tourist family from Mr. Plumptre. They operate within very different technological infrastructures of travel, sightseeing, and documentation. The modern family's knickknacks include not only a VCR but Walkmans to turn Cypriotic beaches or sceneries into soundscapes, and a Polaroid camera for instant snapshots. On their return home their credit card statements will help the family retrace their itineraries through different sights, restaurants, and shops. On the surface they inhabit a radically different tourist world from Mr. Plumptre's, but in some ways they all travel within the same mindscape of modern tourism. They share the urge to narrate, to depict, to memorize, and communicate.

Down in the basement I find an old holiday album, which I produced as a twelve-year-old. It describes a family trip across Sweden and starts with a pasted-in map where the route is carefully drawn. Snapshots, admission tickets, hotel labels, and picture postcards document each step, along with the author's running commentary. It documents a vacation *and* shows the project "our family," an institution that became very visible during those summer months of intensive interaction. Many children take vacations very seriously, and albums like these tell the story of learning to be a tourist.

I don't think I ever made another album like that, but my basement is full of relics and remnants of a tourist life. There are a few dusty boxes of slides and thirty reels of eight-millimeter film from the 1960s. Most of the slides are of landscapes, carefully selected and situated, while the moving pictures endlessly emphasize just this: movement. People always wave and clown around on these early reels. From later stages of my tourist career there are a few videotapes and box after box of snapshots in color, patiently waiting for placement in nice holiday albums—it'll never happen, though. A few early souvenirs have also made the downwardly mobile trip from the living room into the collection of basement junk.

There are many basements or attics like mine all over the tourist world. A constant theme in tourist jokes is the insatiable desire to share vacation memories with others—all those terrible winter evenings of enforced slide shows, leafing through friends' albums or sitting through never-ending family videos. There is even more ironizing over how Mr. and Ms. Tourists' urge to document their own vacations end up being of no use, all those forgotten albums or videos never shown. The argument often runs thus: people are so obsessed by recording and documenting that they don't have time to experience what they see. When Germaine Greer travels on a group tour through China, she never stops complaining about her fellow passengers on the train. She calls them "the packages" and describes them as having one eye glued to the camcorder's sight and the other fixed on the guidebook as the fabulous Chinese landscape rolls by.[1]

If Mr. Plumptre had put away his Claude-glass and the Cyprus tourist had let his camcorder stay in the bag, could they have devoted their energy to enjoying the landscape? Against the "must" of documentation they had to weigh the "must" of uncluttered attention. Tourist life is as always filled with unwritten rules and conflicting notions of the suitable. Those tourists who instead decide to buy the ready-made holiday videos of the sightseeing trip in Paris or the helicopter tour of Hawaii risk another kind of criticism. If you insist on bringing a holiday video home, it should at least be one *you* made.

The critique of the urge to document misses an important point. The pleasure may not be in gathering up mementos to display next winter but just in creating them: letting the video roll, jotting down a few lines on the back of a postcard, keeping a travel diary, clicking through a roll of Kodachrome. However much energy goes into the production of these narratives and whatever their fate, producing them was an experience in its own right.

Viewed from this angle, the phenomenon of tourist narratives over the last two centuries includes a range of artistic creativity that in other situations would be unthinkable. Here is an arena where nonartists and nonauthors do not hesitate to try their hand at producing a watercolor, a photo narrative, a travel diary, a video documentary, or a collage of shells or dried flowers. Here you may become your own director, scriptwriter, or scenographer.

In this history of representations there is a constant interaction between the tourist amateur and the professionals of the trade: travel writers, poets, landscape painters, filmmakers, and *National Geographic* photographers. The forms of this interaction and the genres emanating from it shift constantly as reproductive technologies or trends emerge or wear out, setting up hierarchies in modes of representation that label some souvenirs tacky or give them new life as kitsch. A new technology of watercolor sketching, easy to carry along and very suitable for amateur gentlemen, allows pioneer tourists to dabble a bit in art. The snapshot trivializes the scenic landscape photograph, the oil-painted sunset turns into a picture postcard. The photo album replaces the sketch book and in turn yields to the video library. Certain forms of representations have staying power, others disappear quickly, and still others make a comeback.

VISUALIZATIONS

The picturesque, the sublime, and the panoramic framed the landscape and offered different modes for taking it in. They all contributed their own elements of fixing, delineating, and organizing an eventful situation, a moment of vision. They produced specific forms and conceptual frameworks for communicating feelings and experiences. Many of the adjectives we still use to describe tourist events and sights belong to a vocabulary developed in these traditions. In travel advertisements this continuity is striking. Here roads still tend to be winding, forests lush, brooks babbling, villages sleepy, views from the hotel breathtaking.

In art history the picturesque stands between classical and romantic painting. In tourism it is something else. In his reading of the *Guide Bleu* Roland Barthes mused over the diluted definition of the picturesque, which "is found any time the ground is uneven."[2] As a concept or rather as a cultural articulation of tourist sights and sensibilities, the picturesque has been a survivor, often ridiculed and endlessly redefined, but it is still with us. We can follow its travels over two centuries and its adjustments to new settings, for example, when it crossed the Atlantic. We saw how the standards of the picturesque changed in the confrontation with the American landscape, as "the American sublime" came to represent the cult of technological wonders and breath-taking natural sights.[3] In the same way, new genres of urban picturesqueness developed when the concept found its way into town.

The language of the picturesque is thus an early example of transnational standardization, as it became a filter for evaluating and ranking, which could be used almost anywhere. Somehow the globalization of the tourist industry starts here, with men like Gilpin, who taught the art of learning to look and overlook when traveling.

The history of the picturesque is also a watering-down process. Today we think of the picturesque in terms of a picture, often as a rather worn-out cliché, but as I tried to show, the picturesque for pioneers like Linnerhielm and Plumptre was not "just a view," it was an event, a focusing not only of the eyes but of all the senses, and the same was the case, maybe even more so, with the sublime.

We think of these ways of experiencing the landscape as pictorial regimes in part because the nineteenth century saw the development of technologies to pictorialize the tourist experience in new and increasingly inexpensive ways. The most important tool in this process was the camera and, critical to its global popularity, one of its products: the picture postcard.

WISH YOU WERE HERE

Those who have been unfortunate enough to lose a roll of film in one of the biggest Swedish photo labs will receive a search list, which contains the most popular vacation motifs. You just have to tick off the ones that describe the content of your lost film. Two of the main headings run:

VIEWS (mountains, sea, meadow, forest, alps, lake)

ATTRACTIONS (church, ruin, monument)

Behind this laconic list of Swedish holiday sights lies a long process of selection and framing, parts of which we have already encountered.

Learning to reorganize the landscape into sights and views comes so naturally to most of us that we may find it difficult to understand the kind of relearning that went before it. There are many irritated comments on the Disneyland habit of putting up little flags to signal scenic photo spots, but most of us already carry those flags with us—more or less consciously. Our camera work is heavily preprogrammed. With the help of the nineteenth-century invention of the award system of one to three stars (later expanded into five) spread all over the world, tourists learned to look for attractions that demanded to be seen and photographed.[4]

Nineteenth-century photography remained a relatively exclusive pastime, before the advent of cheap cameras and simple techniques. Photo prints, however, soon became a very important tourist medium, and by far the most important of these was the picture postcard.

Some claim that the first souvenir postcard was issued at the Paris Universal Exhibition of 1889 and depicted the Eiffel Tower. From then on the medium developed into a booming industry, and the decades around the turn of the century proved to be the golden age of the postcard. In 1904 the Swedish population of about five million people mailed over forty-eight million postcards. Exchanging and collecting picture postcards became a favorite hobby, and addicts could subscribe to special magazines for collectors.[5] Many attics still hold old postcard albums from that period. This collection mania may be difficult for us to understand, exposed as we are to all kinds of visual media, but at the turn of the century printed images were still a scarce resource. The picture postcard, as a cheap and attractive pictorial medium, filled a void, a hunger for images, and thus became a very important means to visualize the world. The Swedish term for picture postcards is *vykort* (literally, "a card with a view"), and the term reflects the complex relation between the new medium of photography and visual perceptions at that time.

Looking at a hundred years of Swedish postcards, we can follow very distinct subgenres and favorite motifs that developed rapidly. They became a condensation of the truly Swedish, an emotionalized territory. Photographers, many of them specializing in the new genre, learned the rules of composing attractive views, and mistakes were

Figure 11. The early 1900s were the years of the postcard craze. Here visitors to the Industrial Fair in Stockholm, 1909, are busy scribbling. (Photo Stockholms Stadsmuseum)

quickly corrected by the market. The tourists for their part got confirmations or redefinitions of ideas about beautiful or attractive views. The three-star prospects were not only listed in the guidebook but could also be bought in the form of postcards in the nearby souvenir shop. As a new mass medium, the postcard made sure you brought the view home or shared it with friends through the mail. The genre had a great influence on the development of amateur photography among tourists.

The motifs of picture postcards in many cases show great continuity, especially in the genre of landscapes. A couple of years ago I bought a standard set of slides in a Swedish souvenir shop, simply labeled "Sweden I" and "Sweden II." A number of its views had been scenographic "classics" even a century earlier. This gallery includes Lapland waterfalls, a little red cottage by the lake, timber floating (a trade long since gone), Dalecarlians in folk costume rowing to church, Saami herding their reindeer down a mountain slope, and, of course, a midnight sun.

In an international perspective the sunset has been *the* most popular postcard motif over the last hundred years. This scenery has many local variations; a Swedish, a Moroccan, or an American sunset may be staged in different ways, but the basic structure is the same and is a product of tourist experiences as well as landscape painting.

In an account of her African fieldwork the anthropologist Manda Cesara recollects a remark one of the locals once made about his peculiar European friend who sat endlessly on the porch, sundowner in hand, waiting for the setting sun. "Why should anyone sit and watch the sunset?" he asked.[6] The same bewilderment could be found among Swedish countryfolk who observed the first waves of urban middle-class tourists in search of scenic spots. Why go through all that work of climbing up the hillside just for a view?

The sunset panorama satisfied many emotional longings. Observing the view alone or with silent companions became a form of aesthetic worship, a profound experience of serenity and wholeness. The absolute stillness, the dying day, the landscape opening before you, all that could give a feeling of total belonging or quiet ecstasy. The experience often felt like "time standing still" or "natural time." It could work like a ritual of belonging, returning to a mythical past or a more authentic existence.[7]

Feelings of nostalgia, of homecoming, traveling back in time could also be part of it, as well as a feeling of closure.

The element of melancholy and longing could also take the form of a phrase that now seems rather worn. A Swedish sunset from 1909 bears the scribbled subtext: "If only you had been here this evening!" The definition of the sunset as an intimate or romantic situation intended for loving couples or close friends took the form of "Wish you were here." The sunset came to represent not only a specific scenery but a specific mood. From time to time this link has been made even more obvious by the addition of printed subtexts to the view, specifying the mood. In the early 1990s a popular Swedish sunset version carried the text "Missing you." The combination of picture and text could communicate moods and feelings that many found difficult to verbalize.

In nineteenth-century landscape painting the sunset was a favorite genre, which was gradually trivialized to the extent that it was redefined as vulgar—with too glaring colors. Filmmakers turned the sunset into a cliché as more and more heroes and heroines walked right into that happy or melancholy ending. Travel writers had their problems too:

> I do not think I shall ever forget the sight of Etna at sunset; the mountain almost invisible in a blur of pastel grey, glowing on the top and then repeating its shape, as though reflected, in a wisp of grey smoke, with the whole horizon behind radiant with pink light, fading into a grey pastel sky. Nothing I have ever seen in Art or Nature was quite so revolting.

As Martin Stannard points out, this piece from Evelyn Waugh's *Labels: A Mediterranean Journal* from 1930 can only be read as parody of one of his contemporary travel writers, Robert Byron's description of Stromboli from 1926—or a thousand other descriptions of Mediterranean sunsets.[8] Sunset representations became the icon of bad art and tired prose, but the more humble medium of the picture postcard could keep carrying this motif.

Sunset viewing is still a popular ritual for many of us. On the long sandy shores of the Danish west coast cars drive out on the beaches and people gather in small groups or remain inside their vehicles for silent communion with the sun. The next minute the cars are all gone, but the view is on sale next door. On California beaches you can experience a similar scene, and a really good sunset may also produce enthusiastic applause from the onlookers. But for really top-quality sunsets you have to go to Hawaii:

> Visitors chasing the perfect sunset can find it in Wailea. . . . People become connoisseurs of Wailea sunsets. They rate them, collect them on film, discuss them as one might a vintage burgundy or a new car. . . .
> The Renaissance Wailea Beach Resort has elevated sunset-watching to an art form with the simple device of a few hammocks strategically hung among some palms. While your friends cuddle up with a mai tai in hand and romance in mind, you can shoot them against the setting sun.[9]

LIFE IMITATING ART?

The tourist postcard represents a powerful medium for organizing and presenting ideas about vacation preferences, tastes, and attractions. The same scenic preferences may confront you in the travel brochure you read at home, the guidebooks brought along, the stops made during the sightseeing trips for photo opportunities, and the cards available at the souvenir shops. There is a strong process of reinforcement here, which in part may account for the marked conservatism of scenic viewing.

An example from a booming scene of package tourism shows the process at work. One of the most reproduced images of Morocco comes from the colorful setting of "the Dyers' Lane" in the old artisanal section of the market in Marrakech, where bundles of yarn in all conceivable shades are draped across the lane. You will find this scene in tourist brochures, on travel posters, and in postcards racks. During the guided tours in the maze of this huge bazaar the guide will stop when you approach the lane and signal that here is a good spot for a photograph. The problem is that the mass tourist invasion to this part of the market has altered its look. Souvenir shops, as well as changes in production, have driven the dyers out of the lane, but in order to live up to tourist expectations, a few bundles of colorful yarn still remain draped across the walls.

In the background the water peddlers in their exotic red outfits wait with their brass cups, not to peddle water, for which the market in modern Marrakech is dwindling, but to act as a folkloristic backdrop in your photograph for the fee of a couple of dirhams. The sound of their brass bells is no longer a signal for the thirsty traveler but a reminder to the tourist that she or he is approaching a scenic spot. In Marrakech the water peddlers are a necessary cultural prop. Postcards and guidebooks immortalize their presence. The point to be made here is, of course, that once scenery has been institutionalized through various media it becomes in a way frozen and taken out of time. An element of mise-en-scène becomes necessary to make it stay that way, as local life changes. Here as in many other situations we observe the power of the representation, as the norm of authenticity that reality will have to try to live up to.

The picture postcard is, however, not a stagnant genre, simply reproducing old images. It also makes fun of itself and tourists; the comic postcard, the ironic or kitschy postcard, the period postcard are all traditions with a rather long history. Anti-genres, discarding worn clichés in favor of new artistic or ethnographic traditions in professional travel photography, set up new norms, which mirror an urge to get away from anything that smells of the arranged, of fakelore, or of the classic sights. The fact that a dangling camera (photo opportunities!) has become the sign of the vulgar tourist poses a problem for those who feel a need to distance themselves: should they carry a camera at all? but otherwise, how can they bring back pictorial evidence of actually getting off the beaten track?

THE SCIENCE OF THE SCENIC

At least two centuries of scenic viewing thus condition our selections and evaluations of tourist settings and sights, but their work is not always conscious. A good example is the strange tradition of landscape evaluation measurement techniques that became very popular in environmental studies and planning for some decades, especially during the 1970s.[10]

Scores of studies appeared, with titles like "Eye Pupillary Measurement of Aesthetic Response to Forest Scenes" or "Modeling and Predicting Human Response to the Visual Recreation Environment."[11] Hoping to create tools for natural resource management and planning, from wilderness aesthetics to scenic roads design, many of these studies put enormous amounts of energy and some pretty spectacular number crunching into what are good examples of social science trivia. They reflect a period in tourist and leisure management when hard facts, models, and clear taxonomies were in demand. How do we predict tourist preferences and measure visitor satisfaction? Studies like these demonstrate the prevailing strengths of the lessons of the picturesque. The most favored mountain scenes turn out to be those Gilpin would have preferred, like a grove of trees foregrounding a lake scene with a mighty mountain in the background or, in the words of the researchers, "the positive effect of a perimeter of immediate vegetation."[12] Other results announce that people with camping experience have higher emotional responses to woodland sceneries or that older people with a longer education prefer scenic natural beaches.[13]

Another study in the same tradition (which is still with us) asked 2,826 Danes to rank 52 different forest photos. The winner was a deer on a winding path in a sunlit forest clearing, but when a tractor replaced the deer, the same scenery ended up next to last.[14]

This science of the scenic represents the ultimate pictorialization of nature experiences. Nature as a two-dimensional picture postcard, not to walk in or smell or touch or listen to but just to look upon. And obviously, the nineteenth century brought a focus on the power of vision with many new technologies, from the panorama and the stereoscope to the camera. But an increased ocularization of tourist life into the "tourist gaze" does not equate with the hegemony of the surveilling or controlling (male) gaze. Rather there was a period of intense experimentation, juggling very different modes of seeing that came to coexist. Sightseeing elaborated the art of fixing, framing, and positioning a view, as well as the techniques of scanning, and it also explored the art of glimpsing and glancing—the furtive, disinterested, or distracted look. Later in the

Figure 12. A Swedish postcard photographer at work in the 1960s. He carries along a model in folk costume as well as a collapsible fence and a couple of goats, to create a suitable scene. (Photo Leif Forslund, Falun)

twentieth century the tourist industry learned to develop "eye candy" for the consuming gaze, which wants to touch and feel.

The abundance of pictorial (and increasingly affordable) representations, from the watercolor to the video cassette, also produced a materiality or concretion of the visible: this is what we experienced and remember. In our narratives we also depend heavily on the well-developed language for describing visual impressions that many of the other senses lack. And we are, of course, not just looking; other senses interact in this making of a vision. It is only that the other senses have not kept up with this verbalization and technologization of the visual.

SOUVENIRS

> Mass-tourists ask little except the same sort of food that they eat at home; the English for example, scorn any meal that does not include potatoes—to hell with rice and spaghetti! And who wants wine, when he can get beer? They don't object to a little local colour, especially flamenco-strumming by pretended gipsies, and gaudy souvenirs; dolls in provincial costume, inlaid Toledo steel paper-knives, plastic castanets dangling coloured ribbons, leather wine-bottles, olive-wood bowls and boxes, bullfighting posters with their own names printed between those of El Litri and James Ostos. . . . But they shy away from any closer approach to the real Spain.[15]

Robert Graves is commenting on the tourist scene in Majorca and the very touchy issue of souvenirs. This is a territory where different tastes and interests, as well as outspoken verdicts, continually clash. As a child I remember the meaningful glances passing between my parents when my sisters and I chose among the treasures of souvenir shops. Although nothing was said it was obvious that our taste was childlike and immature. Our grandmother, on the other hand, loved souvenirs too and had the dangerous habit of bringing home real bits and pieces from three-star attractions, stones from Bethlehem, marble fragments from the Parthenon. She followed the example of the young Englishman who wrote home to his mother in 1861 that he had been to see the Sphinx and had broken "a bit of its neck to take home with us, as everyone else does."[16] We could not help worrying about our grandma's participation in this mass movement, which in the long run would clean the world of classical monuments.

Like many other children of my generation I loved souvenirs, and the ritual of acquiring one from each place was important. Pocket money for school excursions should preferably always include money for ice cream *and* a souvenir, and we always expected our parents to bring us home a token from their latest trip abroad. Growing older, I experienced how the genres of souvenir collecting change along the life cycle. Collecting tacky souvenirs was a student exercise in kitsch, and later on souvenirs became bottles of funny-smelling local liqueurs, a lucky stone from a memorable day at a beach, all kinds of objets trouvés. For me the magic of the souvenir still works.

A burgeoning souvenir market developed in the eighteenth-century world of the Grand Tour. Earlier I mentioned the export industry of Italian landscape paintings, but there was also a great demand for archaeological finds, which soon tempted the locals to start forging them. Just like later generations of tourists these pioneers wanted to bring back something material: a piece of the landscape, and in Naples there was a brisk trade in pieces of lava.[17] Local artists and artisans started to work exclusively for the tourist market: new forms of "native crafts" constantly appeared.

At Niagara early tourists dug up bones from the battlefields of the 1812 war to bring home. Native Americans soon got caught up in the tourist trade, as providers of the authentic. Here as elsewhere the genres of "native crafts" and "local souvenirs" soon became blurred. In 1850 you could buy items cut from local rock and wood, beaded moccasins, bark trifles, baskets, leather cigar cases decorated with dyed elk's hair, and also miniature canoes.[18] At Niagara the tourists opened up a market for imported souvenirs, everything from prints to trinkets of all kinds. Here we may witness the start of the globalization of souvenir production. Instead of buying a piece containing the magic of local materials, you can buy an object made into a local souvenir by the magic of naming, from "Niagara Falls" in poker-work, produced in New York sweatshops, to the pens, ashtrays, or T-shirts from Taiwan of later periods.

Although souvenir shops have been denounced in every possible way over most of their history, they persist and thrive. Susan Stewart's classic study *On Longing* is one attempt to explain that popularity.[19] She points out that souvenirs carry the magic of place, whether bought or found there, and this magic evaporates if they do not come from the faraway place—as in the devalued experience of receiving a friend's postcard mailed after the homecoming. She discusses the processes of fetishization and miniaturization, but the most convincing part of her argument is about their power to produce narratives.

The theme of miniaturization is equally absorbing. The tiny beaded canoe, the folklore doll, the Statue of Liberty piggy bank, they all hold, as Gaston Bachelard states, a strange attraction as a medium for daydreaming, as a way to experience what is large in what is small.[20] Small things are easy to carry home, but they are also "good to think with," they often function as narrative coat hangers.[21] Their three-dimensionality is important in relation to the flatness of all the texts and pictures that otherwise make up our vacation leftovers.

The evocative power of souvenirs rests in their seeming unchangeability, all those objects that have no other function than to store memories. Cups that are not for drinking out of, painted cutting boards that never will come near a loaf of bread, funny hats that won't leave their pegs. But they are of course constantly changing, and their seductive thingishness may obscure the fact that they are vessels for travel in time and space. One of the best treatments of this theme is the folklorist Henry Glassie's text on Mrs. Cutler's kitchen dresser in the Irish village of Ballymenone. On the dresser there is a parade of souvenir plates, mugs, a doll in a kilt, a dippy duck, "a glass wee man with an ass and a cart," porcelain figures of saints, little brass ornaments, and much much more. Glassie describes Mrs. Cutler's running commentary on her souvenirs, her constant care and rearranging of them. They are always on the move: "their meaning lies less in their manifest content than in their magical capacity to bring events and human beings to life in the mind. . . . The art of ornaments does not lie in them, as part of their fabric. They become art in mind and manipulation."[22]

These souvenirs may look trivial but the kinds of narratives and memories they trigger are astounding, opening up this tiny kitchen to the world. So in answering the question, what is a souvenir—a fetish, nostalgia, an object without utility value, a narrative trigger?—the answer is: maybe. To me the most striking characteristic of a souvenir is its openness, its readiness to carry the mind in all directions. There might be millions of tiny brass Eiffel Towers distributed over the globe, but no two of them carry the same meanings.

MEMORIZING

"Travels, to be good for anything, must be literary," was the opening editorial statement of the new American *Magazine of Travel* in 1857.[23] The close relation between souvenir and story-telling reminds us that there are many minor genres of travel narrative, which tend to live in the shadow of the major genres of travel books and poetry, guides, or edited diaries. As in the visual representations, the minor ones live under the constant influence of the major ones. They emerge, for example, when you ask people to narrate their life histories as vacationers—Mrs. Cutler's running commentary is one. But the minor genres exist too as subtexts in photo albums, holiday diaries never meant for publication, guest book entries, stories told during coffee breaks at work after the return home, or reminiscences with family and friends.

Analysis of the major genres of travel writing forms a rich literature.[24] Surveying the British output on the Mediterranean in the nineteenth century, John Pemble lists the key words of the titles: *Sketches, Notes, Diaries, Gleanings, Glimpses, Impressions, Pictures, Narratives, Tours, Visits, Wanderings, Residences, Rambles,* and *Travels.*[25] Behind the tone of improvisation or informality, which may serve as a protection against comparisons with the great travel writers, and with all its changes of form and format over the last two centuries, travel writing has rather stable genres and styles of writing. Leaving this well explored field, I briefly explore one of the minor ones, the messages on the back of vacationers' postcards.

"This space may be used for communication" was a direction often printed on early postcards. Gradually the space allotted to text expanded to the modern standard of half of the reverse, which has made postcard writing into a minimalistic art with its own traditions and standard formulas. The function of its text links it to vacation greetings. But to whom do you mail cards and why?

In a world where telephones and e-mail have encroached on the traditional territory of letter writing, postcards are still a popular (and less demanding) medium. You mail cards to people you'd never dream of sending a letter to. There are rules of reciprocity—the network of people who *expect* to get a card from you. They will also know what to expect in terms of stock phrases and selected topics. A classic vacation postcard with palm trees and blue water from Majorca has an equally classic reverse:

Palma, 9 August 1966

Hello there!

Just want to send a sunny greeting from a wonderful place. We bask in the sun, swim, and have great fun. Hope you're having good weather and are all right. Here it's 25° centigrade in the water and we'll miss that when we get home!

All the best,
Ruth and Herbert

The discourse on the weather and stock phrases like "Wish you were here," "Having a wonderful time," "We are fine, how are you?" have their parodic parallel in the subgenre of holiday cards with preprinted messages and empty spaces for adding the desired adjective: weather here is . . . , food is . . . , mother-in-law's temper is . . .

But this genre is not without its surprises. Reading the messages on the backs of early twentieth-century postcards, I am struck by the lighthearted tone, the many (and sometimes rather daring) jokes. It is a world of jolly phrases, exclamation marks, and a good deal of sexual innuendo. In this sense it is also a folklore genre, which has shown quite a continuity over the last century.

The postcard is a private message, ready to be read by others. If postcards in the past often ended up in albums, many vacationers' greetings of today tend to end up as public exhibitions. Some of them land on the front of the fridge or the kitchen bulletin board, but many are exposed at work. During the last few decades they have, at least in Sweden, been one of the most common forms of decoration in the office, the canteen, or the locker room.

In tourist research much of the analysis is based on quite different sorts of texts, belonging to the major genres. Historical reconstructions in particular (like mine) depend heavily on what a rather select group of tourists has produced, which tends to result in a narrowing down of the tourist experience. First of all we again encounter the oculocentric tendency. It is on the whole much easier to describe what's in front of us than to verbalize other kinds of sensations. The conventions of narrative also tend to crowd out all those other experiences that tell us we're away from home and not passive spectators: an itching sunburn, tired feet, insects, a rumbling stomach, a hangover from last night's fiesta, or nagging kids. The breathtaking sight needs to be recorded, but what about boredom, disappointment, or the sudden wish to be somewhere else?

Second, the grand travel narrative may create a false continuity. The enduring rules and conventions of travel narratives may obscure much more varied and changing tourist experiences, just as the visualizations of sights do. A good way of bringing these, often unwritten, rules up to the surface is to turn to a text that makes them explicit, like *The Travel Writer's Handbook: How to Write and Sell Your Own Travel Experiences* (1992).[26] Here we find advice about emplotment, the need for colorful detail, "a hook" to pull readers in, and a slant to fascinate them, as well as anatomies of good travel stories.

Third, there is the social position of the travel writer and his or her urge to narrate. Some groups have a stronger urge to narrate and elaborate than others. The traveling middle classes, and especially the trend-setting groups of academics, writers, and artists, are the trade's stars, and thus their representations often become "the tourist experience." Their sketchbooks, travel diaries, guidebooks fill out much of the landscape, whereas those groups who do not feel a need to record or elaborate their experiences or lack the possibilities are muted in the process. A Swedish writer was struck by the old country folks he encountered in the 1960s, who just sat silently in the landscape. There was this old farmer who used to sit on his porch every summer evening or stare out of the window during the winter, slowly sinking into the landscape. When asked why he was sitting there, the laconic answer was "It's nice" but, as the author added, "The question seemed to make him embarrassed."[27] In 1843 the American Margaret Fuller described a similar experience. She was standing on a hill with a friend, watching "one of the finest sunsets that ever enriched this world":

> a little cow-boy, trudging along, wondered what we could be gazing at. After spying about some time, he found it could only be the sunset, and looking too, a moment, he said approvingly, "that sun look well enough."[28]

DÉJÀ VU

"Can I learn to look at things with clear, fresh eyes? How much can I take in at a single glance? Can the grooves of mental habits be effaced?" These are the classic questions of Goethe from his Italian journey in 1786–88, which tend to turn up again and again in reflections on tourism.

One of the grand narratives of tourism argues that we can never recapture the freshness of Goethe, Lord Byron, John Muir, or those other great pioneers. Our vacation experiences are hopelessly cluttered up with sediments of associations, clichés, and images: "The problem is that life rarely feels real. If I am having a picnic with my friends out on the cliffs in the Åland archipelago, life suddenly disappears and I begin to think that everything we are doing is part of a beer commercial." This journalist's memories of the previous summer unfold against the backdrop of an immensely successful Swedish beer commercial. The TV spot plays seductively on the theme of the perfect summer memory out in the archipelago. Young and tanned actors fool around in the waves, and stage an improvised picnic next to the boathouse. This is a nostalgic flashback to summer and fun, by a young couple who revisit the island in the melancholy of the autumn.[29]

The journalist's reflection on fiction invading life is the start of an interview with a Swedish author, who voices the often-heard standpoint

Figure 13. It is no coincidence that Kodak campaigns from quite early on focused on women—hoping to create a mass market for its new technology by attracting women's interest. (Advertisement from 1925, courtesy George Eastman House)

that the basic definition of twentieth-century life is that we live in a world in which boundaries between reality and fiction are dissolved. Earlier generations did not have to face the problem, she argues. Maybe a walk along with Linnerhielm in the garden of Forsmark would have made her less sure of her opinion. The mix of reality and fiction has as long a history as the daydream, the flight of fantasy, or the religious vision. Vacationscapes develop out of the interplay between the physical and mental landscapes through which we move simultaneously.

The anthropologist Arjun Appadurai sets up "landscapes" to capture this interaction in the ways cultural flows help build new, transnational worlds, where fantasy and images are an important part of everyday social practices. He talks of people on the move (ethnoscapes), of mobile capital (finanscapes), technologies (technoscapes), ideologies (ideoscapes) and finally the flow of information, images, and narratives (mediascapes).[30] His approach is useful for a discussion of tourism. How are such different "scapes" produced and changed over time and integrated in everyday practices?

There is a constant play between experience and technologies of mediation here. Tourists always experiment with new forms of mediations and technologies of movement, perception, and sensing. On the Swedish west coast island I visit every summer, people still talk about how confounded the locals were by the visitors down at the manor in the middle of the last century: Could you believe it? Those ladies with their hair let down sat in the grass down by the shore reading books!

"Those ladies" transformed the landscape into a multimedia space through other techniques of virtual reality than ours. Their flight of fantasy in reading novels blended with the experience of being out in nature, and a similar thought probably inspired the visitor to a Catskill lake in the 1830s who exclaimed: "What a place for music by moonlight!"[31] And a modern teenager with a Walkman can set music to the landscape she moves through.

We now consume music and texts out in the open and—paralleling the last decades' increase in our media consumption of images—we also carry with us a wider range of fore-sights, and increasingly so in the form of pre-visualizations. They may be everything from landscape paintings to scenes from vacation advertisements, to which we compare our actual landscape experiences, as well as all our past landscape experiences. The question is whether this massive pictorialization produces an overstimulation or just a wider range of possible associations.

When the sightseeing bus cruises along we observe the vacation landscape through the smoke-colored Claude-glass of the panorama window. What is new, what is continuity since the days of Mr. Plumptre? What does it mean to appropriate the landscape through the Claude-glass, through the sight of the camcorder, through the car window, or resting on a walking stick? Through intense reading of classical authors, romantic poetry, years of MTV-viewing, or leafing through package tour catalogs?

The 1996 vacation dream on the seashore drew on a sedimentation of mass-mediated messages, texts, and images, as well as personal associations, memories of great and not-so-great vacations. But how much of this mix is shaped by the actual historical conditions? Quite obviously, there are striking similarities and differences between the person sitting on a rock by the water with a television commercial on his mind in 1996 and the one standing in front of the Älvkarleby waterfalls in 1787 and in his memory leafing through the engravings of picturesque views he has in the library at home. What kinds of fore-sights and preconditions are at work here? How are landscape experiences mediated both by each individual's past history and by the technologies of representation?

The question of what we carry along into a tourist experience also produces the problem of wear and tear. The history of tourist experiences illustrates that many of the processes of change are more micro-processes of a somewhat cyclical nature. As new sights and attractions, new forms of tourist activities and leisure come into vogue, they run through processes of exploration, followed by institutionalization and sometimes commoditization, and may then appear worn and tired and trivialized. The intimate, picturesque view may grow stale or feel claustrophobic. Landscapes seen as barren and uninviting may take on a new aura as their very simplicity and nothingness become an asset. In all such developments we need to focus on the wear and tear. Why do we grow tired of experiences, how do souvenirs come to seem tacky, what makes a sight boring?

An answer to this question calls for a return to the question raised earlier: what is an experience? If we look at the semantics of the word in different languages, there is a common emphasis on movement. Experience derives from experimenting, trying, risking, the German *Erlebnis* and the Swedish *upplevelse* from living through, living up to, running through, being part of, accomplishing. Again the focus is on personal participation, we have to be both physically and mentally *there*.

"To have an experience" calls for a situation with a beginning and an end. In the everyday flow of activity the experience stands out, it is marked and distinctive. It is something we enter and exit, and the production of experiences—especially out of the ordinary ones that can be furthered by rites de passage—is a situating that involves both time and space.[32] Experiences always take place, but in ways that combine the realities of both the grounds we are treading and the mental images present. We neither have nor can be given experiences. We *make* them in a highly personal way of taking in impressions, but in this process we use a great deal of established and shared cultural knowledge and frames. And yet we share experiences only through representations and expressions. Here is the famous hermeneutical circle: experience structures expression and expression structures experience. Our associations are culturally conditioned and so are our afterthoughts, the ways in which we reflect on and express consciousness. What is possible to express, how can it be expressed? The anthropologist Allen Feldman pushes this argument even further: an event is not what happens but what can be narrated.[33]

In the history of tourism there is a strong normative element in discussions of experiences. They are not only framed, localized, and memorized, they are also weighed, measured, and ranked. They can be described as rich and poor, deep or shallow, full or empty, strong or weak, to name some of the metaphors used. How do we know when we have had an experience or even a peak experience? Is it possible to prepare ourselves for it, to stage it or rehearse it, to open our senses to it? Or is it precisely the opposite way: rich experiences do not come prepackaged, they take us unawares, spontaneity is their hallmark? Questions like these seem to have always haunted both tourists and the tourist industry and they carry an element of catch-22. On the one hand, the wish for deeper or stronger experience means a focus on opening up the senses, being prepared, but on the other hand the peak experience should be spontaneous. It should sneak up, take us off guard, unprepared, like a sudden shiver running down the spine. How then is the cultural capital of preparation, of background knowledge to be weighed against the importance of freshness, the longing for a clean slate, an "unmediated" experience?

This dilemma may produce a tourist angst, which also has to do with the comparative framework of the narratives and experiences of those others: Goethe or the neighbors across the road. Will my holiday experiences live up to their standards? Cyril Connolly talks about that guidebook-produced "inadequacy of our feelings," when "the Acropolis just resembles a set of false teeth in a broken palate."[34] In 1856 the American travel writer George Curtis wrote that "people love the country theoretically, as they do poetry. Very few are heroic enough to confess that it is wearisome even when they are fatigued by it." The reason for this was, he thought, the idea that "we ought to love it, and we ought to be satisfied and glad among the hills and under the trees."[35]

The histories of Niagara and Yosemite demonstrate this anxiety, and the continuous mental wear and tear of our presence at tourist sites. As guidebooks and fellow travelers provide a wealth of subtexts to each panorama, we have to develop new strategies in order to make it into a strong and undisturbed personal experience.

A classic example is Nathaniel Hawthorne's sketch about the tourist who, approaching Niagara in 1834, shut his eyes to avoid seeing the falls and instead hastened to his hotel room to build up the right mood. But his anticipations proved to be too much: when he stepped out to admire the falls, they turned out to be an anticlimax.[36] Other travelers could describe their own disappointments or ironize about high-flying expectations.

In 1872 Isaac Bromley visited Yosemite and set out for the experience of the Grizzly Giant in the Mariposa Grove of giant sequoias. He had been "working up pretty carefully," supposing that he would be inspired to "soar on the wings of fancy, and all that sort of thing," only to find himself not inspired at all. There was nothing he could think of "except for lunch, and as for soaring, nothing in the world could make me soar except my unfortunate horse, and he had done it already so that I could hardly turn in the saddle."[37]

Narratives of disappointments like these, as well as denunciations of "shallow experiences" or "tourist traps," tell us at once about tourist angst and about strategies of heightening the experience of a well-established attraction: intensification as a countermove to trivialization. One of its most striking examples is the nineteenth-century cult of concentration and stillness, so central in the sunset experience. Here is an emphasis on solitude and serenity, but also on focusing, which develops in many arenas of aesthetic consumption. During the early nineteenth century people start hushing others in concert halls and art galleries. The focus of the senses should be directly forward, taking in the music, the acting, the artwork, without distractions. The ears must learn to absorb as well as the eyes.

James Buzard includes the cult of stillness in his discussion of strategies of intensification among nineteenth-century visitors to southern Europe. What he calls the "authenticity effect" can be furthered not only by stillness, but also by the elements of nonutility, saturation, and picturesqueness.[38] For the ambitious tourist intent on putting all the elements to work, the strategy calls for the timing of visits at propitious moments but also for the stillness of a spectator: allowing yourself to be drawn into the scenery. The emphasis here is on the dreamlike qualities of a strong experience. The nonutility element links the effect to an experience of unreality or the theatrical; a great tourist sight should not be contaminated by everyday banality. The fourth element, saturation, is bound up with the two earlier and has to do with a situation or scenery that is "drenched" in significance, full of associations and reminiscences: a dense experience. And finally, picturesqueness has to do with the scenic qualities discussed earlier.

Buzard's discussion deals with a specific era and a specific narrative community of tourists and cannot be generalized, but some of these mechanisms of alterity are still important, although often in transmuted forms. And in certain settings the virtue of nonutility resembles its opposite, the authenticity of an undisturbed everyday reality: village and town scenes where the locals go about their daily business as usual. The picturesque faces competition from other aesthetic norms and so on. Returning to the advertisement for Blue Village, we find quite different techniques of intensification, making sure to activate the body and all the senses. Here the great experience results from diving into, climbing, and tasting the landscape, exploring the sensuality of scenery as well as the sexuality of a partner. A Moroccan tourist slogan from 1998 is typical of this urge for total involvement: "An adventure for all the senses!"

Behind all these changing techniques of intensification there is, of course, a strong normative element present, namely, the idea that we ought to create experiences—they are good for us! Furthermore we should be able to communicate them, represent them in words or images, drawing on available narrative genres for recapitulation, some of which are more tied to specific historic eras or cultural settings than others. Our own experiences are influenced by the narratives of others— other persons, other places, other moments. Sometimes in the midst of a landscape experience or at a tourist attraction I find my mind wandering to the questions of how this moment can be transformed into a memory, a souvenir, or a good story. As tourists we often devote a great deal of energy to the experiences of others, admiring or ridiculing them or even questioning their status as a "true" experience. "Authentic experiences," promised one Danish tour operator, and it is an easy promise to deliver. Whoever had an inauthentic experience?

My argument is that tourism is a rewarding laboratory for exploring the production and transformation of experiences. Here we find the microritualizations of framing the right time and place, the turning of experience into event or occasion by markings, but also the demand to activate all senses.

It is the interaction between certain landscape characteristics, mindsets, and tourist technologies of movement and representation that produces a vacationscape. Some landscapes have special attractions for certain visitors because they carry a special potential of making room for mindscaping. The picturesque idyll contained all kinds of props to set thoughts flying, while a romantic like Thoreau appreciated landscapes uncluttered by human presence and local history, because they gave room for his imagination.[39] The mighty roar of Niagara could produce a special awe, a sense of liberation that set the mind working in other directions, just as the deafening stillness of the vast panoramas of Yosemite or the Grand Canyon helped to create a space for transcendence.

The grammar of landscape experiences includes all the different tourist forms of "taking in a landscape": to traverse it, pass through it or past it, to dwell in it, sense it, be part of it, or balance at a viewpoint and watch it unfold in front of us. The tendency to talk about landscape in terms of settings and scenes, something to approach, enter, or look at, obscures the fact that landscapes are produced by movement, both of the senses and of the body.

A historical perspective can also show continuities and links backwards in time, illuminating the didactic processes that help certain scenes convey specific cultural messages or moods; in other words, how they territorialize emotion. The way we react to a piece of landscape today is often the result of a long process of institutionalization, a development that has condensed a scene into a cultural matrix, an icon.

Because of this condensation, perhaps only a detail, the merest hint, can paint a landscape of the mind. A swaying palm tree or a tilted cocktail glass in a tourist brochure can be enough to conjure up a reader's whole world of holiday moods and carefree tropical dreams; the image of a single tree fills us with patriotic ardor or profound homesickness.

Any landscape experience blends the unique and personal with standardized preconceptions and cultural conventions. Here we are, tourists now, looking out over a beach, a meadow, or a mountain, enjoying particular tourist props with a swarm of earlier experiences, images, and associations we have collected. In this very moment history and the present collude in ways that are difficult to verbalize or even make conscious. We stand still in the same vacationscape with our feet firmly planted on the ground, but our minds travel far, in diverse confrontations between experiences past and present, daydreams, preconceptions, and afterthoughts. We follow the same beaten track and move through different mindscapes looking for different things. We may devote a lot of energy to deconstructing the conventions, associations, and cognitive frameworks of the tourist experience and still not be able to map it. In the ambition of the tourist industry to prepackage and market experiences this dilemma becomes very obvious. Experiences are hard to direct and predict. Their variability also prevents a unilinear narrative of the making of vacationscapes. What we get in such a narrative is often a normative history of what people ought to experience, which begs the question of who is setting the rules and who is supposed to live up to them in given situations.

NOT IN VIEW

What kind of people tend to get out of focus or never get into the narratives of tourism? There are several noticeable absences here. These first chapters on the sightseer's life look mainly at the Phileas Fogg prototype rather than the Robinsonian quest, but they also point up a marked tendency to describe the sightseeing experience precisely in these gentlemanly terms: the white male and middle-class gaze, tourism as a colonial quest. The tourist pioneers were mainly upper-class males, and as travel came within reach of new groups, the discussions about right and wrong, good and bad experiences intensified, as well as remarks on the need to educate the newcomers. We have already seen this concern in nineteenth-century male reactions to female tourists, ranging from the paternalist to the sarcastic.

Gender visibility has less to do with the numbers present in different arenas than with the extent the male frame of travel and sightseeing created a normative framework, defining the desirable, the noteworthy, the exiting.[40] The male desire for "the abroadness" of adventure—out there, away from home, unattached—made travel a mental as well as physical space for elaborating masculinity. The history of tourism illustrates the ways in which polarities of male and female are both reproduced and transformed.

As women gradually staked out a claim in tourism, it became one of the public spheres in which middle-class women could experience some freedom of mobility and also create a space for aesthetic expression.

Some men saw their presence and participation as a threatening feminization of certain tourist activities and arenas. When women moved in, men moved out to find new settings for male adventure. In the same ways there is a constantly changing gendering of tourist technologies. During the twentieth century women have come to write more travel diaries, paint more watercolors, and mail more postcards than men, who do still tend to control the camcorder.

Today, women make up the majority of tourists in most fields, and especially in the classic field of cultural sightseeing. The ideal type of Mr. Fogg may still be with us, but the reality is different. If researchers have not always observed these changes, the market knows and acts accordingly.

For those who are used to the classic division of labor in tourist marketing, of active men and passive women, Japanese tourism supplies a different picture. Here the dominance of women, especially young women, is striking. They are on the all the covers of travel catalogs, swimming in Thailand, shopping in London, photographing the Eiffel Tower, strolling through an art gallery, or enjoying an exotic meal. Today young, unmarried women constitute the key target group in Japanese tourism marketing. They have time and money for travel, and the industry knows that they will also shape the vacation patterns of their future families. One of the still rather few studies of this change is Marilyn Ivy's discussion of how young Japanese women entered the tourist world, especially during the 1970s and 1980s. She shows how the journey, away from home and out in the world, reflects changing female experiences as well as ideals of both gender and the politics of nation-ness. There is a tension here between travel as female emancipation—an accepted way of escaping parental control and the rules of domesticity—and the market's campaign to exploit such desires.[41]

If there has been a striking imbalance in the representation of female experiences in the history of tourism, class is subject to a similar bias. In the early quest for the picturesque, the addition of a representative of "the simple people" could enrich the scenery. A single individual, a rugged shepherd, a peasant resting in the shadows, or a fisherman by the brook, a silent detail in the landscape (rather like the hermit in the

English garden) fitted in quite well. But as a collectivity the lower classes were certainly not picturesque. When the working class appeared on the tourist arena later on in the nineteenth century, complaints were loud and frequent. The classic elite tourist focus on stillness and serenity made flocks of common people a disturbing element; they lacked, it was argued early, the sophistication to handle the sacredness of the wild. Complaints often focused on noise, from the accordion to the ghetto blaster disturbing the peace of the sunset. The following British observation from the early twentieth century is not untypical:

> The excursion train used to vomit forth, at Easter and in Whitsun week, throngs of millhands of the period, cads and their flames, tawdry, blowsy, noisy, drunken; the women with dress that aped "the fashion," and pyramids of artificial flowers on their heads; the men as grotesque and hideous in their own way; tearing through woods and fields like swarms of devastating locusts, and dragging the fern and hawthorn boughs they had torn down in the dust, ending the lovely spring day in pot-houses, drinking gin and bitters; or heavy ales by the quart, and tumbling pellmell into the night train, roaring music-hall choruses; sodden, tipsy, yelling, loathsome creatures, such as make a monkey look a king, and the newt seem an angel beside humanity.[42]

The many middle-class comments like this one underline the ways in which elites define new social groups of tourists as intruders, disturbing elements, or deviations from the established norms of public behavior. The perspective from inside the excursion train is different.

In Europe the outings of working men and women had a long tradition, often sponsored by clubs, unions, and societies, and the emigrants brought this tradition of collective outings to the United States. A German immigrant girl, Agnes, who worked as a maid and dressmaker, was one of the many who used the growing fleet of pleasure boats in New York at the turn of the century. In 1903 she enthusiastically described the many boats trips she took with her friends: "If we go on a boat we dance all the way there, and all the way back." Coney Island was her favorite destination: "Ach, it is just like what I see when I dream of heaven." Agnes was aware that the middle-class people she met through work frowned on this way of turning river transport into a festive event, dancing, partying, and flirting. "The trouble is that these high people don't know how to dance. I have to laugh when I see them at balls and parties," she said.[43] From a working-class perspective the middle-class tourists simply did not understand how to have fun or relax. They looked like anxious and overcontrolled spectators for whom the easygoing collectivity of the day tourists was a provocation. For the tourists themselves it was the many forms of shared fun—dancing, singing, picnicking, fooling around—that formed a central part of the vacation experience.

As the language of class becomes more muted later in the twentieth century this middle-class resentment against collectivity lodged in other metaphors. In tourism it survives in the notions of the vulgar tourist, as we shall see later.

Another absence or deviation, often intertwined with class, has to do with ethnicity. When the first Swedish mountaineers conquered the highest peak in Lapland, the Saami guides were not part of the group photos or named in the celebratory accounts; after all they were just paid helpers, not sportsmen. In the more marked ethnic situation of the United States the absence of ethnicity is even more striking.

Like the Saami, Native Americans were delegated to very special roles, if they were not made invisible. Yosemite is a good example of this. The "discovery" of the valley was actually made by the Mariposa Battalion pursuing a band of Miwok-Paiutes in 1851. The tribe was captured and taken out of the area to a new reservation and members of the battalion took the opportunity to design names for the fantastic scenery they encountered during the chase, with a mix of Miwok-Paiute terms and English words.[44] Lafayette Bunnell, a member of the battalion who wrote down his account of the campaign later, demonstrates a very ambivalent attitude toward the tribe. He has no qualms about removing its members from their land; compared to the white tourists who would come in their place they lacked, he decides, a sense of beauty: "In none of their objections made to the abandonment of their home, was there anything said to indicate any appreciation of the scenery." Bunnell claims that he, as a grand gesture, told the chief of the band that he had decided to name a lake after him and is surprised that this doesn't seem to please him. Bunnell continues: "From this lake we were leading the

Figure 14. The tourist Indian invaded the mountains after the local tribes had been displaced. Great Northern Railway brochure (cover), 1925, written to promote vacations in Glacier National Park (Montana Historical Society Library, Helena)

last remnants of his once dreaded tribe, to a territory from which it was designed they should never return as a people."[45]

Although small groups of Miwok-Paiutes continued to try to make a living in this new tourist area, it is striking how rapidly the Native American past was erased, apart from the select namings made by the white explorers. Yosemite, this American garden of Eden, was presented as virgin land, a true wilderness. The irony was, as Rebecca Solnit shows, that when the first tourists came to Yosemite they found the oak woods in the meadows along the winding river a truly picturesque view in the accepted British sense. What they didn't know was that this scenery was a garden not of Eden, but of a long tradition of horticulture. Generations of Miwok-Paiutes had produced this specific landscape by regularly burning parts of it, by securing good conditions for oak trees, which produced the acorns gathered for food, and by keeping the undergrowth under control, in order to be able to hunt deer and other animals for food. With the tribe gone the picturesque landscape started to become overgrown.[46]

The tribe's forced evacuation from the nation's playground was necessary in order to clear the place for the invasion of a new tribe: the romantic image of Indian life. Its mystic and poetic rhetoric had very little resemblance to those few, impoverished Miwok-Paiutes who remained and tried to make some sort of living among the tourists. Their replacement was the Indian of summer camps, Boy Scouts, outdoor crafts, and popular fiction, as, for example, in organizations like *Seaton's Tribe of Woodcraft Indians* from 1902.[47] Later on the tribe's culture was further reorganized into "live Indian exhibits," for example, with crafts being demonstrated by contracted Miwok-Paiutes.

The landscapes of tourism have other forms of ethnic invisibility. In an ongoing study of Solvang, "the Danish Capital of America," Anders Linde-Laursen shows how this tourist attraction in southern California, where 1.5 million visitors come each year to consume "Danishness," depends on the invisibility of those members of the community locally called "the Mexicans." Chicanos as well as migrants from south of the border make up the labor force that keeps this attraction running but, in order not to disturb the blondness of this theme-park town, they work unseen, backstage.[48]

But what about the ethnic mix among tourists? The theme rarely surfaces in the literature on leisure and the history of American tourism. An early example of an ethnic conflict was the anti-Semitism that Jewish vacationers encountered, from the turn of the century and onward. Already in the 1870s hotels could state bluntly "Hebrews need not apply" or "Israelites not accepted." During later periods this discrimination took on more subtle forms as for example in one Miami hotel in the 1940s, which used the postscript "As always, restricted clientele."[49] (The famous Borscht Belt of Jewish summer resorts in the Catskills grew out of this tourist discrimination.)[50] If Jewish families were not welcome in many Palm Beach hotels, African Americans were to stay invisible, elsewhere. From the 1940s Cleveland Amory writes about "the resort's traditional, though unwritten, curfew law which forbids any colored person, not employed in a Palm Beach home, to be on the streets after dark."[51]

African Americans would feel out of place in many parts of the tourist world. Even the roads were likely to be an unsafe and unwelcome environment: in his autobiography, Chester Himes recounts how in the 1940s, even as a successful author driving a new car, he was forced to travel straight across the country, from New York to California, avoiding most of the stopovers along the route.[52] As an African American man he was an unwelcome guest in the transit culture along the highway.

The striking whiteness of tourism, from seaside resorts to national parks, may also acquire a nostalgic element. The British anthropologist Judith Okely describes the contemporary celebration of "Constable country," a return to the landscape and culture of early nineteenth-century England made famous by the painter. One of its white middle-class appeals, she argues, is that it presents a version of life "when England was England." The nostalgia for old tourist landscapes may often include a nostalgia for a time when "people knew their place" and no immigrants strolled down by the riverside.[53]

The dimensions of class, ethnicity, and gender problematize what the tourist experience is about, and above all the kinds of "freedom to" or "freedom from" that motivate different groups. These tensions also enter the Robinsonian quest for "getting away from it all," which the next chapters explore.

part 2

Getaways

Cottage Cultures

Why do people need a vacation? Linnerhielm and many of his contemporaries did not travel in search of rest and relaxation. For these privileged gentlemen leisure was part of everyday life. In the industrial society of the nineteenth century the idea of leisure as compensation developed. A 1903 guide to the Catskills elaborates the arguments:

> We need change, and cannot live on monotony or systematic routine. Every one of the five senses need a new diet and a change of regime. This cannot be had in the atmosphere or horizon of the town home, even with the entire cessation of work and business. All must be changed— the air, the scenery, the environment, the room, the food, the people we meet, the sounds we hear; to make the rest complete and secure the ben-

109

efits desired. These things we have learned during recent years in the ethics of a Summer vacation, which are being studied by careful observers and scientists.[1]

It took roughly a century for vacations to become an opportunity for (almost) everybody in the Western world, from the 1850s to the 1950s. This gradual expansion to new social groups brought heated debates and struggles over priorities. Does everybody really need a vacation? Workers, housewives? What are vacations good for? How should you spend this new freedom? To understand the making of these "ethics of a Summer vacation," we have to move further back in time.

In 1682 the German Countess Aurora von Königsmarck wrote what looks suspiciously close to a tourist brochure, a collection of letters entitled "Les divertissements de Medevij." The intention was to have copies of the letters distributed to stately homes in order to attract the aristocracy to a new spa at Medevi, then a remote rural spot in southern Sweden.[2]

The twenty-year-old Aurora portrays a world of summer pleasures in baroque forms, in which there is scarcely time for the actual taking of the waters alongside all the gallantry, curtseys, visits, suppers, Roman camps, knightly tournaments, and masquerades. If the author goes overboard in her attempt to lend a continental air to Medevi, it should be said that for most nature lovers in the seventeenth century the boundary between ideal and reality was extremely fluid. Swedish nature—boorish, untidy, ugly—had to be Latinized and made as beautiful as the hills around Rome or Florence. With the help of suitable props and enough imagination, stony hillsides and straggling forests could be refurbished into a northern Arcadia. One of the hills at Medevi was conveniently transformed into Parnassus and peopled by Swedish nobles, dressed up as shepherds and classical gods, surrounded by bleating lambs. This is a double-exposed landscape, a piece of Swedish scenery viewed through a Mediterranean filter.

Medevi developed into a success. During the eighteenth century it became *the* place to visit during summer for aristocrats and intellectuals—the cream of Stockholm society. Still, it remained a very humble copy of the fashionable spas on the continent, just a group of timbered houses in the wood, placed around the spa pavilion. (Much of its rustic eighteenth-century atmosphere remains today.) Interestingly enough it was this simplicity that turned it into a very early experiment of utopian summer living.

In the summer of 1742 Countess Tessin sits in one of the small cottages, which she shares with the king's chamberlain and a few other aristocrats of high rank. She is writing a letter to her beloved husband, Carl-Gustaf, who is in Paris as the king's ambassador to the French court. She reminds him of the many happy summers they have spent at Medevi, with "horse rides, dancing, improvised parties, pranks, and practical jokes" and tells him that she has met an old peasant woman who said, "we're never going to see such fun again as the year when Count Tessin was here."[3]

In Paris, Tessin was exposed to the rigors of French court etiquette, but even the attempts at playing pastoral games, which were popular French aristocratic pastimes, seemed very regimented compared with the informality of Medevi summers.

So what made families like Tessin and others from the Swedish elite forsake the comfort of their Stockholm palaces or country manors and travel to the end of the world—far away from everything? Why were they ready to live together in very simple conditions in these small cottages, next to the wretched invalids and the sick who were crowded together on the other side of the road—intent, like their aristocratic counterparts, on the beneficial effects of "taking the waters"? Obviously, the waters weren't the area's only attraction. In some ways, Medevi became the first Swedish summer camp. Here the alternative utopia of a simpler summer life took shape: a new kind of cottage culture.

The secrets of Medevi started with the ritual move from the territories of work, court ceremonies, and urban life. Traveling to Medevi was a journey to elsewhereland—a magic act of transformation, which could turn a cabinet minister or a countess into a summer child. In 1731 the author Olof von Dalin writes from Medevi on the delights of rural summer life: "its endearing innocence, pleasant simplicity, and agreeable freedom compared to the false artificiality of Stockholm, with its cringing, foolish display, and forced mannerisms."

Out here in the country a more sensual and authentic person could emerge—both more childish and irresponsible. The stiff urban adult was given a chance to be born again. At Medevi informal pleasures were supposed to rule with improvised happenings and masquerades, such as the staging of a mock peasant wedding or a Turkish embassy. People flirted, gossiped, kept running in and out of the cottages, gambled, and mused over the antics of the common people. In a treatise on the benefits of taking the waters, Count Tessin wrote: "A mobile man, who uses the spa for the health of his body, should walk, should dance, should swing, should move."

Some of the magic of the summer vacation had begun to work, but the institution of an alternative summer world developed slowly and took many forms. Here I follow the trail from Medevi to the making of "cottage cultures," which have had a strong tradition in both Scandinavia and parts of North America.

I start with the European experience of colonizing the seaside and look at the ways in which summer communities developed along the Swedish west coast and then turn to the rituals and routines of summer cottage life as it evolved on both sides of the Atlantic. What interests me is a new kind of Robinsonian social life out on the coast, as well as the cultural confrontations between this rather sheltered upper- and middle-class summer world, the local populations, and the growing number of mobile tourists.

TAKING THE WATERS

Medevi was a very rustic version of the fashionable spas on the continent, which had developed as either drinking spas or hot springs, where medicinal baths could be taken. There is a long tradition behind these spas, but their peak period occurred in the eighteenth and nineteenth centuries—all over Europe and North America.[4] During this period the traditional inland spas got competition from seaside spas as the medicinal benefits of sea bathing came to be stressed. Alain Corbin follows this transformation in his book *The Lure of the Sea: The Discovery of the Seaside,*

1750–1840.[5] He points out how the search for the sublime also came to redefine the wilderness of the seaside as a tourist destination, but above all how the new seaside spas developed into the innovation of the seaside vacation.

Many of the early spas, such as Bath and Brighton, its variant on the Channel coast, were frequented by the aristocracy and were characterized by heavily regimented social interaction and an obsession with hierarchies and rituals. An endless program of assemblies, dances, receptions, visits, and card parties organized the season. Against this strict regime the simplicity of Medevi may seem to us more modern, an early example of a new cult of informal summer life.

The seaside spas colonized a territory seen as devoid of aesthetic qualities. Its scenery was of little interest to the early tourist pioneers. Linnerhielm passed through the Varberg region on the Swedish west coast in 1803 and found the landscape barren and repulsive, with no beautiful views. During an earlier visit to the coast a bit further north he stated: "All the islands or promontories that can be seen are rocks; and these are totally bare and not even picturesque. Throughout the whole journey, not a single beautiful place was seen."[6] Other inland visitors agreed with him: the coastal landscape was wild and foreign, disorderly and inharmonious—a depressing landscape. "Not even picturesque" was a harsh judgment, which showed that the romantic search for a wilder nature was in its early stages: the coast was still too wild. And large sections of Scandinavian coastlines, close to the seaways, had been stripped of timber and left naked; grazing sheep kept new vegetation at bay. Visiting the new spa in Varberg in the 1840s, a Swedish author complained that the only green in the landscape was the ribbon of the decoration worn by the mayor. As real-estate agents later discovered, this condition produced a great number of lots with excellent sea views.

When the first sea spas were established along the Swedish west coast during the first half of the nineteenth century it was not the pleasures of the landscape but the medicinal benefits of seawater and the healthy, bracing air that were the attractions.

For many visitors the first confrontation with the seascape made a strong impact: the vast horizon, the barren cliffs and beaches, the

Figure 15. British nineteenth-century seaside resort with pier and bathing machines. (Photo The Bridgeman Art Library, London)

movements of the water—in the language of the sublime such a land-scape could also be seen as having a new aesthetic potential. Out here on the rugged coast you felt close to the dramatic forces of nature.

The new magic of the seashore in northern Europe developed in several stages, as Corbin reminds us. The early cult of the sublime was followed by the romantic quest for the sensualities of walking along the shore, feeling the wind in your hair, tasting the salt on your lips, crossing dunes, climbing cliffs. Standing on a rock at the outermost shore facing the mighty sea became a classic romantic pose. Add to this the new interest in maritime lore, the romancing of smugglers' caves, old pirates' lairs, and the celebration of seafarers braving the elements.[7]

Artists had a crucial role in this redefinition of the seashore, not only by starting to paint seascapes in new ways, but also by settling along the coast in colonies, often becoming the first summer pioneers on both sides of the Atlantic.[8] The special light, the play of sun, water, and mist in the landscape, and the cheap cost of living and the quaintness of the local folk attracted them. In 1870 a popular Swedish magazine published a fictitious letter from an artist to his colleague:

> I have decided for a time to abandon civilization to be with nature. I wish you could see me and be with me, to hear the harmony that I hear and to feel the same bliss that I feel. This is how I am living: a simple room in a meager cabin. This room has two windows; through one of them I can see cliffs, through the other the sea. Imagine this scenery peopled with ragged, ruddy old salts, defying the tossing waves in their boats, or sitting outside the cabins in the sunshine, mending their fishing nets. Nothing can be more salutary for the mind than this stillness combined with this majesty of nature.[9]

The enthusiastic artist had many kindred spirits in Scandinavia. Toward the end of the nineteenth century colonies of artists formed in remote coastal settings, where coastal features now became attractive and paintable. Scandinavian painters returned home from their artist colonies in Rome, Paris, and Düsseldorf.[10] The coast that had previously been defined as far too chaotic now became harmonious, the dismal open spaces became restful, attractive in their clarity and simplicity.

The very emptiness and simplicity of the landscape made room for finding yourself, entering a trancelike or meditative state of mind. There was a new space of freedom here, freedom from the fetters of civilization, the stress of urban life, and colonizing it started out as a very male project: getting away from it all. Here is another typical gentleman's daydream, this time from a Danish magazine in 1866:

> Would you consider running under a happy breeze over to the Swedish or Norwegian archipelago, romping among its rocks and islands, hunting seabirds and seals, hearing the breakers roar against the cliffs, as you lie secure in your boat behind the island—or dreaming about the still, silent night, when the lighthouse shines alone on the cliff above your head, while the boat lies silently on the gleaming black surface, and the only sound you hear is the faint cry of a bird and the beat of its wings as it hovers over the mast? The still, silent night, in which the voice within us is heard loud because nothing from outside can disturb us; instead, everything brings that voice forth. If you cannot conceive such days and nights, then you have no freedom or strength and feel no emotion or poetry, and you do not belong on the sea, and you need no pleasure boat; but if you are the lucky owner of this gift, then set off if you can.[11]

COME ON IN

The new interest in the seascape was intertwined with medical discourse on the healthiness of the maritime environment: brisk walks along the beach, exposure to the sea breeze swaddled in blankets, and of course slow immersion in seawater. This last ritual was surrounded by a great deal of medical advice and rules of propriety. All over northern Europe bathing machines appeared along the fashionable beaches, allowing an occupant to step down into the sea, sheltered from the views of others inside its wooden structure, after a horse had pulled it out into the water. The cold water was part of a cure to toughen both body and mind: the shock was good for you. Brave men among the seaside tourist pioneers threw themselves into the waves as an act of virility but, as Alain Corbin points out, it was good to have women around to admire that bravery.

Most of the days were spent resting, and, Corbin observes, the contemplative experience out at the seashore was of benefit to invalids. Doctors ordered their patients to the sea and installed a constant reflexivity; the seaside resorts became sanatoriums: "The invalid knew he must analyze himself endlessly, if he hoped to achieve his own recovery."[12] In this way, new forms of awareness were installed. Out at the beach you learned to listen not only to the waves and the wind but also to your body. The experience of just relaxing in a canvas chair or on a beach blanket and absorbing the landscape, which today is so central to beach life, started here.

Bathing in the sea thus began as a direct extension of water cures, and even if the bathing machines fell from vogue by the end of nineteenth century, bathing itself attracted an extensive medical cosmology that prescribed how, where, and when people should enter the sea. This genre of literature started in the eighteenth century and peaked during the latter half of the nineteenth century, as sea bathing became more popular. An example of this genre is a little Swedish publication entitled "In Bathrobe: Hygienic Hints for Bathers" from 1890, in which a doctor gives detailed medical advice. He reminds his readers of the importance of bathing in a calm frame of mind, "thinking neither of difficulties with servants nor of stock-market rates," in order to attain the goal of bathing: the undisturbed harmony of one's mental forces. There are strict warnings about developing bathing into a sport and throwing oneself into the waves more than once a day. "Exaggeration like this normally has a harmful effect on the nervous system." The doctor also has a detailed program for the bather's everyday rhythm, the time for rising, for bathing, for invigorating walks, and so on. Open-air bathing was still a subject of controversy. In 1909, for example, a Danish writer maintained that bathing in the sea can be downright harmful for the body.[13]

The history of sea bathing is often described as a Victorian innovation, hedged in by all sorts of precautions and rules of privacy and modesty. There was, however, a wide range of earlier and parallel traditions of skinny-dipping or taking a plunge, just for fun, and—against the scenery of bathing machines in orderly rows and dignified bourgeois letting themselves slowly down into the water sheltered from the looks of others—more uninhibited scenes.[14] The Victorian reinvention of sea bathing also meant disciplining it, which included a strict monitoring of female behavior. A lot of paternal advice reminded women to control and cover their bodies down on the beach, and to be aware of the risks they took as frail beings going into the water. Maybe the best thing was to abstain totally from learning to swim, and leave this pastime to the men.[15]

The official picture of decorous Victorian bathing contrasts with a much more liberated reality from the Swedish west coast at the turn of the century. A newspaper report from the beaches at Halmstad in 1906 paints the following picture:

> It was all a swarm of men, women, and children, horses and dogs. For the more modest ladies, bathing is not entirely a pleasure. A long row of naked horsemen gallop along the beach. Shaking and trembling, the ladies balance their way with downcast eyes, until they successfully reach some sheltered place.[16]

There are many other examples of a more uninhibited beach life. As seaside tourists started to explore the waves, not as a prescribed cure but as a secret pleasure, a new freedom of movement and body developed. Life at the seaside was natural and unpolluted in several ways, bathers now recognized; it was far removed from the fumes and refuse of cities and industries and it was pure: clean water and fresh, invigorating air, but it was also a refuge in which to enjoy a true life—simple and natural.

This liberating quality is mainly a product of a growing critique of the demands of city life, its stressful, inharmonious character. Out at the coast you could experience a freedom not only from rules and obligations, but also from crowds and noise. The seaside was not a string of pleasing vistas and walks, but rather a new kind of emotional space, an experimental zone where you could question the norms, habits, and routines of bourgeois city life and stretch them a bit, even transgress them. A new polarity between country and city, between summer and winter life was emerging.

The development of resorts mirrors this gradual transformation from health to fun. All over Scandinavia seaside resorts emerged in line with

Figure 16. Mölle was a fashionable Swedish seaside resort that deliberately used daring postcards of mixed bathing in its marketing strategy. (Photo Peter P. Lundh from around 1910, Höganäs Museum)

the British and continental fashions during the nineteenth century, but the Scandinavian experience could never live up to the haut monde of those fashionable spas and resorts. Other circumstances also contributed to create a somewhat different seaside tradition up here in the north as compared with England, Germany, and France.

SPAS, HOTELS, AND BOARDINGHOUSES

"You don't mean to say you're staying here in town in the middle of the summer!" This surprised and disapproving comment was addressed to a Helsinki girl by an elderly acquaintance who bumped into her in the Finnish capital. Around 1900 it was already considered self-evident in Scandinavia that the bourgeoisie should leave town to spend summer in the countryside, preferably on the coast.[17] A Danish medical book from the same time points out that any well-off city dweller should naturally spend the summer in a bathing resort, "far away from the polluted city air."[18]

This Scandinavian conquest of the seashore developed through several stages. The first seaside spas were highly exclusive vacation institutions, where the local press often noted the arrivals of prominent guests. A closed, elitist world was forming here, in the pattern of continental spas.

As the leisure element grew stronger, many of the traditional nineteenth-century spas were gradually reorganized into seaside hotels, emphasizing vacation pleasures more than health cures. This mix of health, fun, and sport is still stressed in a travel guide to the west coast from 1925. One resort describes itself like this: "mild climate, fresh, hardy air, marvelous beaches for bathing, beautiful walks, wonderful sunsets, tennis—sailing—dancing, full licenses to serve alcohol, bathing doctors." Another one, which labeled itself the oldest bathing resort in Sweden, lists the following advantages: "Magnificent scenery. Paths along the shore and through the forest. Radioactive health spa. Hot and cold saltwater baths. Social amusements, sailing, fishing. Music every day in the park."

The large, fashionable seaside hotels, which tried to live up to the standard of their continental models, never acquired a dominant position in Scandinavia. At the turn of the century there was already a belief that life at the seaside should be simpler and more natural than in the continentally inspired hotels or, as one summer visitor wrote from a small resort on the west coast:

> We avoid the annoyance of seeing a lot of mannequins in countless out-fits, avoid incessant, expensive society events, and in general all these compulsory conventions that spoil life for most people at the larger bathing resorts. Social life here is nice, familiar, unconstrained—every-one does what he or she pleases, and the small coteries of young people amuse themselves in the fresh, artless way that is possible only in sim-ple, unpretentious scenery.[19]

It was in fact the modest seaside boardinghouse—an often caricatured institution—that became a Nordic specialty. The boardinghouse was much less fashionable but still had its strict rituals. Precisely because vis-itors mingled so directly and so intimately with strangers, distinctions became important. Each visitor learned his place both in the dining room and among the different coteries, and new arrivals were closely ob-served. The first entry into the dining room was a nervous debut role played to an inquisitive, cautious audience. A typical Danish seaside novel from 1890 describes this sensitive moment:

> The new people sharing the table . . . inspected each other with furtive glances to see how high they could value each other. The situation was not a little reminiscent of the way in which, at children's balls, the boys gather along one wall and the girls along the other before the dance be-gins. They had a burning desire to speak to each other, but they did not know how to set about doing so.[20]

Half a century later, a Swedish journalist describes the same mood:

> The first minutes in a new dining room are terrible! Everyone looks at you and tries at the same time to look as if they were not curious. You yourself bow blushingly and slightly too humbly, and the other guests bow back, gravely and reservedly, as if they were expressing condolences.
>
> All the others have napkin cases or napkin rings of precious material or metal, and you think to yourself how strange it is that you never re-member to take one along.[21]

A guest in a Danish boardinghouse during the 1920s recounts a breach of decorum when a young lady at table two, who normally had to be content with simpler service, suddenly raises her voice and says: "Would it not be possible for the *good* cheese to reach our table at least once?" A deathly silence fell on the dining room: "It was not one angel that passed through the dining room, but a whole regiment of them." A nervous waitress hurried over with the cheese, which was then passed round without anyone else daring to touch it, after which it returned to its proper place at the table of honor.[22]

What did you learn as a boardinghouse guest, apart from knowing your place and finding your napkin ring? The picture of a thoroughly controlled and hierarchical boardinghouse life became an easy foil for the caricatures of later generations. The boardinghouse also provided training for society building in miniature. Families had to learn how to live along with other strange families, which led to the first-night nerves that are often described. But the weeks in the boardinghouse were not primarily a matter of dressing properly for dinner, or taking the items from the smorgasbord in the correct order, but of building up a different and collective leisure time with croquet tournaments, masquerades, boating excursions, practical jokes, and improvised evening entertainment. It was not etiquette but rather the renunciation of as much as possible of the etiquette of urban winter society that was the exciting challenge, and summer life at the seaside was shaped by the tension between the ingrained conventions of winter life and the longing for a simple, sensuous, corporeal life.

For many women, boardinghouse life could be liberating in some ways. Married women escaped the responsibility of the housewife and hostess, while unmarried women could find their own place—without male chaperones—in the boardinghouse collective.

A HOUSE WITH A VIEW

Next to hotels and boardinghouses, settlements of summer houses had slowly been growing along the Swedish west coast since the end of the nineteenth century. Building one's own house by the sea was at first a project restricted to the wealthy upper middle class, and the new settlers had strong preferences about where to build.

In the coastal villages close to the town of Varberg summer visitors started to buy up land and property in the early twentieth century. Their preferences amazed the local population, as the highest demand was for locations that hitherto had little economic or aesthetic value: the wind-blown hills of heather and the rugged cliffs. All of a sudden it was locations with a view of the sea and the coastline (even better, facing the sunset) and the walking distance to the beach that shaped the demand. In the local economy the beach was only a source for seaweed to fertilize the fields. Swimming was unheard-of as a pastime—most of the locals who earned their livelihood from fishing never learned to swim. They, like farmers, preferred to have their houses well sheltered from the wind behind a cliff. The idea that you should be able to contemplate a maritime panorama from your parlor was alien to most of them: you got more than enough of the sea during your daily work.

The new summer houses, whether they were the little wooden palaces built early in the century or the more functionalist boxes erected in the thirties and forties, had one thing in common. The glass veranda, and later the functionalist picture window, was the focus of the house. Thus a whole new settlement pattern emerged during the first half of this century, based on the scarce resource of views: views of the sea, the horizon, and preferably the sunset. Tourists learned to look west.

Today "the view" is still an important asset for local summer visitors in the region, although in the real estate market a house with a view has become a scarcer asset. The rapid reforestation of the coastal area has made the landscape less open, which means that many summer guests devote quite a lot of energy to keeping the vegetation at bay or fiercely oppose new developments that would "block my view."

The pioneer generations of summer cottagers were recruited from the urban elite, but during the twenties and thirties the social base was broadened. The middle class of civil servants, academics, and office clerks built themselves less imposing summer houses, but the relative austerity of the new summer settlements reflected more than a need to economize. The new generations saw themselves as representing a more modern attitude to summer life and were eager to distance themselves from what they saw as the artificial and overceremonious traditions of the summer pioneers. They would ridicule the rituals and habits of the Victorians: ladies with umbrellas strolling along the beach, men in white suits drinking brandy and admiring the sunset from the hotel veranda.

The new middle class was out to colonize the summer in a different way: in practical clothes, in sporty styles and with healthy habits. Summer life should be simple![23] It was good to live without all the amenities of urban civilization. Playfulness was the order of the day, and each summer day was filled with activities: hiking, biking, sailing, swimming, badminton, and boccie. Summer life was the healthy antidote to an over-civilized urban winter existence, and vacationers could relearn the art of being childish and playful. Amazed children could watch their serious winter uncles take off their jackets and vests to do somersaults in the grass, play hide and seek down at the beach, or frolic in the waves.

The quest for simplicity also meant a growing interest in traditional houses. After the Second World War old farmhouses and fishing cottages became much sought after, and you could always tell if it was a summer visitor or a local who lived in the house, by judging the scarcity of the window decorations. In the new middle-class aesthetic, moderation was supposed to rule.

These cottage communities along the coast expanded rapidly, and hotels and boardinghouses emptied in the 1960s as families preferred the privacy of their own summer cottage or a rented house. By the 1970s there were half a million vacation homes all over Sweden, most of them on the coast, distributed among a population of a little more than eight million Swedes, and roughly the same number of pleasure boats.[24]

Summer visitors bought up whole coastal communities, house by house. Those who could not afford or find an old house built new ones, but often in the style that symbolized the perfect Swedish vacation, a little red painted cottage, with a flagpole firmly planted in the middle of the lawn.

MEETING THE LOCALS

The class confrontations that took place in the boardinghouse dining rooms paled in comparison with the encounter with the local populace.

The invasion of the coastal communities in the decades around 1900 gave rise to odd confrontations, in which the urban upper class came face to face with marginalized and isolated poverty. Many of these coastal communities were among the poorest in the nation, and it would be hard to think of a greater social, cultural, and economic divide in Sweden at that time.

The "genuine" people were at first seen as exotic scenery, as in the artist's letter cited above. In an 1858 handbook of bathing resorts on the Swedish west coast, the local population around Varberg appears in less picturesque terms:

> For long stretches the eye sees no other human dwellings than a wretched croft or fisherman's hut surrounded by some sunburned, half-naked children playing in the sand with the pigs. If one sees any adult representatives of the local population, they are of the kind that one would expect in such scenery. No fire in their eyes, no life in their souls, no quickness of thought can be detected. The nature in which they live has stamped her impression on them. They are a breed of profound destitution, of bitter privation, of meager spiritual means.[25]

Later the view of the locals became more complex.[26] The yearbook of the Swedish Touring Club for 1903 speaks of "these simple but healthy and worthy people of the lower classes," a population not yet harmed by the diseases resulting from civilization. Out here in the archipelago, people who had spent the winter dealing with "dissatisfied, whining, and nervous upper-class types" could find relief for their souls.[27]

But the attitude to the naturalness of the lower classes was ambivalent. The lack of culture could be offensive and even threatening, especially since the visitors' own children could learn unmannerly behavior from the locals. A newspaper article from 1872 complains about "the impudence" of local children and their "unsuitable manners, language, and behavior" and asks summer visitors to protect their own children against such influences.[28]

The picture of "the others" thus became ambivalent. Some middle-class visitors felt that their own presence should have a healthy civilizing effect. Good manners and etiquette, it was hoped, would spread to the rude cottagers. Others discovered a world with different cultural values—for them the life of the local population gave rise to critical self-reflection: some in the urban elite could see themselves as "overcivilized" and anxiously bound by conventions.

The local population created their own picture of the summer visitors, in a richly embroidered folklore. People along the coast told yarns about idiotic urbanites and hoity-toity ladies. There was the story of the visitor who did not want to charter a boat but insisted on sailing himself. He heaved a huge stone into the boat as ballast and then watched in surprise as first the stone and then the boat sank to the bottom. "It appears to have made a hole in the bottom," he said in wonderment to the local audience on the jetty. "Looks like it," was the laconic response. This narrative tradition often has the form of the trickster genre, with the quick-witted villager outwitting the unpractical, pompous town-dweller. In another of these stories, the local people are irritated by the fact that visitors are allowed to take their dogs into the restaurant. The restaurateur cuts off the criticism by saying, "Of course domestic animals are allowed," which gives some boys the idea of returning, dragging a reluctant cow into the dining room.

The encounter became even more concrete through the special form of shared accommodation that developed along the coasts of Scandinavia, where those visitors who did not choose the boardinghouse or could not build their own cottage rented rooms in the homes of the locals. Theirs was a cheaper and more informal kind of vacation than life in a hotel or a boardinghouse. It could also be a more programmatic idea of living close to the common people. A Dane remembers her officer father's argument from the early twentieth century: "Every spring my father was on reconnaissance to find out where we should spend the summer. We were to get to know our country and the common rural life . . . and live together in healthy nature."[29]

The locals in need of the money moved out to a shed or down into the basement. On the Swedish west coast as in some other regions, there was an old rural tradition of moving out to summer quarters, to live under more primitive conditions, which made such a rental arrangement fit in easily. Many locals remember having urban guests as something exciting. All of a sudden you had these fancy town people in your own yard. The social boundaries had to remain, though. In some cases local kids were allowed to socialize with the guests, but they had to know their place. From their close observation posts the locals could contemplate the exotic habits of townspeople. A Norwegian remembers his childhood in the 1920s:

> We looked forward to the arrival of these holiday people. But we were never together with them. They lived in a world we could only dream about. We hid behind bushes and trees to watch nicely dressed children play and use the gramophone on the veranda. But we were ashamed of our dialect, our clothes, and above all our shoes, and never dared to come forward.[30]

Illustrating this strange confrontation of two worlds apart, a Swedish west coast fisherman exclaimed:

> Oh, how we bent our backs for the summer guests! They came in their white linen suits. The difference was obvious, but there was no influence on the lifestyle of the locals. They could not afford it. And what would it have looked like if a woman from here was seen wearing an upper-class hat? No, it wasn't possible. They were two different worlds.[31]

Even if the locals adjusted perforce to the habits and wishes of the summer visitors, in most bathing resorts people followed the advice that a fisherman's son received from his mother: "Let them have theirs and we can have ours!"

For another fisherman the strongest memory was of the immense difference in standard of living. The summer guests brought tinned food and gave local kids their worn-out tennis shoes. When the guests left, you searched the house and the garden for leftovers from their luxurious holiday life.

The locals needed the money but felt very much like the underdogs in this relationship. Their resentment was rarely overt. Visitors could complain about the uncommunicative or sulky attitudes of the locals, their laconic and sluggish reactions, but usually failed to recognize their hosts' silent resistance. Their villages and even their homes were occupied by an alien culture in sandals and suntan lotion, with hearty laughter, plenty of cash, and a friendly interest in the life of the coastal people. The vacationers' wish to "come close to the people" blinded them to the condescending nature of this project.

But the cultural encounter on the coast also created a new cultural reflexivity. During the summer months both parties glimpsed a diametrically different way of living and thinking. The coastal population met an urban world that would otherwise be infinitely distant, while the bourgeoisie had their self-image shaken. Even the most secure men in their careers might suddenly feel inferior. Compared with the fishermen, they were clumsy and fumbling when they took on the practical challenges of summer life. In the same way, the locals came to feel less inferior as they recovered from the invasion. Women in particular took the initiative in the new vacation economy: it was mostly they who looked after the renting of rooms and the running of kiosks and cafés. For many locals it was also a symbolically important change when their own living standards became so high in the 1950s and 1960s that they no longer needed to move down into the basement or the garden shed. Now they could stay where they were and rent the shed to the visitors instead!

OLD AND NEW GUESTS

Quite early in the twentieth century the ideology of the healthiness of summer life by the sea led to the construction of a number of summer camps for working-class children from inland cities. Working-class families were still rare visitors to the coast in the 1930s, but with the new statutory two-week holidays in 1938, more and more workers made their way to the seaside. Boardinghouse life was not a working-class alternative—it remained a middle-class arena—but some industries and labor unions sponsored guest homes for their employees and members, where they could spend a week or two together with co-workers and their families. In this novel form of collective holidays, the days filled with games, excursions, swimming, and the evenings with community singing, card playing.

At first workers could be hesitant: Was it really a good idea to spend vacation time with co-workers? Wouldn't it just be endless shop talk? But the critics were wrong: a new collectivity of families emerged, as well as new summer skills such as fishing and boating.[32]

A strong sense of freedom came with the first statutory holidays: the mind-boggling thought of having two whole weeks at one's own disposal. To be able to pack a tent and equipment on bicycles and set off out to the coast remains a powerful memory for this working-class generation. It was an intoxicating sense of freedom, as if the world had suddenly opened and their horizons had widened. Down at the beach occupied by the middle-class cottagers, working-class families pitched their tents. With the growing prosperity of the postwar years, workers exchanged their bicycles for cars. A new and much more mobile tourism emerged on the coast:

> Motoring has turned bathing guests into nomads. They derive their summer pleasure from a vehicle and a tent. They go into the water wherever they find it, not concerned about whether or not a village there can give them a summer address. No bathing attendant writes down names, no one knows where the bather goes. People throughout the inland, in cities, villages, and factory towns, rise like a flock of birds and alight to soak up the sun and paddle anywhere the beach invites them.[33]

This is a 1958 statement about the new kinds of tourists who were invading the west coast. Campsites emerged everywhere in new and—in the view of local authorities—far too uncontrolled forms. The reaction of the tourist business to the postwar expansion and the increasingly mobile tourism was mixed. For the traditional middle class the new invasion represented a threat to their own very comfortable holiday pattern, with fixed weeks in boardinghouses, regular guests each with their distinctive napkin rings, and well-worn paths for the daily stroll.

When the Swedish Tourist Traffic Association held its meeting in 1959, this new conflict dominated the debate. Camping and self-catering tourists were to blame for the financial ruin of the traditional tourist institutions. And, local propertyowners warned, "nomadized car families" made a "holiday slum" when they flocked to popular areas.

After the feverish boom in early motorized tourism, camping sites slowly started to become differentiated. Many aimed for a family clientele, and the restless and party-seeking youths had to go elsewhere. The concept of "wild camping" came to denote not only improvised sites, but also the uncontrolled youth life out there on the margins of the tourist landscape. The media already had a long tradition of horrified comment about what really went on inside and around the tents:

> Lying on the beach there are extremely undressed young people in groups or in pairs, watching with indolent, pale eyes the placid progress of the natives as they row past. Empty berry cartons and wrappers for chocolate and chewing gum float on the water, opened cans, broken bottles, and more things like that testify to the ingestion of food. In the background can be glimpsed the tents, low, cramped shelters big enough for two people in lying or possibly sitting position. In one group the listless silence is broken by a shrill girl's voice . . . whose tones emerge from a portable gramophone. The holiday-making city youths are getting back to nature.[34]

This text from 1941 represents a genre with great stability. It sounds rather like the complaints from Yosemite, cited earlier. Another characterization from 1943 describes the campsite visited by city youth as "a zoological garden rather than anything fit for human beings."[35] The threatening aspect of wild camping was above all the fact that it created an alternative arena for youth life outside the control of adult society, and the media shock stories from the campsites continued on through the 1960s and into the 1980s.

By that time "respectable" campers hardly ever used tents. Until the 1960s the trailer had been an exclusive object—a modernist symbol of mobility and adventure. During this decade growing working-class affluence made the trailer a much more popular (and less prestigious) object, and in the new trailer camps a sedentary pattern evolved. Families tended to settle down and return to their own reserved campsite every summer, confirming their status as regular guests by slowly but surely privatizing their surroundings, building fences, starting to lay out small gardens. Many campsites thus changed from transit posts for nomads to homes for steady regulars, but the social tensions in the summer landscape were still there.

We encounter very similar tensions in most cottage cultures over the world. The history of the summer colonization of the Swedish west coast has some local and specific traits, but it also illustrates general patterns found on both sides of the Atlantic.

COTTAGE CULTURES

A cottage is "a humble rural dwelling," according to the dictionary. A summer cottage has a much wider range of forms, from a shack in an allotment garden to "The Breakers," the famous resort cottage in Newport Beach, built in 1895, with the motto Little Do I Care For Riches, And Do Not Miss Them Since Only Cleverness Prevails In The End, written over the fireplace (in French). It has four floors and seventy rooms (thirty-three of them for servants).[36] The strange retention of terms like cottage and cottagers in the American palatial resort tradition of the financial elite is, however, a different story. Here the term summer cottage refers to a rural second home in Europe or North America. It can be anything from an actual restored rural cottage to a farmhouse, a Victorian villa, a hunting lodge, a functionalist box, or a small prefab cabin. The kind of cottage communities that developed along the Swedish west coast have many striking parallels around the world, but they are rather unevenly distributed. Not surprisingly, most of them are found by the water, on seashores or lakesides or in the mountains, and preferably not too far away from the urban centers where the owners live. Roughly 25 percent of Swedish households own a cottage out in the country, and figures are very high for the other Scandinavian countries too. Slightly lower but still high are the figures for France (about 16 percent). Strikingly enough, in Britain, the country many often think of as the classic site of the summer cottage tradition, only a few percent own second homes. There is also a strong cottage tradition in Eastern Europe, as in the Russian *dacha,* which covers anything from a small shack with a kitchen garden to exclusive mansions built for former *nomenklatura.* In the United States second homes approach 4 percent, and the tradition started along the New England coast. In Canada it first focused on the lakes in the Ontario highlands, within easy reach of Toronto.[37]

Culturally, the summer cottage traditions of Canada, the United States, and Scandinavia have striking similarities of lifestyle and symbolic aura. They mostly developed out of summer vacations in hotels and boardinghouses. Ownership of a summer home was at first an ambition of a narrow elite, but during the early twentieth century its social base broadened and, as pressures on recreational space increased, narrowed again in many tourist regions. In 1891 the *Nation* noted the American drift from resorts to farm houses, cottages, and rural villages in accordance with the English tradition: "summer migration is seeking the rural quietudes and moving away from the old centers of mere fashion. . . . The greatest resorts are becoming the summer homes of the class, while the remote places are sought for by the mass."[38]

"The mass" here still referred to the upper middle class of professionals, academics, and managers, who came to dominate the new cottage cultures. The new settlements followed the "back-to-nature" tradition with an emphasis on privacy and a family-centered vacation life—away from the holiday crowds. In Scandinavia they could celebrate a peasant culture heritage and in Canada, more often a frontier past.

In these cottage cultures a very distinct summer world developed, a world of days spent down at the beach, of informal visits and parties in the evening, a great many physical activities such as canoeing, sailing, fishing along with summer sports such as croquet or badminton, hikes to wild berry patches, expeditions by sail or oars to nearby islands. Institutions like bazaars, fairs, and sailing regattas gave summer life a marked structure.[39] Life at the cottage contrasted to the ceremonial-ridden resort life but soon added its own routines and rituals.

One of the most striking characteristics of these cottage cultures had to do with rhythms and temporalities. Most of the year the vacation cottages stood closed: "shutters fastened, porch chairs inside, rank growth of weeds outsides" as Earl Pomeroy described seaside communities on the American West Coast.[40] The start of summer was marked by the grand ritual of leaving town, not for a couple of weeks but for the whole summer. One condition of this departure was the long school vacations typical of North America and Scandinavia; the other was the presence of an adult who did not work outside the household (traditionally, the

Figure 17. Immersed in nature, the members of this American family pose in front of their summer cottage. By now the hammock symbolizes carefree vacations, and so their grave looks probably reflect a formal occasion but could also signal the strains of a family vacation. (Culver Pictures, Inc.)

wife). The family usually spent several months at the cottage, while the wage earner (the husband) visited for shorter periods.

In earlier periods, the summer migration by rail or steamboat was quite an undertaking. Here is a situation from the archipelago of Stockholm around 1910: "As schools ended in June, you moved with all the household goods, from furniture and bedding to silverware, service, and potted plants, onto overloaded steamboats resembling gigantic removal transports." On arrival the house had to be wakened from its hibernation, and the summer cleaning also became a ritual of alterity. You got a whiff of the strange smells of winter before opening up the shutters, letting the summer air in, taking the covers off the furniture, collecting the dead flies along the windowsills, and making sure the mice had left their winter lodgings.

With the car, the move got easier but the ritualization of the journey remained. I remember the family expeditions to our summer house in the 1950s. I cannot help wondering about the amount of stuff we managed to cram into the Volvo. Packing the car was a tense experience, with a lot of bargaining and pleading about what was necessary to bring or not. "Do you really need *this* for the summer?" my stressed Dad would constantly ask the rest of us. (In the end you had to smuggle some of it in.) Finally, overloaded and usually late, the car took off with four kids, a dog, and a number of potted plants precariously balanced on top of the bags. The eight-hour drive from Stockholm to the west coast had its own microrituals and traditions, from the moment one of my sisters always chose to get carsick to the ceremonial lunch at the same old restaurant, preferably with the same menu as last June. We had to keep up the traditions of the drive, in detail. "Hey, we always stop here!" There were constant references to landmarks passed or things that had changed since last summer. We were driving back in time, to the territories of all those early summers. Approaching the coast, we got ready for the standard game: who could spot the ocean first. When we were nearly there Dad had to stop the car to let us kids race down the road to the summer house. Just driving into the grounds wasn't enough of a return to summer.

People usually have strong memories of such comings and goings. On arrival there are the rituals of reclaiming the summer ground. Children fly through the knee-high grass to inspect their territories; the rooms wait, dozing, as if frozen in time, every item left as it was last summer. A year has passed, but in some ways the rhythms of summers deny this. In Ursula Le Guin's collection of stories from a northern California seaside resort, a woman inspects the kitchen of the family beach house, experiencing this strange time warp:

> Everything is circular, or anyhow spiral. It was no time at all, certainly not twelve months, since last October in this kitchen, and she was absolutely standing in her tracks. It wasn't *déjà vu* but *déjà vécu*, and all the Octobers before it, and still all the same this was now, and therefore different feet standing in her tracks.[41]

In the same way the departure at the end of vacations has its own rituals. End-of-summer parties set the mood: the melancholy atmosphere of leave-taking, walking the grounds for the last time, closing shutters, taking a last quick dip . . .

The return to summer also means changes in rhythms and movements. Bodies revert to summer modes of loafing or pottering about, described in metaphors of winding down, shifting gear, relaxing, taking it easy, or as a cottager in the Catskills put it in 1926, "At the little hill farm we bathe our souls in a delicious now. The straining forward for a better tomorrow is stopped a bit."[42]

Clocktime becomes less important. Life is supposed to have fewer deadlines. Routines are broken by the many comings and goings, as guests, kin, or members of the household travel back and forth between town and country. Waiting for the wage earner to return from the city is an important part of this rhythm. In a description of "the husband train" in the Catskills around 1910, "Passengers were shouting the pet names of their wives or children; women and children were calling to their newly arrived husbands and fathers, some gaily, others shrieking as though the train was on fire."[43]

"The husband train" operated throughout the world of cottage cultures, until the family car relieved its ritual comings and goings. Many children remember the long summer spells with Mom as times of freedom, followed by the explosion of activities when Dad arrives and the family is reunited. In summer cottage memories from the first half of the twentieth century, the Saturday evening ritual of stressed family fathers returning from town and "winding down" on the veranda or down at the beach at sunset stand out very clearly. But then next morning activities start. In the standard middle-class division of labor dads are supposed to provide endless projects, expeditions, heroic tasks: Don't just sit there, let's do something!

The car and the five-day week transformed many summer cottages into weekend cottages, but the shuttle between city and beach often remained, although in less dramatic forms. The middle-class othering of city and cottage life developed strong polarities during the last century. In the city, work kept up its usual rhythm. At the cottage the category of work disappeared, or rather out there work *became* leisure. Some could spend a good deal of the summer working on the house, the boat or the garden, but this was not city work—it was a hobby. The most marked polarization, however, is that of an aesthetization of summer life.

SUMMER AESTHETICS

> When we see a modest cabin standing upon a rock, beside a lake or river, we think it beautiful. The same cabin standing in town or city would be a shack, affronting both aesthetic sense and civic ordinances. . . . A summer house should *look* like a summer house, and invite us to recreate ourselves in an easy, summery way, and then we will find it satisfying to the eye and call it beautiful. Whoever has lived in a cottage for a weekend or a month or a summer can look at a picture of it only with longing, must feel the slap of water on canoe and the tug on the fishing line and even smell the burning birch log. Such a house is not simply a house. It is the concrete emblem of a whole class of experiences.[44]

This is a 1970s Canadian version of cottage aesthetics, but the pattern is international. Summer houses should look different, feel different, be used differently. Many of them also have names. Both in Canada and Sweden you find romantic names like "Eagle's Nest" or more whimsical ones. The most common Swedish names have been those dedicated to the summer goddess, the sun, as in *Sunny Slope, Sunny Side,* and *Sunny Glade.* Such names can be seen as a magical invocation of a holiday utopia of endless sunny days

The centrality of the summer cottage as a utopian territory can be understood from the perspectives the French philosopher Gaston Bachelard develops in his book on the poetics of space, where he explores the microchemistry, the psychic state of the home, its potential airiness and weightlessness, the way it opens itself to daydreams and time travel.[45] Bachelard has a tendency to generalize or rather dehistoricize the meanings of home, but his approach works fine for this specific type of dwelling.

Summer cottages become very mobile dream spaces, because most of the year they are inhabited only by longings and memories. They also present a homology between design inside or outside the structure and everyday life in or around it. "The right summer place is as warm and familiar as a comfortable old cardigan," to quote an American enthusiast from 1997.[46] Simplicity and carefree life must go together.

The making of this dream house has many starting points. The British cultural historian Nicholas Green reports on some of them in the early Parisian exodus to *maisons de campagne* in the mid-nineteenth century. He studies advertisements and the marketing of rural property. First of all there is a focus on the dual life, accessibility to Paris is always stressed. Surprisingly little information touches on the layout of the house, its internal aspects, the number of rooms, or the like. Instead it notes a different structure of exteriority and interiority and stresses the eye of the house, its position vis-à-vis surrounding country views on the one hand and on the other the healthy enclosure within, the sheltered garden with its gates and walls: "These were features to conjure up an intimate and private world. They promised *safety,* especially for women and children, and they implied *immersion* in your own sensations and experiences."[47]

The idea of immersion is very central to cottage cultures, letting yourself be drawn totally into a different world, with new aesthetics. At the turn of the century the cult of simplicity was already very evident. "Life is still very simple at the beaches of the northwest coast," wrote the California magazine *Sunset* in 1914.[48] But this simplicity of summering became programmatic and would become even simpler. In Swedish summer cottages white was the color of summer; light colors and light materials, such as wicker furniture, dominated the house interiors. Decorations were supposed to be simple and restrained. Compared to the urban dwellings of the bourgeoisie this was a very striking difference indeed.[49] Later generations took this theme further. They matched the house's simple decor in the informality of dress and socializing: walking barefoot in the grass, improvising outdoor parties, never dressing up. (In Swedish seaside communities it was said in the 1960s that you could easily tell the summer visitors from the locals—the first group wore overalls even on Sundays.) Summer birthdays were often organized on quite a different scale from urban celebrations. There could be improvised theatrics, music. In Sweden the flower garland became the symbol of summer celebrations, adorning the locks of aging executives as well as young girls.

In reminiscences of summer childhoods seemingly trivial details conjure up this universe of otherness. Eliot Porter came from a wealthy Boston family. In 1912 when he was ten his father bought a Maine island as a summer retreat. There was a constant coming and going of guests, ferried over in the family's motorboat *Hippocampus.* The large household assembled for each meal at the twelve-foot table without a tablecloth. His father presided at the head of the table, sliding the filled plates down the well-oiled surface, with guests trying to steer the passing plates along. Glasses of milk were spilled and dishes upset at times, "but the custom was never abandoned," he remembers. In a family with otherwise very strict rules for children, this ritual became a summer adventure.[50]

The cult of simplicity, naturalness, and informality could also mean abstaining from modern conveniences as they became available in summer life. Sticking to the kerosene lamp or the hand pump was part of the lifestyle, not mowing the lawn but letting wild flowers grow. Taking an improvised shower or washing up outside on a rickety bench was a cultural statement, something to enjoy. Later generations could battle about keeping cottages TV-free or not. Coming back to the cottage can thus serve as a reversal in time.

Cottage cultures develop a strange mix of the ephemeral and the long-term. Summer life allows relaxed improvisations—you can make do with simple solutions, cheap materials, temporary arrangements—and yet cottage aesthetics emphasize continuity and stability. The same old silly souvenirs or dried flowers are still there, not to be moved around. Piles of old magazines and mystery stories must line the bookshelves. It is great to walk about in that old straw hat, the one that once was Grandpa's, or to find that worn sweater. (In some ways this is a summer aesthetic of anti-aesthetic, and children in particular become the guardians of unchanging summer life.) In town you can redecorate or switch houses, but to rebuild or sell the cottage, that is something different. The past is thus constantly present in the materials and routines of summer.

The focus on continuity also tells us something about the intense emotional commitment to summer homes. In 1925 *The Great Gatsby*'s narrator calls them inessential houses, but his words ring false. Emotionally, second homes often come first. This strong commitment may also have to do with the increase in the careers of urban mobility. For many people the summer place becomes the territory of rooting, of digging in. You eagerly explore local history and traditions, becoming as local as possible. Local knowledge turns into cultural capital and distinguishes old summer guests from new ones; it may hold jealously guarded secrets about good fishing grounds or berry patches, or well-developed contacts with the "real locals." The term "my wild-strawberry patches" has in Sweden become a metaphor for favorite but secret summer spots. Swedish cosmopolitans who have international careers that take them around the world often make great efforts to have a little red cottage back home, complete with "wild-strawberry patches." Their identities may be intensely transnational but also intensely local, and at the meetings of the local history society they may appear as the most fervent guardians of that local heritage.

This focus on carving out an emotional space in the summer landscape, elaborating a cultural capital of belonging, also raises the question of other visitors as intruders. That "old cardigan" only fits some. A Swedish woman puts it like this:

Being on someone else's land has always made me feel uneasy. Few places are as occupied as other people's summer places, since they are so obviously someone else's homes. Silently unpacking in a strange room and sitting, bouncing a little on a newly made bed to try it out. Hearing voices outside the window, those who feel at home in this place, that still makes me sad. Why does one never grow up?[51]

US AND THEM

What can I tell you about the Moon-Azures?

They own the original Clew homestead with its crooked doorframes and worn stairs, Dr. and Mrs. Moon-Azure from Basiltower, Maryland. I was born in that house.

The Moon-Azures come up from Maryland every June and go back in August. They scrape nine layers of paint off the paneling in the parlor, point out to us the things they do to better the place. They clear out the dump, get a backhoe in to cut a wide driveway. They get somebody to sand the floors. They buy a horse. Dr. Moon-Azure's hands get roughed up when he works on the stone wall. He holds them out and says admiringly: "Look at those hands." A faint smell comes from his clothes, the familiar brown odor of the old house. His wall buckles with the first frost heaves.[52]

E. Annie Proulx's short story "Electric Arrows" gives the locals' perspective on the urban cottagers. The Moon-Azures fence in their new land and also its history: "Dead Clews belong to the property and the property belongs to the Moon-Azures." They are always out on country walks, their hands full of wilted branches, and with an insatiable appetite for local knowledge. When's the right time to pick blackberries? How did the old sheep marks look? Is this facing west? How's the hay coming along?

The Moon-Azures encounter a local resistance movement in forms that recur in many other battles in cottage cultures. In community politics summer guests often stand for the politics of nonchange, which many of the "real" locals can find exasperating. In Swedish fishing villages the cottage people may be all for safeguarding the traditional fishing, but when the locals want to modernize their equipment and expand the harbor facilities, these changes may be seen as unwanted. One summer guest complained about the new rows of blue plastic barrels that local fishermen used for developing mussel farming out in the bay. "If only they could have chosen a more natural material," she sighed. In one of the more fashionable resorts on the American East Coast the summer cottagers tried to prohibit automobiles in 1906, but this time the locals rose united.[53]

The tensions sometimes surface as outright confrontation, sometimes as silent resistance or withdrawal. A study from a Vermont village highlights this. Here the locals were fighting a very active battle to keep the summer people from taking over the place. In an inversion of the example quoted earlier, where summer visitors worried about local culture corrupting their children, the school principal told the visiting researcher, who asked if he could have a job as a substitute teacher, that local people felt that their children got enough outside influence from the summer tourists. They wanted to minimize that influence during the rest of the year by hiring only local teachers.[54]

In the same manner the inhabitants cleansed the school's texts celebrating local life of references to that other life of tourists, summer camps, leaf watchers, holiday fairs. Theirs was a very conscious attempt to keep two cultural worlds separate. A common local attitude was that "those summer people" will never understand what a village like this is like. For example, they would never endure the tough winter or spring's mud season.

Changes from summer affluence to winter austerity feed the animosity that many cottage communities still experience. When the summer visitors leave, the packages of goat cheese, sun-dried tomatoes, and other urban treats disappear from the counters of the local stores. Many shops close down, and the intensity of summer work may give way to the long period of winter unemployment. The locals find themselves walking around in a community where most of the old houses stand dark and abandoned until next year.

Summer resistance to visitors may adopt the sullen, taciturn tactics of avoidance or the kind of trickster jokes mentioned earlier. A favorite

Maine story tells of the resorter on the road from Bangor to Bar Harbor who stops his car and asks a local if this is the right way:

> "Don't know," replies the native. The resorter then inquires how far it is to the nearest town where he can at least ask the way. "Don't know," the native replies once more. At this the resorter is exasperated. "You don't know a hell of a lot, do you?" he says. The native shakes his head. "Nope," he says. "Ain't lost."[55]

Folklore like this often becomes migratory legends to be retold and cherished in many local settings, but at times it gets co-opted by the "other" locals, the old summer guests, who like to think of themselves as part of the local resistance movement against "those tourists."

Some researchers argue that cottage communities tend to construct "two nations" in the same rural place, with confrontations between very different local cultural images, as in the Vermont case.[56] Usually the situation is much more complex, as we have seen in the Swedish examples.

WHO OWNS SUMMER?

My own childhood memories of the 1950s echo this complex social landscape of invisible boundaries and silent hierarchies. Down at "our beach" most families had their favorite spots, territories marked by blankets, toys, and picnic baskets. We thought of ourselves as the old ones— why, some families had even been there for a couple of decades. The "new ones" did not have to be newcomers, their newness was defined by their otherness. They were successful businessmen, who built fancy new houses with impeccable lawns and rhododendron bushes. We silently envied their kids who had all kinds of expensive gadgets, from mopeds to speedboats and water skis, but had to console ourselves with the thought that they did not fit in. The other intruders were the day tourists or weekend campers. They brought fancy portable radios to the beach, which played too loud. The women sometimes sunned in their pink underwear, which seemed rather frivolous. Class was a word no longer used in the 1950s, but it was always present. People could talk about nice families, nice children, nice activities, or hint about what did not belong in this summer world. In questions of ownership what concerned the cottagers wasn't just property. They worried about the ownership of summer life and its safeguarding through a specific lifestyle.

In the constant discussions of who and what belongs in the summer world of cottage life, distinctions are made and remade. On the whole the classic cottage cultures are not only run by the middle class, they tend to be dominated by the kind of middle class that owns more cultural than economic capital (often manifested in a long college education). The battle against intruders in the summer paradise of cottage life during the twentieth century could often be the battle against "the nouveaux riches." Confrontations may focus on issues like allowing speedboats or water skiing, or vetoing attempts at conspicuous consumption. In many ways this was a battle between different bourgeois lifestyles, as well as between "old" and "new" elites. In his 1948 book on the last grand resorts in the United States, Cleveland Amory summarized the conflict like this:

> Today's resort old-timers believe firmly in a curious theory of resorts. This theory is that, generally speaking, the following groups have come to the social resorts in this order: first, artists and writers in search of good scenery and solitude; second, professors and clergymen and other so-called "solid people" with long vacations in search of the simple life; third, "nice millionaires" in search of a good place for their children to lead the simple life (as lived by the "solid people"); fourth, "naughty millionaires" who wished to associate socially with the "nice millionaires" but who built million-dollar cottages and million-dollar clubs, dressed up for dinner, gave balls and utterly destroyed the simple life, and fifth, trouble.[57]

The patterns of development along the New England coast are a bit more complex than this outline suggests. Dona Brown documents the early history of Martha's Vineyard, which today may belong in the Newport category but had a more humble beginning. It started as a Methodist summer camp meeting in the 1830s and by the 1850s had developed into a tent city of campers. Gradually the camp meeting atmosphere changed into a summer vacation community, with families building summer cottages. Still the community prided itself on being something different from

Newport, dominated by industrious and hard-working shopkeepers and artisans. The word "cottage" here signaled the importance of a simple lifestyle, as well as domesticity and informality.

On Martha's Vineyard the Wesleyan Grove was transformed into Cottage City, a type of secular vacation community that spread all over the New England coast. These cottage communities also provided privacy, a shelter from the growing category of working-class sightseers, whose seaside vacation was a day or weekend excursion by steamship, train, or trolley. Toward the end of the nineteenth century a new landscape of beer gardens, picnic groves, and amusement parks developed close to the big urban centers.[58] The increased pressure on beaches and recreational space developed the kind of tensions between "the sedentary" and "the mobile" summer visitors that we met along the Swedish west coast. Cottagers saw day tourists, sightseers, bikers, and later auto campers as intruders in *their* summer world. "Every precaution has been taken to guard against the invasion of excursionists," the Kennebunkport Seashore Company in 1886 assured prospective buyers in this new resort, well knowing that excursionists by then had become the code word for working-class tourists.[59]

A century later a woman remembers the ways in which local summer guests reacted in the 1970s to the sightseers from the nearby factory town, who took the boat out to "their" island on the Swedish west coast:

> We called the boat *Spyfjorden* [i.e., "Puke-fjord"], because it vomited out people and we were lying on the beach looking at the clock: "Good God, they will soon be going back, how nice. Then it'll just be us again."[60]

In another Swedish beach community one of the cottagers watches the visitors:

> They unpack everything, lunch boxes and cool bags and beach balls and water wings and five parasols and everything. And they lie there on the beach all day with their screaming kids who want ice cream and lemonade and this and that, while we who live near the beach, we mostly stay at our houses, and we go down for a swim and go back up to the house again and it's enough to make you smile when you go down for a dip and see all this.[61]

One pattern of avoidance is found in the retreat into privacy among the old and wealthy cottagers or, as a Long Island summer resident in Southampton put it: "I don't spend much time in town either. Summers, the streets are crawling with motorcyclists and backpackers sleeping all over the place. At least they haven't corrupted the sea yet or the gorgeous beach out here . . . "[62] The class dimensions in these confrontations change with different times and settings. For many families who own summer homes, privacy has been a chief concern: during your vacation you should be able to enjoy peace and quiet in the seclusion of an empty beach or on your own plot. For them the dense settlement and the intensive socialization on the beach, in the picnic area, or in the trailer camp represent an alien life. That people choose the camp life not only out of economic necessity but also because they enjoy the intense and informal social life is sometimes difficult to understand for the middle-class householders whose perspective often dominates the nostalgia for those earlier golden days, of peace and quiet and informal togetherness.

Control of territory is thus a touchy issue in cottage cultures. A Canadian observer mused over this tendency in 1946:

> Merely to dwell alongside a lake is good, but it is not everything. The true ideal of summer residence is to OWN a lake, so that you may dwell by it and nobody else can. . . . What he wants is to be able to walk all around the blessed thing and say to himself. "This is mine. If I liked I could drain it dry and nobody would stop me."[63]

Fights over beach access, rights of way, keeping views clear plague cottage cultures. In many Swedish west coast fishing villages the old paths usually went across the yard close to the kitchen window. To watch other locals pass by and wave from the window was a nice break, but urbanites buying up the property had a totally different idea about such close encounters and insisted on barring the paths. When affluent Germans started renting and buying summer property in western Denmark, they provoked summer "locals" by their tendency to put up signs saying No Trespassing or Private Property on terrain of familiar and informal rules of rights of way.[64]

Figure 18. Tent camps like this on the shores of Long Island, N.Y., were a source of irritation for "old" summer visitors. (Photo from 1937, Culver Pictures, Inc.)

Another change in the social mix of cottage cultures follows real-estate prices. In Scandinavia the relative abundance of land as well as the late urbanization made it easier for lower middle-class and working-class families to acquire a summer cottage. Many inherited land from their rural families or bought land cheaply through relatives. Some farms or locally owned houses now look like circled wagon trains as kin return and set up their trailers around the old buildings. Today, seaside locations are becoming scarcer in Scandinavia, as in the United States, through a similar development—a pricing out of the less affluent.

The history of seaside settlements is the history of fine distinctions, of definitions of "us" and "the others" that change over time and among different groups. The sites of Swedish west coast tourism do indeed present a very complex and fluid social landscape. The "locals" range from well-to-do farmers to impoverished fishing families, the visitors from urban elite to working-class youth. Their identities form and reform as they draw distinctions and boundaries: city folks against locals, old tourists against new, houseowners against campers, and so on.

Now at the end of the twentieth century on both sides of the Atlantic, such distinctions lose their meaning. In many seaside communities it is hard to draw a sharp line between locals and summer guests. Who are the locals? The retired urban couple, the returned local boy, the commuting young family? It is a social landscape in which the classic categories of old and new, urban and rural, insiders and outsiders don't work.

Whatever the combinations, cottage cultures will be contested territories. Who has a right not only to a house, but to a corner of the beach or to the view? To whom does summer really belong? The local population, old summer guests, and weekend campers walk the same territory but often move in very different mental landscapes.

DREAMSCAPES

"Visit *The Beach House* and you won't want to leave ever!" reads the blurb on the front of Georgia Bockoven's bestselling novel. On the back the text continues: "The beach house is a peaceful summer haven, a place to escape mundane troubles. Here, four families find their feelings intensified and their lives transformed." The novel unfolds in a small beach community next to Santa Cruz and uses the vacation home as an arena for conflicts, relationships, and, above all, romance. As each family returns to the beach house for a new vacation they enter a magical landscape:

> Judy dug in her pocket for the key and opened the front door to the beach house. Instead of going in, she stood at the threshold and stared inside. Light from the evening sun spilled into the room, gaining entry from a missing slat on the shuttered window. Dust hung suspended in the stagnant air, silent and waiting.[65]

With this opening paragraph Georgia Bockoven places herself in the company of the host of writers skillfully using the dreamscapes of cottage cultures. But their central position in the symbolic vacation universe may give us a false idea of their actual frequency. Summer cottages are houses we live by, rather than live in, to borrow a metaphor from the historian John Gillis.[66]

Within the context of this rather limited middle-class world, summer cottages appear to be a natural part of going on vacation. "Everybody" goes canoeing from their lakeshore cottage in Canada, "everybody" loves their little red cottage by the seashore in Sweden. Even in contemporary images of cottage life it is hard to know the boundaries between nostalgia and present-day realities, especially since lifestyle producers of the marketing world constantly exploit this longing for bygone summers. We are moving in the territories of "imagined nostalgia," where you learn to miss things you never had.[67] "Remember that warm glow your family shared by the campfire?," says the advertisement for gas-fire installations, which promises to bring the glow back again if you promise to remember.[68] Of course I remember. Or do I?

A tiny segment of vacationers in the Western world actually own a summer cottage, and the classic era of long, slow-winding summers was an experience limited to few, but still the cottage experiences fuels many of our holiday dreams and fantasies. Why is this? What kind of longing makes summer cottages such good fantasy spaces, used in daydreams, in fiction, and in advertisements?

It is a utopia shaped by several kinds of longings. First of all it is the nostalgia for paradise lost, the idea of a golden age, when summer life was simple and affordable, and families took long vacations. Such longings feed on the many descriptions of "traditional" summer life of wonderful picnics, sailing, straw hats, and white linen dresses. They depict a very local world in intensely transnational ways. Contemporary market actors like Gant and Ralph Lauren are very skilled at exploring this nostalgia.

There is also the nostalgia of the melancholy mood. One of the main characteristics of summer vacations or summers on the whole is their hopeless brevity. Here is a utopia that we start to lose already at the beginning of our vacation. Summers are always drawing to a close, we watch the signs, we feel the mood, rather like the schoolkid in David Updike's short story "Summer":

> It was the first week in August, the time when summer briefly pauses, shifting between its beginning and its end: the light had not yet begun to change, the leaves were still full and green on the trees, the nights were still warm. From the woods and fields came the hiss of crickets, the line of distant mountains was still dulled by the edge of summer haze, the echo of fireworks was replaced by the rumble of thunder and the hollow premonition of school, too far off to imagine though dimly, dully felt.[69]

This bittersweet sense of summers always passing too quick also fuels the strong element of nostalgia for those seemingly endless school vacations in a distant past. When people are asked to describe their cottage childhood or favorite summer memories, the language often becomes very sensual—there are a lot of smells and sounds as well as sights.

Searching for a key metaphor in the cultural organization of this traditional cottage life, I would opt for the centrality of *returns*, of motion backward in both physical and mental terms. The question then is of course, returning to what? Eliot Porter came back to his summer island in 1963, after eight years of absence:

> At last, unbelievably, I was on the island. It had not changed; everything was the same. The trees towered as they always had. . . . The grass path up to my house was still not trampled down into a worn, brown carpet as it would be by many treading feet through the summer. The odors of

spruce, fern, and salt were heavy in the air. Suddenly, all tension was gone out of me, and I felt content. All I wanted to do was lie relaxed in the grass and look up at the tree tops and the sky.[70]

The nostalgia of return is a very active and creative part of cottage life. Somehow, summer seems so easy to remember. It is not only a return to nature and the blessings of a simple life, but also for many a return to childhood. In 1941 the New York journalist E. B. White went back with his young son to the cabin by the lake in Maine where he had spent his childhood. As they went fishing together next morning, a dragonfly landed on his fishing rod:

> It was the arrival of this fly that convinced me beyond any doubt that everything was as it always had been, that the years were a mirage and there had been no years. . . . I looked at the boy, who was silently watching his fly, and it was my hands that held his rod, my eyes watching. I felt dizzy and didn't know which rod I was at the end of.[71]

All kinds of things remain the same, but in this mental journey they are, of course, changed subtly. "To be back again" is a theme also exploited by the advertising world. In the early 1990s the Swedish State Railways ran a very successful campaign, in which the message was "Take the train back to the summers of your childhood." Traveling *back* to the country, the train ride constituted movement in time and space: a nostalgic ritual.

The dreamscapes of all those cottages, beach houses, lakeside lodges, second homes, have an enormous mental energy condensed into them. Even if the closest we will ever get to the real thing is a weekly rental of a Santa Cruz beach house, a time-share condo, a trailer campsite, or visits to the cottages of friends or relatives, we hope to reenact the classic cottage culture scenario of the perfect summer getaway. Or if we ourselves never had "cottage summers," the least we can do is to provide that experience for the kids—they should have good summer memories, which means a feeling of ritualized continuity. Or perhaps the dreamscapes of perfect summers may serve to make us remember that we don't belong to that landscape:

It is during summer that we are struck by the insight that we don't own anything. No, I don't have a house by the sea, we realize, surprised. No veranda either to the east or to the west. . . . It is during summer we discover that we don't have a territory. Or rather that the customs and habits, which rule the country in which we live, aren't ours to dispose of. That we speak and enjoy ourselves as aliens.[72]

THE PERFECT SUMMER

The attraction of cottage cultures may be that they provide a very safe and workable utopia where people can explore different sides of themselves or their relations with others or with nature. It is a secure laboratory—or is it? Alone with children, women could develop a somewhat different life and could also come in contact with the local world of women who often had a stronger position vis-à-vis their husbands. For children, cottage culture could bring a chance to experience new sides of their parents, sliding plates along the table, clowning on the beach. The adults had a chance to rekindle their childishness, while the real children developed secret territories and experiences of their own in a wider landscape, not policed by parents, teachers, or other adults all the time. For many middle-class kids, the more egalitarian relations among the locals, between adults and children, men and women, represent a fascinating alternative society.

But the women in the summer cottages were also the ones who had to pay the price for the cult of simplicity. The symbolic value of not having running water meant extra toil. The men, for their part, tried to develop the model of the vacation Dad who has to be able to handle anything from a leaking roof to a treasure hunt. As I pointed out earlier, their practical skills rarely matched those of local men, which was a touchy issue.

The cottage world can thus become a testing ground of conflicting projects. The men may feel like visitors to a female-dominated universe of flower garlands and picnic baskets or feel they can't live up to the expectations of the vacation Dad. And the women can feel imprisoned in a male world of endless practical projects and quests, like the woman in Margaret Atwood's poem *Bored*, who is "bored out of her mind" as she helps in her husband's do-it-yourself schemes: she patiently holds the log while he is sawing or the string while he is measuring, weeds out the garden he planted, or just sits still in the boat he is rowing, the car he is driving . . . [73]

The cottage utopia, charged with so many assumptions and yearning daydreams, creates a constant tension between winter anticipation and summer frustration. Often the few vacation weeks fail to live up to the heavy load of those winter expectations. The other side of cottage life is claustrophobia, too much pottering about or an overdose of togetherness. Summer families and summer relations should by definition be easygoing, effortless, conflict-free, and for precisely that reason they may turn out different. Atwood's bored heroine "could hardly wait to get the hell out of here," and many other writers have used the summer cottage as a scene for personal crisis or family fights. Summering makes people more naked—both open and vulnerable—as they discard old defenses and winter conventions, and this in combination with too much white wine during the long evenings on the porch can be a dangerous mix. Summer is the time of kin reunions but also of conflicts between generations and sibling rivalry: who controls summer life in the shared cottage? Middle-aged children all of a sudden find themselves defined as kids again, as their aging parents tell them what to do and how to do it.

Ove, a middle-aged Swede, is one of those who feel nervous as summer vacations start. He begins to long for the stable routines of work back home in the city. To the interviewing journalist he says:

> Don't make me into a nail-biting careerist who sits and counts the hours until I can step back into the office again. But there's such a hell of a lot of things that have to be done in the summer that I can never have a real vacation.

There are so many demands on him, he feels. Weed the flowerbeds, paint the windows, see old friends, make new ones, get close to the children, be a better lover, rest, become someone else.

> It's as if I were two people. The happy Holiday Ove in shorts and the dull Office Ove in a suit. The whole of society is permeated by huge ex-

pectations of everything that should happen in the summer. It can only go wrong.[74]

The nineteenth-century author George Sand is said to have claimed that people could be classified according to whether they aspired to live in a cottage or a palace.[75] And many observers describe cottage summer life as a critique of civilization, an idea of an alternative to the stressed and complicated urban everyday. Polar opposites and ideas of cultural compensation alike miss the way these different lifestyles constitute each other. It is rather the break between the two homes, the two settings, which integrate them. It is a very well integrated alterity. Cottage life anticipates the return to the city palace, whether an apartment or a suburban home.

One of the secrets of the marked transformation between these two polarities lies in the role of movement—not so much to a different geographical location, but to a different social space of "elsewhereness." It is not the length of the journey that is decisive but the ritual passage itself. The physical move is a precondition for the transformation of the winter person into a summer person: the notion of a freer, simpler life, and also a more childish life, in Medevi as well as in the trailer camp. The journey to summer is for many people also a journey through time, back to childhood. The journey makes people culturally prepared, giving them a chance to switch to a different emotional register. Movement underlies the programmatic demand for a total change of regime found in the 1903 arguments for vacations. The air you breathe, the food you taste, the sun you enjoy is the same, but everything feels different, tastes different. Movement should open you up, intensify your experiences, make you sensual.

This Robinsonian quest for another life need not be long. One Saskatchewan wheat farmer had a summer house fifteen miles away across the Canadian prairie. Here he would go to relax with a beer and watch the hawks as well as his farm in the distance. The second home created a different space for other thoughts and activities.[76] In a Swedish fishing village an old fisherman's wife told me how intensely she once longed for that day in early summer when the family moved from the dwelling house across the yard to the shed. Their life there in the summer kitchen was primitive and simple, but above all it displaced them. It was different and freer. The short distance across the yard became an adventure.

The Mediterranean in the
Age of the Package Tour

> The whole Mediterranean consists of movement in space. Anything entering it—wars, shadows of war, fashions, techniques, epidemics, merchandise, light and heavy, precious or commonplace—may be caught up in the flow of its life blood, ferried over great distances, washed ashore to be taken up again and passed on endlessly, maybe even carried beyond its shores.[1]

A walk along a Mediterranean beach through the cultural flotsam and jetsam is rather like an excavation of the world of tourism in the spirit of the French historian Fernand Braudel, quoted above.

In the sand lies the ribbed blue cap of the standard plastic 1.5 liter bottle of mineral water, without which no Mediterranean tourism is possible.

155

("We recommend that you do not drink the local tap water," tends to be the opening remark of tour guides.) Next to the cap is the black rubber mouthpiece of a snorkel, an empty tube of NIVEA suntan oil (factor 25), a broken pink miniature sword that perhaps once defended a Tequila Sunrise, half a blue-and-white German health sandal, torn apart by countless treks from the beach to the pool bar, lumps of waste oil from the many cruise ships, and of course plastic in every conceivable form and fragment.

Plastic is the element that ties this new Mediterranean economy together—it is carried by winds and streams from coast to coast. Pieces of plastic, blown apart by the wind, dried brittle by the sun, are interwoven between stones and grass, flapping in the breeze, sailing over the beach, from the thinnest fragments of the thousands of plastic bags in which holiday apartment guests collect their morning bread down in the *super-mercado* on the Costa del Sol, to the thick yellow plastic that tears loose from the roofs of tomato greenhouses in Lesbos or Minorca.

What could Braudel do with the material gathered in the sand? His grand history of the Mediterranean in the sixteenth century breaks totally new ground, developing a kind of social, economic, and mental history, where the major actors are not kings, generals, or diplomats, but the sea, the droughts, the winds, the travels of goods and people, the lives of shepherds and sailors. In this 1949 book he pioneers a new kind of integrative history, where the detail—the fate of a rumor, the itinerary of a Venetian skipper, or the effects of a winter storm—leads the narrative to major questions.

The bits and pieces from the tourist trade along the beach tell a fragmented story of how today, as in the days of Philip II, exchanges of goods, ideas, and people or climatic variations and seasonal changes hold the Mediterranean together as an economic and cultural system. Today it is no longer olive oil, Venetian cloth, or pepper that circulates between the coasts and islands—but the complexity is still there.

The Mediterranean in the age of mass tourism produces large amounts of sun blockers, hotel cats, camel rides, margaritas, village fiestas, picturesque panoramas, folk dance troupes, snake charmers, and bouzouki tapes. The tourist industry constantly develops new destinations, communities, and local cultures but within a rather stable and homogenizing framework. Modern tourism in search of the exotic as well as sun, sand, and sea developed here, and if we want to understand the making of package tourism as a giant industry we should start on these shores. The models of tourism emerging here were later exported to other parts of the world, as global tourism expanded.

The birth date of Mediterranean package tourism coincides with the year when Braudel's study appeared: in 1949 the first plane-load of charter tourists landed in Corsica.[2] But the real expansion came in the early 1960s when British, German, and Scandinavian tour operators started on a grand scale. By using a Braudelian approach to trace the flows of tourists—to see how pioneer routes and destinations develop, peak, and disappear, how new routes and favorite destinations emerge—we can track the package tour's institutions and routines.

The making of a Mediterranean tourist industry involved several phases, and each one still has a considerable influence on the industry. Actually the place to start is where Braudel's history ends, with the period of gradual decline of the Mediterranean world during the seventeenth and eighteenth centuries, a time when the economic and cultural focus of Europe was shifting to the northwest and the Atlantic coasts. During the following centuries this imbalance became more and more acute. The Mediterranean world turned into a European periphery, a backwater region, in which the chief exports were emigrants. The new imports, on the other hand, were tourists, as the region became a destination for northern European elites in search of classic culture. The Mediterranean slid back into history, a space for time travel back to the grandeur of earlier eras, classical antiquity or the Renaissance. Spearheaded by the British nobility, the tradition of the educational Grand Tour through France to Italy began. What started as a slow trickle in the sixteenth century was a firmly established routine by the late eighteenth, when Samuel Johnson made the famous remark, "A man who has not been to Italy, is always conscious of an inferiority, from his not having seen what it is expected that a man should see. The grand object of travelling is to see the seashores of the Mediterranean."[3] The journey south was not only a journey back in time but a search for the roots of Western civilization, and thus an important educational project. And it gave young male aristocrats from northern Europe the chance to polish off their manners in interacting with high society down south. There, three centuries ago, we have to start.

THE OLD SOUTH

On 15 December 1697 the twenty-seven-year-old Swede Olof Celsius is in Florence, as part of his education. He has difficulties in writing his diary because the ink is frozen. Like all travelers, he has been told to avoid the hot and dangerous summer months but is unfortunate to hit Florence in a spell of particularly cold weather. There is ice on the palace garden pond where he is staying, which gives him the interesting experience of skating in Florence for two weeks.

In his first lodgings he finds bloodstains on the bed. It turns out that two young Swedish noblemen had stayed here earlier but have now been taken into custody after a violent fight with the city guards. "It is rumored," he writes, "that these men had made the acquaintance with some ladies and that this was the result of their affair."

Celsius belonged to the new brotherhood of travelers, going from destination to destination in what was slowly institutionalized as the Grand Tour. This journey was meant to finish off their education and it produced a wealth of travel books and guides, sketches and bad poetry. The handbooks gave all kinds of instructions, not all with the kind of German thoroughness of the almost thousand pages of *Die Kunst zu reisen— ein systematischer Versuch* written for young travelers.[4]

Florence was one of the obligatory stops for those on this itinerary, and the young gentlemen often traveled with letters of introduction, in order to receive local hospitality. The institution drew on the fact that members of the thin elite layer in European societies were ready to assist their equals, offer advice, conversation, and perhaps lodgings. Latin still functioned as the lingua franca of this network, in competition with French. Florence thus got used to handling tourists at quite an early stage, but as the number of visitors increased, local hospitality could not always be taken for granted.

In January 1817 the French author Stendhal came to Florence, excited at the prospect of meeting the city he knew so well from books and

Figure 19. On the Grand Tour at the monument of Philopappos, Greece 1821.
(The Bridgeman Art Library, London)

etchings. His mental images made it possible for him to find his way through the streets without a guide. He aimed straight for the famous church of Santa Croce, but its fantastic interior with all the artworks proved too much. He had an "attack of nerves"; dizzy and with a fiercely beating heart he stumbled outside to rest on one of the benches of the piazza.[5] Thus was created what later came to be called the Stendhal syndrome, tourist overexposure, too many three-star sights at once.

Stendhal recuperated and explored the city of his dreams. He found it occupied by too many Englishmen. "Florence is nothing better than a vast museum full of foreign tourists; and each nationality brings with it its own manners and customs," he writes, and tells how the impoverished local gentry take their revenge on "the gilded luxury of Albion," by sharing countless satirical anecdotes on the behavior of these stupid aliens.

Today groups of all nationalities roam the city. Cyril Connolly describes his own latter-day version of the Grand Tour in 1963:

> And now the Florentine week begins in earnest, a round of rain and sun, of churches and villas, work and play. For sightseeing is work and one clocks into a museum like an office, arriving fresh and leaving with jangled nerves, still several rooms behind schedule, yet with the satisfaction comparable only to that felt in wartime, by those "engaged in work of national importance." In a city like Florence, all along our route in fact, one is conscious of a host of predecessors all busy passing judgment until it seems quite impossible to find anything to say.[6]

The true descendants of Olof Celsius and the Grand Tour tradition, however, consist of the young interrailers who roam the city in search of other interrailers and the groups of American and Japanese college students doing the modern version of the Grand Tour. Just as in the seventeenth century, they are here with the blessing of their parents. A season of interrailing or a European tour is still supposed to be a good investment in a middle-class education. It should make your children more cosmopolitan and self-confident. The peregrinators of the 1690s and the interrailers of the 1990s travel to discover both the world and themselves.

The classic era of the Grand Tour was the eighteenth century, a period when increasing numbers of the elites from other northern European countries joined the British nobility. The tour usually involved a trip to Paris and visits to major Italian cities, like Rome, Venice, Florence, and Naples, and to this basic program other itineraries were added.

Above all the tour focused on Italy, with very few eighteenth-century tourists visiting Spain or Greece. Traveling conditions were still poor, with a choice of reaching Italy over the Alps or along the Mediterranean coast. Eighteenth-century Britons kept complaining of voyages in small feluccas, which were vulnerable to hard weather. And sea travel often meant long and unpredictable waiting times for winds to change, storms to settle, or calms to end, just as in the days of Philip II.

The further south you went, the worse the road conditions got. Few tourists ventured as far as Sicily, but one Englishman wrote about his stay there in 1792: "There is not a wheel in the whole country, the roads are mere paths for a single mule and the few huts scattered around are as bad as Hottentot kraals . . . [and] we are sick of Sicilian roads and accommodation."[7]

BEING MEDITERRANEANIZED

After the Napoleonic Wars the social base of Mediterranean travel broadened. The British upper middle class became a dominant group. Unlike their aristocratic countrymen, they could not fall back on the help of local nobility, but fortunately they had Mr. Cook. Having started his tour operations and excursions in the early 1840s, he went continental in the late 1850s. During the following decades he became an institution, laying the foundation (together with his less famous competitors in the business) for mass travel south, by offering both lower prices and well-organized tours, but above all by domesticating the exotic experiences abroad. It seemed as if Mr. Cook's helpful agents were everywhere and always ready to arrange hotel accommodation, guided tours, and rail tickets or solve conflicts whether in Naples or in Smyrna. At his death in 1895 it was claimed that "Cook at present pervades the whole civilized world."[8]

Mr. Cook belonged to the era of the railways. The journey from London to Rome was not much faster in 1830 than in Roman times. It took three weeks and involved travel in stagecoaches or hired carriages. At that time the steamboats had started to provide faster and above all more comfortable travel. A steamer could make that journey in half the time and also made new destinations around the Mediterranean possible. A network of routes led from Malaga in the west to Constantinople in the east.[9] The railways provided the great travel revolution a few decades later. Now you could leave London in the morning and have dinner in Nice the next day.

The new travel possibilities changed the tourist map of the Mediterranean, although Italy remained number one. Spain and Greece lacked the tourist infrastructure and were still less frequented. Palestine was a popular destination for historic and religious pilgrimages, but the colonial presence also made Egypt popular. In 1898 a Thomas Cook pamphlet declared that Cairo has become "no more than a winter suburb of London."[10] This result owed less to Mr. Cook's efforts than to the combination of the Suez Canal and the Orient Line. The latter company claimed to have innovated the cruise, or transportation as leisure.

The 1896 edition of the *Orient Line Guide* advertises both its regular schedule to the colonies via Suez and Mediterranean cruises, extolling the luxuries of modern travel. The ocean liner is a floating palace with a life "in security and luxury."[11] What once was a dreaded voyage is now a vacation in itself. The illustrations show drawing rooms and dining saloons of a reassuring voluptuousness: thick carpets, elegant paneling, and padded velvet chairs. With sports, games, concerts, and dancing nightly, there is never a dull moment and more important, no worries for the tourists:

> The bustle and fatigue of long railway journeys, the discomfort of land hotels, with their poor food and insanitary surroundings, do not exist for them. Their stately ship anchors in the harbour of some foreign city in the early morning, and after an English breakfast on board, they go ashore to explore the sights of the place. They have ample leisure and opportunity of doing so, and after a long day's sightseeing, it is with a sense of relief that they find themselves once more occupying their accustomed seats at the dinner-table surrounded by the familiar faces of their friends. They explore oceans, islands, and cities, and feel all the time they are at home.[12]

Advertisements for cruises a century later show that at least the marketing rhetoric is still very much the same.

With steamers and trains the English colonized even the remotest corners of the south. They seemed to be everywhere, Anglicizing the whole Mediterranean, as both the locals and other tourists complained. With them they brought churches, lending libraries, English newspapers, cricket, and all sorts of strange British foods. The first *ghetto Inglese* was created in Rome in the eighteenth century, and by the end of the nineteenth century there were winter colonies all over the place, even in Algiers. One striking new element in this colonization was the many women who traveled, not only with families but on their own or with female friends. Organizations like Mr. Cook's now made it possible for middle-class women to venture abroad.[13]

Unlike the pioneers of the Grand Tour the new tourists were out to see classical culture and to explore the exotic otherness of the south, to "Mediterraneanize oneself," as an English writer put it in 1911.[14] By going south you became a different person, relaxing from the constraints of overcivilization and urban stress, just like the pioneers venturing out to the Scandinavian coastline. But considerations of health made summer travel to southern climes out of the question.

The focus on health also produced a British medical infrastructure. A listing from 1899 gives the following distribution of English doctors: seven in Rome, seven in Florence, two in Naples, two in Venice, one in Algiers and one in Malaga, and thirty-nine on the Riviera. Italy still held a strong position but the Riviera had now become the most popular destination.[15] Most of the doctors practiced in Nice, a city rapidly learning to accommodate tourism, in a way that illustrates some of the problems of becoming a tourist destination. In Nice we can follow the making of a new pattern in Mediterranean tourism.

LEARNING TO LIVE WITH TOURISTS

During the eighteenth century Nice was an obscure town, an unpopular stopover on the Grand Tour to Italy. The sandy and rocky Riviera did not constitute a pleasing scenery. The British writer John Fielding longed for green England, when passing through this barren coast.[16] Those who passed through Nice along the Riviera complained bitterly about the terrible local traveling conditions. The roads were often too bad for carriages, sometimes even too bad for mules and mountain horses, as one British traveler declared in 1777.[17] Tobias Smollett described Nice in 1763 as a rather miserable place, plagued by poverty, where "all the common people are thieves and beggars,"[18] but its advantage, he found, was that the midwinter sun was as warm as England in May. Already by the end of the eighteenth century there was a small English colony of invalids in Nice, enjoying the mild winter and the healthy air. This English settlement slowly grew and established its rather closed world in a part of the town. Nice was on its way to becoming "the sanatorium of Europe." These *hivernants* created a winter season, arriving in Nice in late October or early November and leaving for northern Europe in April. They spent most of their time worrying about their health or taking part in the growing social life of strolls, carriage rides, parties, dances, and gambling.[19]

For the local city authorities this influx of tourists was a godsend but it also created new problems. Nice is one of the first examples of a city that had to organize itself to meet the needs of a powerful alien group with no wish to fit into local life.

The British wanted to walk along the seaside, while the locals stayed on the inland boulevards of the city, and thus the British in the 1820s took the initiative of building the promenade des Anglais. Locals began renting out houses to *les hivernants* and, as the city was turned over from Italy to France in 1860, tourism started to develop faster. Nice was one of the first tourist places to market its good weather energetically, developing the classic tactic of comparing it to the lack of sun back home. As much as possible was made of the fact that the city could boast three times more winter sun than Paris. And not only that: the sun in Nice was better than anywhere else.[20] Today, this tactic appears all over the vacation world, where listings of the (hopefully terrible) weather conditions back home are supposed to remind tourists of their good luck.

Nice became one of the fastest growing cities in Europe between 1860 and 1914. The tourist industry was labor-intensive and came to depend on cheap labor, recruited mainly from Italy, which formed another ghetto in the city.

Local bureaucrats and property owners faced the challenge of learning what this strange tribe called *les Anglais* wanted and how they could satisfy their peculiar wishes. *Les hivernants* did not have the right to vote, but they could always vote with their feet. How did one make sure that they returned next season? Here was a population waiting to be entertained, and with plenty of time and money to spend. Roughly 90 percent of the visitors along the Riviera in 1890 were classified as *rentiers*.[21] The English and the French dominated in numbers, but the most striking cosmopolitan element was flamboyant Russian counts and grand dukes, who escaped the severe winters of St. Petersburg to build their own cathedral in Nice and drink caseloads of sweet champagne.

In wealth and rank the visitors were far above the local bourgeoisie, and they were here to have fun, not to visit Roman ruins or take care of their health. As Nice slowly developed from a resting place for invalids to a highly fashionable winter playground for the European aristocracy (and royalty), it had to go through some major changes. First of all the tourist demanded modern amenities: water, sanitation, and tidy streets, but it was not only the streets that had to be cleaned up; local culture needed similar treatment. The local carnival had to be cleansed of all vulgar elements of popular culture.[22]

Secondly the tourists demanded entertainment. A pigeon shoot was planned in 1875 and the tourist community itself had a roller-skating rink built. Plans were also made for a casino.[23] The new hotels borrowed designs and activities from the fashionable spas elsewhere and imported entrepreneurs and managers, as well as hotel dancers to entertain the dowagers. There was little local experience of how to please the tourist crowd.

The tourist economy was a blessing, but also a risky business. Nice went through a number of crises as tourists temporarily disappeared. There was a great local ambivalence. Tourists brought affluence to the city, but it was unevenly distributed. Tourist needs always come first, was a common complaint, and in April many of the locals were happy to see them go away.

Step by step the communities along the Riviera transformed themselves into a winter playground. The promenade des Anglais was replicated elsewhere, new plants like the mimosa and the palm tree were imported to become part of the traditional Riviera landscape. Thrills like gambling and later car racing were new additions to the program.

On the pleasant shore of the French Riviera, about half way between Marseilles and the Italian border, stands a large, proud, rose-colored hotel. Deferential palms cool its flushed facade, and before it stretches a short dazzling beach. Lately it has become a summer resort of notable and fashionable people; a decade ago it was almost deserted after its English clientele went north in April.

These opening lines from F. Scott Fitzgerald's novel *Tender Is the Night* start the classic tale of a new kind of tourist life on the Riviera. In June 1925 the seventeen-year-old Rosemarie arrives with her mother at the hotel and explores the intensive holiday life down at the beach. Here she meets Dick and Nicole Diver, the hero and heroine of the novel. She is attracted to their carefree style of summer living and asks them, "Do you like it here—this place?" A friend in the group answers for them, "They have to like it. . . . They invented it."[24] Fitzgerald dedicated his novel to his close friends Gerald and Sara Murphy, who were not all that pleased to find that they were the model for the Divers, though only partly, because the author and his wife, Zelda, also became part of the story. So many details in the book turned out to be lifted directly from the summers the two couples spent together in Antibes, from 1924 to 1929.

Fitzgerald was right. In many ways the Murphys did invent the new summer life on the Riviera, with ample help from their French and American friends, artists like Fernand Léger and Pablo Picasso, writers like Dorothy Parker and John Dos Passos.

In Braudel's history of the Mediterranean the seasonal rhythm plays an important part. Summer was the time of standstill, as the populations withdrew behind closed shutters to survive the heat and the summer maladies, while the more fortunate escaped into the cooler mountain regions. Visitors followed the rule of Celsius and stayed away. Between

May and September there were few tourists to be seen. This marked rhythm would eventually turn upside down.

In the early 1920s the Riviera still closed down as summer approached. "Le Soleil Toute L'Année" the tourist posters pleaded, but winter remained the season. Back at the end of the nineteenth century Nice had tried to develop a summer season, but with very little luck. Only Italians are foolish enough to go to the beach in the summer, as an Englishwoman put it in 1880.[25]

In the summer of 1922 the Murphys and their small children came to visit Cole Porter, who was renting a chateau for the summer in Cap d'Antibes. Gerald Murphy had inherited money, studied at Yale, and was now trying his talents as a painter in Paris; his wife, Sara, had spent a large part of her childhood in Europe. The town was almost deserted, the telephone services were open only part of the day, and the entertainment consisted of a local movie house, open once a week. The weather was hot, but the Murphys found a tiny beach covered with seaweed. "We dug out a corner of the beach and bathed there and sat in the sun, and we decided that this was where we wanted to be."[26]

They persuaded a small local hotel to keep open the next summer. Usually the managers closed on 1 May and went up to the Italian Alps to take care of a hotel for the summer season there. Next the Murphys decided to buy a house, had it rebuilt, and named it Villa America. Here they developed their own version of Riviera vacation life, surrounded by a steady inflow of guests. In many ways Gerald and Sara saw their summer life as a piece of art. With the help of local everyday objects, they decorated the villa. Sara started gardening, Gerald adopted a costume that would become trend-setting: sandals and tanned legs in shorts, the traditional French sailor's striped jersey, and a white work cap.

Here was a new summer life, days at the beach, clowning and swimming, afternoon cocktails by the pool, jazz on the gramophone, sailing cruises, improvised terrace meals, and love affairs. "It was like a great fair, and everybody was so young," Sara remembered. There was a wide tolerance. Sara "didn't care much what people did, so long as they didn't do it out in the street and frighten the horses."[27] Away from your stuffy old home ground, you could experiment with being a very different person.

The Murphy set also made excursions to Juan-les-Pins, which was becoming fashionable at that time. A local restaurant owner saw a film that included a beach party scene in Miami in 1924 and it inspired him to develop a new, American style in entertaining. His venture was an instant success.[28]

The new Riviera life moved from the old winter promenades to the beaches. Apart from swimming, tanning was the new craze. "Sunshine is Life. Come to the Riviera" as a British Rail poster from the 1920s put it.[29] Sunbathing was an innovation from the north, pioneered by the Germans and the Scandinavians. A visitor who took up a villa in deserted summer Cannes in 1924 remembers: "We immediately started sunbathing, which was something new at the time. A lot of sunbathing, exaggerated sunbathing. It was a study, it took time, hours and hours of sunbathing."[30]

Sunbathing and other amusements drew a new blend of money, youth, and bohemian intellectuals and artists to the Riviera. Holiday life was supposed to be informal, fun, and fast. Speeding down the coast road to a casino or nightclub became part of the routine. Unlike the old elite the new bohemians adored local, rural culture, appropriating, mixing, blending it into their own lifestyle. At any time they would choose a local café rather than the stuffy old hotel lounges. *Le Hig-lif* had come to stay. In 1931 the hoteliers of the Côte d'Azur met and voted to stay open over the summer, although many still were pessimistic.

As the new Riviera developed with all the fashionable resorts like Antibes, the old one, Nice, was left in the backwater. It became that boring old city with old people walking the promenade, and it was a city to which the new generation of tourists just went for shopping. Fifty years later retirement communities surround Nice. Their residents are aging, well-to-do English, Germans, and Scandinavians, migrating south. In the 1990s some people still take a swim on the seaside of the promenade des Anglais, if they can manage to get over the six lanes of heavy traffic. The old Italian ghetto, which no nineteenth-century tourist would enter, is transformed into the picturesque old town, where the tourists gather. The new immigrant labor comes from North Africa, and the racist

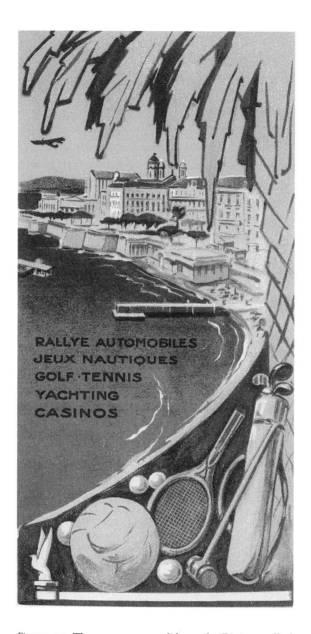

Figure 20. The new summer life on the Riviera called for active vacationers unlike the slow-moving traditional *hivernants,* as this 1935 poster from St-Raphaël stresses. Car racing, sports, yachting, and gambling— here was life in the fast lane! (Archiv für Kunst und Geschichte, Berlin)

National Front has a strong position in local politics. The coast itself has become one of the most heavily trafficked highways of southern Europe, called the *mur de béton*—the wall of concrete.

As in all tourist narratives of a golden age, the new Riviera experience of the 1920s went sour. "Everybody" flocked to the Riviera, trying to emulate the bohemian and artistic lifestyle, Hollywood moguls, *nouveaux riches*, second-rate artists. The disillusioned hero in Cyril Connolly's novel *The Rock Pool* from 1936 walks around in Juan-les-Pins, hating it. Quarrelsome women in cheap beach pajamas in the street, tarts, gigolos, and motorcar salesmen in the cafés, he complains.[31] Gone were the days when you could find a beach of your own, or an inexpensive local meal.

Fitzgerald's book captures this melancholy longing for the golden age of carefree youth, between myth and memory. The Divers return to their old beach to find it totally transformed: "few people swam any more in that blue paradise . . . most of Gausse's guests stripped the concealing pajamas from their flabbiness only for a short hangover dip at one o'clock."[32]

By then the Riviera beach culture was firmly established, waiting to be exported all over the Mediterranean and the world. It was the result of a strange cosmopolitan mix of French, English, and above all American elements, or as Gerald Murphy summarized it: "Even though it happened in France, it was all somehow an American experience."[33]

CHARTER TOUR PIONEERS

If the middle-class pilgrimages to the south in the nineteenth century were based on a combination of Mr. Cook and steam, the real expansion in mass travel occurred after the Second World War. It started with bus travel and spread to charter flights.

After the war there was a pent-up longing to travel. As the economy recuperated there was mounting affluence in northern Europe, which not only included the middle classes but also growing sectors of the working class. The new market made new demands on cheaper and more sheltered travel than the world of Mr. Cook and his agents had de-livered. The bus became the technology that supplied both needs. Northerners took package tours south, which included a long and tiresome ride in a chartered coach—not down to the French Riviera, much too expensive—but to Italy. The beaches of Rimini on the Adriatic were easily accessible by bus and had a well-developed infrastructure as a century-old resort, mainly for Italians.

The bus tour became an institution, which still influences much of the ideals and the rituals of charter tours. Today it is often seen as a too sheltered and boring way of vacationing, meant for older people or the anxiety-ridden petite bourgeoisie. The bus tourists seem to end up on the lowest rungs of tourist hierarchies, a meek flock of sheep never allowed out on their own, sheltered from any contact with reality behind their tinted windows.

In the early 1950s, however, the bus tour to sinful Paris or the beaches of Rimini was an adventure, celebrated in movies and magazines, rather like the ways in which Hollywood celebrated the pioneer days of Greyhound travel. Bus travel developed the image of the "package tour group." Here classic stereotypes, role models, and rituals emerged, and they are still with us. First of all they distribute a set of personages among the group: the darling old couple on their first trip abroad, the photo-crazy engineer and his bored wife, the fussy spinster complaining about bathrooms, the know-all middle-aged accountant always checking the bill twice, the young newlyweds with eyes just for each other, the merry widow casting longing glances after Mediterranean males, the happy drunk in search of new bars, the clowning driver, the dapper young guide, both being mothered by the group and mothering them.

The microphysics of bus travel produced a social psychology of its own. The long haul down through Europe rapidly turned the bus into a second home, a fixed point in a rapidly moving landscape. Braving the new and unknown territories outside, for sightseeing, lunches, hotel beds, or rest rooms, became much easier because of the reassuring familiarity of "our bus," with its own odors and unique little details. The reassuring vibrations, the moderated climate, the tinted windows enhanced this feeling of a safe haven in an unpredictable world. This hominess very rapidly increased as people stuck to a fixed seating order: my seat, my baggage rack, territory usually marked with a sweater, a dog-eared book, sunglasses. Group cohesion, as well as the formation of cliques, developed quickly in those circumstances. A shared knowledge of jokes, sayings, microrituals, and routines was part of this culture-building.

The bus gave the group a suitable size, small enough to create togetherness but big enough for you to avoid undesired contacts. Relations were established in small talk across the aisle, community singing, shared laughter at bad jokes from the driver. The world outside was "them against us," and this also went for other bus tour groups, which were eyed with a suspicious or critical eye during stops. When you finally stepped off the bus at the *penzione* next to the beach you were already a tight-knit community, reuniting every day on the beach, in the hotel lobby, or back again on the dear old bus for sightseeing trips. The bus tour opened up Europe for people who did not have the middle-class money or travel skills.

The warm togetherness of the bus became the positive image of the package tour (there were enough negative ones around, but they belonged to people who never went on bus tours). It blended into the world of air charter and continued to be celebrated and mediated in many forms, although the actual traveling conditions made such a community hard to reproduce and also a less attractive goal as tourists became more travel-wise and individualist in their preferences. Even today tour operators market this romance of togetherness, and still people may cast themselves or their fellow travelers in the classic parts established decades earlier.

SEA, SAND, SUN, AND SEX

As northern Europeans raised their standard of living they often chose, unlike the American workforce, to invest in longer and longer vacations, through both union bargaining and government legislation. Preferring shorter hours to bigger paychecks, northern Europeans, the archetypes of the Protestant work ethic, ended up with the longest vacations in the world. During the seventies there was an average 10 percent reduction in working hours for manual workers in the European Community and the length of paid vacations increased to four weeks.[34]

Here was a new vacation market ripe for development, but only quicker and more comfortable travel could produce a mass exodus to the Mediterranean. The Second World War had left even remote islands with a new asset: airstrips, and charter flights began to open up these island destinations to northern vacationers. The great potential market expanded rapidly with the addition of two other conditions: jet planes and computer reservation systems.[35] As earlier, the British were still the pioneers, only to be challenged by the Scandinavians and especially the huge German market.

If Nice, Antibes, and Rimini were the first steps toward modern vacationing in the south, Majorca became the pioneer air charter destination during the early 1960s. Soon the numbers of visitors were counted in millions.[36] The early success of Majorca was not a simple result of transport economics and the supply of local beaches. The property situation, with the breakup of old, large, and indebted estates, also made it much easier for outside developers to move in and buy up large parts of the seafront. The classic geographical division of labor emerged. Hotels and nightlife on the beaches, mountain villages as sightseeing destinations with restaurants, cafés, and souvenir shops.[37] The only three-star destination that Majorca could muster was the village where Frédéric Chopin and George Sand had spent three romantic months (complaining about the local setting), but clever marketing exploited those few months to the utmost.

The early boom years of Majorcan development caused a heated debate about this novel form of tourism in northern Europe. A look at the Swedish mass-media reports of the early 1960s shows that the reactions were mixed—to say the least.[38]

Critics characterized the Mediterranean vacation as being based on five S's: sun, sand, sea, sex, and spirits (the addition of cheap liquor to the list was a Scandinavian specialty). Newspapers printed irate letters from their subscribers and also carried numerous reports about how charter tourists lost all their inhibitions, almost from the very second when they fastened their seatbelts on the DC-3. The division of labor was fairly rigid: the men did the drinking, the women did the sinning.

Blind-drunk men and shameless women populated the bars and beaches of Majorca and the Costa del Sol.

Sex was to become a central and delicate theme. The condemnation of Latin courtesans often carried overtones of race and class prejudice, as in some of the illustrated novelettes produced for teenagers' and women's magazines. In one teenage weekly from 1960 we meet the blond tourist heroine Annika on her adventures on Majorca—persistently courted by the handsome, mustachioed, but untrustworthy Alfredo, who is finally brushed out of the way by the solid, flaxen-haired Claes. Together the two young Swedes return home to the security of everyday life.

What is striking about the early debate is that it is so concerned with hedonism, with the way tourists indulge their lusts and passions. How could it be that respectable travelers could sink so low during a couple of vacation weeks? Or as one newspaper exclaimed in 1962, "How can Swedish women come home without blushing?"

Another recurring scandal concerned the cowboys in the travel business. There were many reports about cheated and stranded tourists, who found that the new form of adventure could be more venturesome than they had anticipated. A favorite topic was the gullibility of the Swedes, and the dishonesty of shady travel agencies and crooked local hoteliers.

In the early 1960s Swedes and above all Britons and Germans made Spain the main charter destination, with Majorca and the huge resort development of the Costa del Sol on the mainland at the top. The number of tourists skyrocketed from 6 million in 1960 to 30 million in 1975. Seafront property was still relatively cheap and the cost of living low. The iron fist of the Franco dictatorship was usually well hidden from tourists, and the government encouraged the development of large resort areas, which would make it easier to monitor tourist influences on or contacts with local people.[39] Majorca thus became the prototype of the new package tour. Words like playa, bodega, paella, and mañana entered the lingua franca of tourism.

As the numbers of Mediterranean vacationers expanded greatly during the 1970s and 1980s, new territories had to be discovered and colonized. It turned out that Spain had a hidden card, the Canary Islands, far out in the Atlantic. Here you could find a new important resource, a

Figure 21. Ready for adventure. Two Swedish farm girls pose before leaving on their first trip to Italy. (Photo 1956 by Rune Öberg, Museet i Varberg)

warm winter sun. Northern vacationers were getting interested in escaping the north during the cold season for a week if a cheap and reasonably close destination could be found, with the promise of safe sun.

This the Canary Islands could offer, and the development of jet airplanes supplied the other condition. Jets were at first a costly travel experience, for a short period producing a new tourist elite—"the jet set"—which was distinguished by a truly global nomadism: a weekend on the Sardinian gold coast, a trip to the Bahamas, a party in New York. They were recognizable by their casual but expensive outfits and their all-year-round tan, generously exposed in open shirts or low-cut dresses.

Airline investments in new large fleets of jets resulted in overcapacity of seats, which the tour companies could fill cheaply. Suddenly the winter sun was only four to five hours away and the northerners invaded the isolated and sparsely populated island group out in the Atlantic—absolutely in the middle of nowhere.

INVENTING SUMMER ALL YEAR ROUND AT THE CASA SUECA

Majorca had some earlier tourist experience, but in the Canary Islands it started from scratch. The first expansion occurred around the capital of Las Palmas, but soon developers started to look for more virgin areas, especially as the dry, barren, and desertlike coastal areas had the safe supply of winter sun.

A coastal village on Tenerife, studied by Kenneth More in the 1960s, is a good example of this process.[40] In 1955 Los Santos was an isolated and poor village, with around 1,200 inhabitants. The villagers made their meager living in agricultural work and fishing. All communications had to go via the mountains, and in the fifties only a few men braved the three-day walking tour over the range. Trucks came in to pick up the cash crop, tomatoes, and a priest arrived once a month to say mass. There were three part-time bars, a bakery, a kiosk selling staples, but no restaurant, no electricity. Locals sold their day's catch of cuttlefish from their boats, on the beach. Three families owned much of the land and the village was governed by an appointed mayor. The villagers saw themselves as more or less powerless and outside the larger world.

A few tourists ventured as far as the village but found it barren and depressingly poor. No Murphys arrived over the mountains to discover the location this time, but an invalid Swedish veterinarian, looking for a warm and inexpensive place to retire in. After his first visit in 1956 he went back to Stockholm and persuaded a group of invalided friends he had met in hospital to take up residence in Los Santos. Next year the group arrived, rented a house, and named it Casa Sueca (Swedish house). The low cost of labor meant that they could hire ample help, boys to push wheelchairs, cooks, and cleaners. These Swedes were greeted with open arms, they learned Spanish fast and began to involve themselves in community improvement. The village started to change.

The Swedes weren't happy with the local bread, so the local baker asked for a recipe and started making Swedish bread, to please his new customers. The grocer stocked up new kinds of goods, such as canned frankfurters and corned beef.

New Swedes arrived, invalids as well as friends and family. A small pension was built, with a generator, which supplied some electricity until midnight each day. In order to attract more Swedes, a movie theater was built and next to it a small restaurant, in the style of an American hot-dog stand. Suddenly there was a tourist infrastructure in the village and other tourists started to come. The tourist economy entered most households. Paying guests went out to sea for sport fishing or ordered local copies of dresses out of Swedish fashion magazines; an ice-cream machine appeared, which meant that its owner also had to produce power around the clock and made a nice profit selling electricity to the other villagers.

The locals were impressed by Swedish technology and education but thought the visitors were morally depraved; the Swedes talked about the generosity and openness of the locals but also found them backward and superstitious.

A decade after the arrival of the Swedes, Los Santos was a small resort community. A supermarket sold fresh meat, and the several new restaurants offered not only local fish but Danish pork and Polish beef, and there were regular bus services to other communities. But growth also posed problems. In the past garbage had just been left out in the sun to disintegrate, but now the smell from the dumps became a problem, like the noise and fumes from the many generators, and there were half-finished concrete buildings everywhere. Growth had just happened, there was no overall plan.

Coming over the mountains today (or rather taking the freeway along the coast), the old Swedish veterinarian would have the shock of his life. The whole coastal region is now a giant resort, with high-rise hotels everywhere. Some of them still carry the label of fishing villages in travel brochures, but you have to look hard to find traces of earlier settlements. Entering Playa de las Americas, for example, you encounter a row of giant signs: *Bienvenidos! Welcome! Välkommen! Wilkommen!* This is not a resort village, rather a good-sized town, but with a strange structure. Hotel follows hotel, all facing south and centering on their own pool complexes. The traffic consists of sightseeing buses, small rental cars, and delivery vans. There are no workshops or commercial outlets apart from *supermercados*, bazaars, and souvenir shops for tourists. There are no locals apart from the northern European senior citizens who live here the year round. The other locals live up in the mountains and are bused in for their work in the service sector every day. The pride of the town is the local luxury hotel, aptly named Mediterranean Palace Luxe. It is plastered with copies of Greek gods in durable plastic: fourteen giant Apollos of Belvedere around the pool, eight Venuses of Milo in the tennis court, and one Nike of Samothrace guarding the minigolf course.

There is hardly any parallel in the history of the tourism industry to the rapid development of the Canary Islands, whose success largely reflects the fact that it has no season. It is business as usual, all year round. And new forms of retirement communities attract lower-middle-class and comfortable working-class visitors.

NEW TERRITORIES

Thus Mediterranean tourism moved southwest, but also east. The Canary Islands acquired a mixed reputation: all sun and sand, but too crowded and not enough local atmosphere. Greece became an important alternative. In 1951 a mere fifty thousand tourists went there, ten years later they were half a million and in 1981 five and a half million.[41] As the Greek islands got more crowded and expensive, Turkey emerged as an alternative, whereas countries like Tunisia, Morocco, Egypt, and Israel started to market themselves as alternative destinations for winter sun. Morocco especially became a low-budget alternative to the Canary Islands. Here too you chose your own mix of the familiar and the exotic. In the large resort of Agadir you could live in a standard Mediterranean resort setting, but a walk up to the other quarters of the city or a drive out into the countryside presented a very different life. In a similar manner Portugal became a new alternative to Spain in the 1960s.[42]

During the 1980s Turkey—a country with little tourist experience—entered the tourist market. The Turkish government worked hard to attract visitors.[43] The country had to compete especially with its old arch-enemy Greece and promoted a similar mix of sunny beaches and a classical heritage, along with a special bonus: the oriental flavor of the Turkish Mediterranean. In early stages it offered the virgin nature and local color that attracted more adventurous tourists but later—to create a mass market—had to play down the exoticism. Its chief draws were competitive prices and less crowded coasts, which made Turkey a new favorite among families and spurred the rapid development of a Turkish mass market (and since Greece had erased almost all traces of the long Ottoman rule during the late nineteenth and early twentieth centuries, it did not offer tourists the same mix of classical and oriental flavors).[44]

Slowly the Mediterranean tourist map expanded into the old eastern bloc. In the 1960s Yugoslavia, Romania, and Bulgaria started to emulate the successful Western European tourist industry. Yugoslavia, in between the east and the west, was first. The country had a long earlier tradition of coastal tourism since the days of the Hapsburgs, when the Adriatic was a favorite elite destination. In the new era a less fashionable public visited Yugoslavia. East bloc visitors accounted for a good deal, but especially West Germans traveling in their own cars or RVs came to dominate the coast.[45]

In Bulgaria tourist development followed the classic five-year-plan tradition. A tourist ministry at the top set up the main Black Sea resorts,

Golden Sands and Sunny Beach, which started to attract Western Europeans in the 1960s, mainly because of the low prices. A large part of the visitors came from Eastern European countries, for whom the Black Sea represented the only chance of a southern holiday. They had to make do with the poorer accommodation, while the Westerners with their sought-after foreign currency got the best alternatives.

Each resort complex consisted of brigades, which received their detailed planning directions from Balkantourist in Sofia. They placed orders for food and beverages in advance with the central agency, which filled them on a quota basis; any unforeseen influx of tourists left restaurants stranded. Complaints from Westerners not used to the service culture of the East were many—extensive menus but only two main dishes available, slow and rude service. Yet what reason did the underpaid and resentful staff have to work their hearts out to please these wealthy Westerners?[46]

Over the last thirty years we can thus follow how the tourist map of the Mediterranean has constantly changed for cultural, economic, and political reasons. The fall of the dictatorships in Portugal and Greece opened up these nations for new tourist invasions, while the Algerian socialist government kept tourists out. The oil crisis sent prices up and air travel figures down. The wars in Lebanon closed this eastern Riviera and opened up new markets for Cyprus; the Yugoslavian wars brought local tourism to a standstill.

Behind the redrawing of the destination map also lies what in the trade terminology is often called "reaching the maturity stage of the product life cycle."[47] There is a constant wear and tear on tourist destinations. As small fishing villages like Los Santos turn into popular destinations, overcrowding and pollution emerge as side effects. Resorts may slowly undergo "the Torremolinos effect," turning into tourist slums, where the only attraction is low prices, or "Happy Hour Holidays" as some locals call it.

Much of the early exploitation of the Mediterranean coasts proceeded in strict accordance with laissez-faire capitalism of the slash-and-burn strategy: get in, make a profit, get out, and find a new underdeveloped shore. This process often meant very limited investments in organizing fresh water supplies, electricity, roads, and the handling of garbage and sewage. After an initial boom with high profits, local economies had to try to deal with polluted beaches, traffic congestion, water shortages, illegal garbage dumps. All these side effects hit Majorca during its four decades of mass tourism. In 1990 the island claimed to have more hotel beds than the whole of Greece, but by then the Torremolinos effect had reached its shores, and an alarming number of these beds were empty. Majorca had moved down the market. A major resort like Magaluf was dominated by hard-drinking young British, "lager louts" on continuous pub crawls; many restaurants promised genuine British fare only (like fish and chips, sausages, and baked beans).

Here the early speculators had been allowed to buy up many of the beaches and plaster them with hotels. Now hotels were torn down and attempts made to restore the beaches, in a drive to upgrade the area. The project was called "Magaluf's Dressing Up" and included changing the name to Costas de Calvia, planting trees, cobbling roads, building a "Spanish-style" shopping district—all well known tricks of the trade.

Along many Mediterranean coasts and islands we find a similar pattern of seashore exploitation. At the beginning there is just the beach, maybe a small village, and a winding coastal road. The first hotels, restaurants, and shops line up alongside the road with a view of the beach. Step by step the settlement becomes denser and the picturesque road turns into a traffic inferno; the old hotels may still have a sea view but now also a perfect view of endless traffic and a lot of noise. New hotels have to move elsewhere.

Another fate is a change in clientele. The term *ibizzazione* refers to the ways in which destinations like Ibiza in Spain and Kos in Greece become hot spots for "beach & boogie," with a much younger clientele moving in.[48] Although their beaches are pretty much deserted until the disco crowd wakes up in the afternoon, the family tourists and senior citizens go elsewhere.[49] In the 1970s hippie communities settled in many places around the Mediterranean and some are still around. Along the barren coast of southern Crete during the 1980s the old hippie caves became a tourist sight in themselves. People visited the area in the hope of seeing some real cavedwellers from 1968.

Aside from the actual physical abrasion that creates the slash-and-burn effect of Mediterranean tourism, there is mental wear and tear. The whole industry is based on a constant need for discovery: find new and unspoiled destinations as old destinations grow overcrowded, overpriced, or overfamiliar.

PARADISE FOUND AND LOST:
ON THE POETICS OF VIRGINITY

> And suddenly there is Cagliari: a naked town rising steep, steep, golden-looking, piled naked to the sky from the plain at the head of the formless, hollow bay. It is strange and rather wonderful, not a bit like Italy. . . . There is a very little crowd waiting on the quay: mostly men with their hands in their pockets, they have a certain aloofness and reserve. They are not like the tourist parasites of these post-war days, who move to the attack with a terrifying cold vindictiveness the moment one emerges from any vehicle.[50]

> We came down at the seaport of Herakleion, one of the principal towns of Crete. The main street is almost a ringer for a movie still in a third-rate Western picture . . .
> I wandered about in a daze, stopping now and then to listen to a cracked record from a horned phonograph standing on a chair in the middle of the street. The butchers were draped in blood-red aprons; they stood before primitive chopping blocks in little booths such as one may still see at Pompeii . . .
> Every inch of Herakleion is paintable; it is a confused, nightmarish town, thoroughly anomalous, thoroughly heterogeneous, a place-dream suspended in a void between Europe and Africa, smelling strongly of raw hides, caraway seeds, tar and sub-tropical fruits.[51]

These two quotations, the first one from D. H. Lawrence's *Sea and Sardinia* from 1923, the second from Henry Miller's 1941 account of Crete, belong securely to a genre found in travel literature and vacation advertisements (as well as some tourist studies). Through the history of modern tourism in the Mediterranean runs a constant narrative structure: the discovery of virgin coasts, villages, and regions. The genre draws on a long literary tradition.[52] One central element is precisely this Robinsonian opening: the classic landing, the first footprints in the sand, the heroic conquest.

This theme also runs through the promotional texts and guidebooks that borrow their rather stable set of scenarios, clichés, and narrative

forms from the travel literature. Here places are discovered and redis-
covered, and the definitions of the authentic are constantly adjusted to
the current situation. The picturesque fishing village in the travel catalog
with only three hundred inhabitants also houses three thousand summer visitors.

Each year a new travel catalog has to be developed and each year
some new destinations will have to be presented within the Robinsonian
formula: a hidden gem, an untouched village. A typical example from a
1994 Swedish catalog runs like this:

> You feel a bit like a pioneer when you reach Chrysochou Bay . . . the lit-
> tle town of Polis is growing very slowly. A few modern holiday apart-
> ments and hotels have blended in almost unnoticed with the traditional
> setting, and here the tempo is a traditional Cypriot one.

As definitions of virginity change, standards will fall. Here in Polis there
are no big discos, "only a small one," and next door of course "sleepy
mountain villages and deserted beaches." A visit to Polis "will give you
a new and different view of Cyprus."

The rhetoric of virginity constantly creates new definitions of spoiled
and unspoiled, but also the subgenre of paradise lost. Miller notes to his
surprise a cinema announcing a Laurel and Hardy film, whereas
Lawrence laments the coming of modern times. There are also frequent
references to earlier travelers. Miller often refers to "Byron's days," while
other authors will quote Goethe's Italian travels. Modern times are in a
sense always coming, it does not matter very much whether it is 1830,
1930, or 1990. William Thackeray worded his comment like this in 1846:

> Wherever the steamboat touches the shore adventure retreats into the in-
> terior, and what is called romance vanishes. . . . Now that dark Hassan
> sits in his divan and drinks champagne, and Selim has a French watch
> and Zuleika perhaps takes Morrison's Pills, Byronism becomes absurd
> instead of sublime.[53]

The steam whistle, whether of the train or the ship, became a classic symbol for a spoiled tourist setting during the later half of the nineteenth century. Another favorite phrase is used by Reverend Henry Christmas a few
years later: "Those who wish to see Spain while it is worth seeing must go

soon."[54] In this tourist debate metaphors of evolutionary time are common. Usually you are "too late," but then there are villages and coasts where time stands still, has been arrested, or at least moves at a slower pace.

There is a constant nostalgia for an earlier "then," which tends to move around in time, as virginity is made and remade in different generational and social experiences of "the local." In the old days, back in the 1850s or 1980s, "when we first came here, there wasn't even a tourist/hotel/airport/disco" or "life was so very different then."

In the cultural economy of authenticity, timelessness, and exclusivity, new hidden treasures have to be discovered and sampled before they are swamped by invading tourists. That is why so many tourist guides choose the strategy of telling secrets: Hidden Hawaii, Underground San Francisco, Undiscovered Europe. Or, as a brochure on an isolated Andalusian village puts it, "Enjoy the south's LAST paradise, RIGHT at the seashore," and then at the end warns, "One should keep the secret so it doesn't become fashionable. Do not tell anybody where you rest."[55]

Ideas of authenticity may also change. As a tourist on the Canary Island of Fuertoventura you may all of a sudden get an urge to see just a normal urban setting, where locals go to work, shop, or take a drink. The town next to the airport lacks all picturesque qualities but is at least banal enough.

The ways in which narrative forms, clichés, and scenarios cycle back and forth among different genres tell us something about the making of a Mediterranean tourist literature. Many locations have their own imported literary Big Man. In Sardinia it is Lawrence, in Majorca Robert Graves, in Cyprus Lawrence Durrell, in Morocco Paul Bowles, and so on.

THE MAKING OF THE NEW SOUTH

Postwar mass tourism remapped the Mediterranean. It turned the old peripheries—the barren, depopulated coasts and the isolated islands—into centers of economic growth. They are the new foci of a Mediterranean tourist industry, and through them northern European money and tourists flow south on a large scale, producing new settlements and communities, turning deserts into beaches and irrigated hotel gardens. Again, the irony is that their lack of industrial and urban infrastructures, their empty spaces and scorching sun, turned them into economic assets. The cult of the Mediterranean sun required a technology of refrigeration and air-conditioning, as well as enormous quantities of fresh water, in regions where water shortage was already a big problem. The northern European tourists came from countries where water was abundant and used enormous quantities of fresh water compared with the locals.[56] To develop a basic infrastructure of electricity, water supply, roads, and transport systems for tourist necessities—from fresh meat to bottled beer—called for large investments.

Just as Braudel's Mediterranean world of the sixteenth century had floating and changing boundaries that did not overlap with the actual physical space of the Mediterranean Sea, the new Mediterranean sunbelt has been expanding and contracting over its forty-year history. It expanded first to the west, then south and east in search of new beaches, more sun hours, and undeveloped coasts. Basically, the availability of guaranteed sun and sandy beaches within easy reach of northern European airports defined its boundaries and centers. The travel catalogs map out its present reach. In the north it stretches from Hotel West End in Nice to the Panorama Apartments on Mamaia Beach in Romania, in the west from Bahía Playa Hotel in Tenerife to Hotel Dianamar in Portugal's Albufeira, in the east from Sunny Apartments in Alanya, Turkey, to the King Solomon Hotel in Netanya in Israel, and in the south from the Magawish Hotel in Hurghada, Egypt, to the Panorama in Sousse, Tunisia, and Club Med in Agadir, Morocco.

The map changes quickly, as some areas get overexploited or polluted, threatened by war or terrorism. Several factors determine its outer limits: relatively short flying times (not exceeding five hours) from northern Europe, a standardized tourist infrastructure without the necessity of malaria pills and other tropical hazards. The homogeneity of the area is the result of a gradual process of diffusion and economic integration within the tourist industry. In Braudel's history we meet very diverse cultures communicating, integrating, sharing institutions and ideas. In the same way countries as diverse as Spain, the Arab world of the

Maghreb, parts of old Eastern Europe, Turkey, and so on have been drawn into this economic and cultural system, held together by the charter tourist. If we view it as a culture area, what are its main characteristics and how and to what extent has it been standardized?

Returning to Braudel, we start with the basic rhythm in tourist life: the season, the week, the day. In Braudel's analysis of the sixteenth-century Mediterranean world the polarity of seasons is a basic organizing structure: the sharp division between summer and winter life. During the winter much of the economic activity came to a total standstill, and the tourist economy still reflects this break. But, as we noted, the length of the season varies a great deal among destinations and has grown steadily longer each year since the 1960s. In Agadir the tourist season of winter sun runs from October to April, when more attractive destinations start their season. In Cyprus the season runs from April to November, in Majorca from May to September. Then there is the making of an off-season, with cheap prices for senior citizens who want a milder winter and can take the rainy days. In retirement communities on the Costa del Sol, Cyprus, and the Canary Islands the seasonal fluctuations become even smaller. In the 1980s the proliferation of golfers turned out to be a blessing for many Mediterranean destinations. Provided the proprietors could find the water to keep the courses green, golfers stretched the season at both ends—they were used to rain.

But the strongest homogenizing influence in the Mediterranean tourist industry is the unit on which nearly all vacationing builds: the charter tour week. The economics of flight transport structured charter flights on the concept of filling up a whole airplane. Full loads meant low prices, and low prices were (and remain) the basic condition for mass travel. The idea was to develop a limited number of destinations and use them on a weekly basis. Each time a new batch of tourists stepped off the plane in Torremolinos or Herakleion, last week's arrivals stood ready to fill up the returning flight. This was an unbeatable economic feature, which rapidly came to dominate the market totally. It meant that a Mediterranean vacation became a week's vacation—or if you could afford it, two weeks—and created a characteristic rhythm of tourists coming and going at regular intervals. This principle also meant

Figure 22. The tourist boom of the Meditteranean means that most tourists have to get used to vacationing in an eternal construction site, with cranes hovering over most of the popular beaches. (Photo Hagblom, Lund)

that vacationers could get much cheaper hotel rates, as hotels were assured of an even flow of occupants over the week. The idea of weekend tourism all but disappeared, as did the special holidays.

From this basic time unit followed the whole holiday program. What kinds of programs should tour managers market and offer tourists during their week, what kinds of cultural and local experiences? "You can experience a great deal in a week!" as a travel catalog from 1994 puts it, but the question is how much and in what forms.

THE FAMILIARITY OF THE EXOTIC

"Never change a winner" is an old rule in the tourist industry, and there is an amazing continuity in the structure of package tours to the Mediterranean, among localities and tour companies alike. The format gives veteran tourists a comforting or irritating feeling of *déjà vu:* they know exactly what to expect of their week. Again, it is the pioneer experiences from Majorca and the Costa del Sol that set the standards. Transnationalized, the Spanish experience frames the Greek or Tunisian charter week, from the idea of the welcoming drink to the final village fiesta.

At the airport you meet the other piece of transport technology that gives the charter week its basic structure: the sightseeing bus. For reasons of transport economy and scale, charter tourists travel in buses. The start of your local vacation consists of transportation to the hotel and a first orientation about local conditions from the tour guide, dressed in special colors to set him or her apart from other tour operators. In accordance with the Spanish tour tradition she or he will start by introducing the first name of today's driver, who also has learned to put a little box for tips at the door of the bus. The next item of the week is the welcome reception, where a local drink is served free of charge in a hotel lobby or a nearby restaurant. The color and smell of the drink will tell you where you have landed: sangría in Spain, ouzo in Greece, madeira in Madeira, port in Portugal, and mint tea in Morocco.

The package tour grew from the group travel idea: a vacation cum sightseeing program, already familiar from the history of the bus tour.

The air charter week slowly developed its own structure of sights and activities, with a remarkable degree of standardization and continuity. At the welcoming reception the chances are very great that the first item on the list your guide announces will be tomorrow's half-day city tour, when you will be taken around the local sights and stop for a drink somewhere, then follow the other various tours, which often include a visit to a community of local artisans. And if you are on the coast there will probably be a chartered adventure cruise to an inaccessible beach for an improvised beach party with a barbecue and swimming. The grand finale of the week will be the "village fiesta," an important package tour institution.

The idea of the village fiesta developed in the early Majorcan days of package tours. A local farmer or restaurant owner out in the countryside would put on a dinner of local food, plenty of wine, and a folk dance performance. Today village fiestas take place all over the Mediterranean. In Crete and Sardinia you are invited to an evening with the herders, who might sing and dance for you; in Morocco you are brought to a Berber evening. The village fiesta is a package deal in the same way as the whole tour: bus transport to the hacienda (or farm, old castle, or country inn), a welcome drink, a chance to adorn yourself in a piece of local headgear, plenty of food (preferably barbecued pig), wine *ad libitum*, a performance of local talent and a chance to join in the dancing, and then a return trip late at night. The Majorcan model is of course subject to local circumstances and the requirements of large-scale operations. Although tour brochures still market it within a rather idyllic formula of a visit to a genuine local setting, where villagers may offer you their local specialties, maybe sing a song or two, and urge you to join in their local dances, it has grown into something quite different. An example from Crete illustrates a typical large-scale formula. For the many tour operators based around Herakleion a local restaurant owner has developed a Greek evening at reasonable prices. The bus takes you along winding roads up to what is advertised as a mountain inn but turns out to be a large, hangar-like building. At the entrance sits an old Cretan in traditional dress behind a huge mountain of mass-produced hats "in local style," and inside you find a vast terrain of large tables all marked with big labels announcing the name of your tour operator. You will share your local evening with several hundred other tourists, English, German, Dutch, and Danish, but the different nationalities do not mingle. They stick to their tour group.

There are huge decanters of wine on the table, and as soon as your group sits down an army of waiters will start serving you large chunks of grilled meat, together with potatoes—rather in school cafeteria style. In the middle of the room there is a small podium decorated with folklore items and a sign in package tour lingua franca saying VILLAGE FIESTA. In one corner a small band is playing, and on the stage is a group of professional folk dancers. Later on there will be general dancing and drinking, and if the room gets too hot, the whole roof of the hangar is rolled away. Again, this large-scale version has to do with the ways in which tour operators usually choose to operate. Here is a local entrepreneur who can book a group of any size, any day, with parking space for many buses, at a low price and with professional musicians and dancers. Those tourists who have hoped for something smaller and more local will of course be disappointed, but today most tourists know exactly what to expect. It is the carnivalesque quality of the evening, rather than an anticipation of "a genuine village atmosphere," that is the attraction. During a period when the village fiesta was the symbol of holiday tackiness, it was nicknamed "the pig swill" by those who saw it mainly as a chance to gorge on pork and get smashed. Never having attended one of those evenings became an important mark of distinction.

The rest of the excursion program tends to work in the same way. Tour operators choose the same sights, relying on local entrepreneurs to provide food, entertainment, transport, and the like on a large scale and in dependable forms. It is much safer and easier to handle such professional settings than to send your bus out into less familiar territory. The result is a well-beaten track where the excursions offered by competing companies do not differ very much, and it also often limits the highest impact of mass tourism to special areas, villages, and routes.

There is another reason for this conformity, which has to do with the structure of the workforce: the tour guides. Their job has always had a great appeal for the young, as a kind of ticket to sun and fun, which means that wages are relatively low and the turnover rate high. Most guides are in transit; they stay in the job for a couple of years, with little chance of promotion. Companies also tend to rotate their guides between the different destinations, which means that they must be able to switch from Morocco to Greece or Turkey. The similar tour structure and excursion programs make this much easier on the guides. They have standard routines to rely on, wherever you end up, and accumulate little local expertise. Interchangeability is the name of the game.

Whenever the industry develops a new destination, it uses the established formula. What we need is a weekly excursion program: where should we locate the city tour, the beach barbecue, the demonstration of local crafts, and the village fiesta? Do we have a reliable and well-functioning structure of sights? If there are no local crafts on the island or along the coast, the formula calls for developing them. Thus matrixes for sightseeing plans constantly circulate, borrowing and adapting from older destinations.

The weekly rhythm is also evident in the ways the larger tourist hotels plan their entertainment, which tends to be a miniaturized version of the tour program. Thursday evening is "local buffet," Friday snake charmers, Saturday folklore evening. A corps of local dancers and magicians as well as one-person bands tour the hotel circuit.

The fact that Mediterranean tourists sample different destinations gives them certain expectations. "But they don't have much culture here you know," a tourist in Malta complained to an anthropologist, "crafts and things," she added.[57] When another tour company guarantees that its vacation resorts all are surrounded by "rich local culture," they are thinking in terms of the standard guidebook taxonomies of local culture, with chapters on customs, fiestas, arts and crafts, historical buildings, and monuments. Entrepreneurs in Malta developed a new more flamboyant kind of folklore dancing to meet the expectations of those tourists who had been to Spain or Greece. In this way there is a constant standardization of cultural difference.

On sparsely populated coasts, with a weak infrastructure and relatively few "local cultural attractions," the making of a well-functioning excursion program can be more problematic. Such was the case in the tourist development of Lanzarote, a barren—but guaranteed sunny—Canary Island with a small local population. Here a cultural infrastructure of old ruins, historical monuments, crafts, and picturesque local villages was absent, or rather was not of the type suitable for mass tourism. With the help of thousands of tons of sand, as elsewhere in the Canary Islands, developers could redress the lack of good beaches, but they had to make more creative arrangements to set up suitable destinations for the weekly sightseeing schedule, for example, the use of Moroccan cultural imports, such as the marketing of carpets and Berber crafts.

Lanzarote also illustrates the problem of developing a new attraction, organized on a large scale. The island has plenty of desert-like areas, and with Morocco close by the idea of offering camel safaris as part of the weekly program came up. This called for the import of camels, and a large stretch of desert sand, with easy bus access and ample parking space. Furthermore, to make the venture profitable but keep prices down there had to be a steady daily flow of customers. The camel safari quickly degenerated from an exploration of the wilds into a lemming migration along a deeply tramped bit of desert road with the subsequent disappointment: "Was that it?"

In the same way that a distinct weekly rhythm synchronizes tourist communities, each day within this culture area has its schedule. Every morning, thousands of pool attendants from Hotel Atlantico in the Algarve to Pasha Bay Apartments in Alanya start cleaning their pools, administering the correct daily dose of chlorine. Down at the beach tractors sweep the sand and beach attendants bring forth umbrellas and chairs for hire.

The first guests emerge to claim their favorite chairs, go to the hotel buffet, or visit the local supermercado or bakery for their morning bread if they are staying in the condos. The buses tour the hotels to pick up the excursionists. Later on in the afternoon bars open for "after-beach drinks" or a happy hour. Hotels start preparing their evening programs of buffets and entertainment, while the discos wait for the later hours. In the suburbs of Agadir and Antalya folklore troupes and snake charmers load their stuff into their minivans and set off.

PRODUCING THE PACKAGE

> Bernard took a bus to the local shopping centre and went into the first travel agency he came to. The windows and walls of the shop were plastered with brightly coloured posters depicting tanned young people in skimpy bathing costumes and paroxysms of pleasure, fondling each other on beaches or jumping up and down in the sea or clinging to gaudily rigged sailboards. There was a blackboard on the counter with holidays listed like items on a restaurant menu: *Palma 14 days £242. Benidorm 7 days £175. Corfu 14 days £298.* While he waited to be served, Bernard glanced through a heap of brochures. They seemed extraordinarily repetitive: page after page of bays, beaches, couples, windsurfers, high-rise hotels and swimming pools. Majorca looked the same as Corfu and Crete looked the same as Tunisia. It made the Mediterranean seem the centre of the world in a way the early Christians could not have foreseen.

As Bernard, the hero in David Lodge's novel *Paradise News,* observes this vacation world, he registers the conformity that turns up not only in the rhythms of season, week, and day, but also in the Mediterranean world's material setting and in its lingua franca.[58]

This shared material culture is the result of the constant borrowing and adaptation of different elements. Hotel architecture may pay homage to local style, but the basic structure is a rather extreme functionalism that has to do with the tourist economy of sun and views, as well as with local property prices. Hotels and vacation apartments are designed with a precise geometry to secure maximum exposure to the sun and the sea. Nowadays there is often a price tag on each room or apartment: how many sun hours on the balcony, how good a view. The fact that many tour companies today design their own standard vacation villages, following the style of the pioneering Club Med, increases this conformity, which can be seen even in the smallest details. There exists, for example, a standard plastic chair found in pool bars all over the Mediterranean. The layout of vacation apartments is also heavily standardized, down to the content of kitchen utensils found in the top drawer on the left. As tourists tend to circulate between different destinations during their package tour careers, they develop rather stable anticipations (and demands) about what kinds of equipment to find in their apartments or hotel rooms.

Standardization is also striking in the tourist cuisine. Outside the local taverna in Makrigialos in southern Crete big block letters announce this laconic menu:

HAMBURGER, SANDWICH, TOAST, SOUVLAKI, CHOPSTEAK, OMELETTE, PIZZA, POTATOES, GREEK SALAD

This menu is on offer nowadays in most corners of the Mediterranean, as a tourist cuisine has emerged, from fast food and barbecues on the beach to the fancier evening meals, which tend to be dominated by a blend of French, Italian, American, and Spanish cuisine. A lot of local brandy goes into the pan for flambés and there is a sizable import of sparklers to decorate desserts and make fancy cocktails. The meal itself is often an international composition. A traditional Greek dinner, served in Rhodes or Tenerife, might include Danish imitation feta cheese, Taiwan bamboo skewers for the souvlaki, and Amstel beer brewed on license.

Over the years a lingua franca has developed: Cars for Hire, To the Beach, Banana Split, Bungalow, Steak Diane, Fully Air Conditioned, Bodega, Schnitzel. English and German battle for hegemony in most areas. In international settings like these, words—especially longer texts—are hard to follow. Economical use of images and icons is better. Restaurants show their menu in color photo displays. Neon signs and logos draw on the iconography of an international vacation world. A palm tree, a tilted cocktail glass conjure up a whole world of fun and freedom. In this lingua franca there is frequent borrowing from other famous vacation spots: Pizzeria Miami, Hotel Palm Beach, Riviera Cocktail Bar, Hawaii Disco, Café California.

Today a global economy supplies the Mediterranean tourist communities with images, goods, and services, especially as most of the isolated regions have very little (or the wrong kind) of local produce. Along the Agadir beach tourists search for shells from the sea, but the naturally occurring shells are small, so the tourists are followed by local peddlers, who offer much grander shells for sale. These shells find their way from

the Pacific to the small-scale sellers through a complex web of market relations, as does the silver jewelry manufactured in India and the door-
mats that other peddlers on the beach are hawking.

The list of imports is endless: tons of coconut oil for tanning, thousands of white Fiat Pandas with sun tops and Suzuki mopeds for hire,
air-conditioned Volvo buses, Midnight Sun Finnish Butter in individual
portions, Mr. and Mrs. T's Bloody Mary Mix from Stanford, USA, drums
of German Béarnaise essence, langouste from the Atlantic, and giant
shrimps from Southeast Asian farms.

But it is not only local produce that is lacking; there is also a shortage
of specialists to man different jobs in the tourist industry. There is a vast
migration (often seasonal) of managers, waiters, shop owners, tour
guides, American disc jockeys, German hairdressers, Indian bazaar owners, Danish nursery school teachers for the kids' clubs, French scuba diving instructors, and Somalian beach peddlers.

The structure of this huge industry draws on flexible production systems, with "lean" and "flat" organizations, small investments in permanent staff and infrastructure. Because the products are experiences,
sights, events, and adventures, their turnover is much faster than in industries that still produce material commodities. The whole complex
system rests not on a factory structure but on a small and heavily com-
puterized home-based tour company, buying services and products all
along the chain of the tour, including airport clerks, bus drivers, local
guides, hotel accommodation. It is this weaving together of the basics, a
seat on the flight, a hotel bed, local transit, an excursion program, and
some local ground service, that enables the industry to keep down the
costs and have a very small hired staff. The competition is razor-sharp,
as it was relatively easy, at least in the past, to establish yourself in the
business (and to go bust). Computer reservation systems also allow for
an increasingly personalized programming of travel wishes.

For the big companies the competition tends to focus on price levels
and try any trick to keep costs low. At times their tactics include paying
local staff very low wages and making sure to get a percentage from
restaurant and shop owners, car rental firms, and others who recruit
clients from the incoming tour groups. Local hotels also find themselves

in weak bargaining positions versus the big tour operators. To be dumped from their catalogs means severely limited market possibilities.

Some big companies go for vertical integration, producing resorts on the "all-included-model" of Club Med, but most aim for a minimum of investments locally. Smaller companies look for specialized niches, in everything from golf tours to archaeology trips.

The overall effect is a stunning standardization on some levels. Although many companies work hard on marketing their own individual profile, their output is pretty much the same. A glance at the various information folders in the hotel lobby at a place used by different companies shows the similarities. They enthusiastically declare their unique profile by offering the same sightseeing tours, travel hints, and local attractions as their competitors.

COSMOPOLITANS, NATIONALS, AND LOCALS

One factor, however, hampers standardization and large-scale integration, and that is national habits. Despite the very impressive international mergers in this industry, national boundaries are still strikingly important. Britons demand British guides, excursions, and kids' clubs; Germans demand German staff. The only successful attempt at crossing national boundaries seems to be Scandinavian: a Swede is prepared to have a Danish guide speaking in the new language of tourist Scandinavian (and vice versa). But on the whole tourists want to stay with their compatriots, and there is surprisingly little mixing of nations. On the contrary. Mediterranean tourism tends to enforce the stereotyping of those other nationalities.

Walking in a local tourist minimarket—a rather special form of convenience store—you will see this international division of labor even more elaborated, as the shopkeeper has to cater to the special home-brand nostalgia that might hit the visitors: German coffee, Swedish candy, Danish cheese, American chewing gum, English cocoa.

A certain heterogeneity also reflects the different history of Mediterranean regions—not forgetting the colonial past:

Cyprus gives the impression of being more Westernized than Greece and the influence of the British way of life cannot be overlooked. In contrast to Greece, water for bathing in the better hotels is available at all hours of the day and night; there are no fights with dripping taps and the meals are served hot. Despite heavy traffic there are no loud arguments about right of way and one does not encounter the proverbial Greek unpunctuality.[59]

This characterization in a German tour guide tells us both about the colonial past of Cyprus and about German preferences. Small details show you that you are staying in a territory that once was part of the British or French empire or sphere of influence. In Morocco or Tunisia the Frenchness is visible in many ways: the waiter's handshake, the croissants for breakfast, the blue coat of the pool attendant, the ways in which figures are written on the restaurant bill, the size of the coffee cups. (As France and Italy are the only Mediterranean countries with a long tradition of extensive native tourism, the French and Italian Rivierias have kept much more of a national style—in everything from food and entertainment to hotel routines.)

But the tourist industry has also distributed different nationalities unevenly over the Mediterranean region. The English have gathered in Corfu, the Germans dominate Crete, while the Scandinavians are numerous in Rhodes. At most destinations, however, different nationalities mix and go in for a great deal of national stereotyping.

Athens 1850:

that universal nuisance, the all-seeing English traveller—the traveller of that class who scribble their names on the walls of temples, write witty criticisms in the stranger's book at inns, are always paying too much and raving about extortion, depreciate everything that is not like what they are used to, swallow an infinite quantity of dust, and return home with as much knowledge and worse morals than they took with them.[60]

Italy 1900:

There are the usual American tourists here, the most senseless type of human nature, being quite insensible to beauty or decorum and with the manners of shop-boys, who ramble through the gardens of the ancient world with as little knowledge of their value as beasts have, defiling all and trampling all. . . . They should be kept at home, for they have no business in these ancient lands.[61]

Sardinia 1995:

It's a good thing there are so few Germans here. They come and take over the whole place, demanding everything, acting like kings, coarse and loud-mouthed. One at a time could work, but not in groups. Once I got so angry that I walked up to one of them at the pool and said, "You have already lost two world wars, so why don't you quiet down." He wasn't happy about that.[62]

In 1994 a popular British television commercial for Carling lager showed a young, muscular and tanned Englishman entering a Mediterranean hotel terrace, watching a bunch of fat Germans scramble for the best poolside chairs. He nonchalantly throws his Union Jack bathing towel over the heads of the Germans, who in amazement watch it unfold on top of the best chair—and, of course, inside it is a can of ice-cold lager. In the morning hotel battle Britain has been successful again! (The negative stereotypes of Germans focus on their hegemonic position: they are everywhere and oh, so visible, so loud, and so affluent!) And yet, during my many years of tourism in the Mediterranean I have seen only two nationalities who put little national flags on their sun deck: Norwegians and Swedes.

Among local inhabitants there exists a similar stereotyping of different nationalities.[63] The Germans are tidy, the Swedes fussy, the English funny, and the French haughty, but then there are other catogorizations that cut across nationalities, the *windsurfero* and the *black feet* (hippies), who appear to be a truly cosmopolitan mix, and not very popular among the locals either.

As in the case of the cottage cultures the social relations, hierarchies, and taxonomies are complex. Who is a local, who is a regular? In the Andalusian village of Zahara, the Spanish stand owners who come for the season are called tourists, but a different kind. The same goes for those who have been living in retirement for years in Los Santos compared to the ones who are just here for the week. How long a time does it take for you to become a regular? Those who come for two weeks may appear like local experts to next week's incoming group.

But neither the old nor new tourism of the south enhances contacts between locals and visitors. The old *ghetto Inglese* duplicates its boundaries all over the region in different nationalities and subcultures. Many people manage to live for years on the Costa del Sol or Cyprus without developing many local contacts; they are quite content with their tight-knit network of compatriots.

Susan Buck-Morss explores the kind of Othering that goes on in Mediterranean villages swamped by tourists. The schoolteacher in her Cretan village talks of the village "being stuffed with tourists until, like an animal force-fed, it becomes sick to the point of bursting."[64] This feeling of having no control over what is happening to your village echoes in many other studies.[65] The first tourists are an adventure, a promise of economic betterment in coastal regions, where the prime source of income after the Second World War had been migration north in search of jobs, or a meager living from farming or fishing. As the influx grows, people find out that land with next to no apparent value or just the value of its olive crop now brings a very good sale price. Those who by chance have coastal properties are the luckiest, and in many cases these were not always the wealthy farmers. Investors and developers from the outside move in, and all of a sudden they control and plan everything. Multinational chains build hotels, outsiders run souvenir stores, tour companies fly in the guides. The new wealth is usually unevenly distributed and most locals end up in low-paid service jobs.

The old community disappears or rather has to retreat, as the tourists take over. The strategy of creating a tourist front and then making sure that there are backstage territories and arenas for local life has become common in many Mediterranean regions. The problem is of course that when tourists get tired of the phoniness of the local front, they start to search for the "real" local culture behind the curtains.

Tourist are an economic resource but also a source of constant tension. What kind of people are these tourists who seem to drink all day and swim naked down at the beach? There is also the sexual traffic, which becomes problematic in many ways.

MEDITERRANEAN MADNESS

In Cyril Connolly's novel *The Rock Pool* from 1936, the English hero Naylor finds himself affected by the different moral universe of the Riviera:

> He knew nothing about Mediterranean madness, of the altered tissues which are associated with the *zone nerveuse*, the arid foreshore of that iodine-charged littoral . . . [a] balminess, which usually appears not only as great moral toleration, but as an almost drunken ethical laxity.[66]

Already in the days of the Grand Tour the south had an aura of romance, adventure, and sexuality. The amorous Swedish gentlemen that Olof Celsius talked about had many parallels. Going south meant entering a different moral territory. As early as the 1720s British newspapers complained of the conduct of British male tourists: "the whole account of their travels is generally no more than a journal of how many bottles they have drunk, and what loose amours they have had."[67] Traveling in male company could turn the Grand Tour into a kind of mobile stag party, something to brag about after returning north again. The amorous escapades of culture heroes like Byron and Goethe fostered male fantasies about the south as a territory of sexual possibilities, but these territories offered mainly servants or peasant girls. And in a city like Nice the changing tourist clientele during the latter part of the nineteenth century led to a marked expansion of female prostitution. "The horrible and cancerous, the evil of the easy women" had entered the city, following "the swallows of winter," it was noted in 1876, thus placing the problem safely outside local culture.[68] But there were other forms of prostitution in the city. In 1898 Oscar Wilde commented on the different Mediterranean tradition of male homosexuality, calling local boys in Nice the noble army of the boulevard: "The fishing population of the Riviera have the same freedom as the Neapolitans," he added.[69]

As the middle classes entered the arena in growing numbers the discussion about the sexual politics of the south became more heated.[70] Now as more women were among the travelers the focus shifted to the ways in which they had to be protected from Latin courtesans. There is a striking continuity from the moral warnings and narratives of the nineteenth century to the 1960s stories mentioned earlier. The swarthiness, the mustache, the affected airs, the insincerity. In the novel *The Dodd Family Abroad* from 1854 the differences between British men and southerners are outlined in these terms:

> *Our* civilities are like a bill of exchange, that must represent value one day or other. *Theirs* are like the gilt markers on a card table: they have a look of money about them, but are only counterfeit. Perhaps this may explain why our women like the Continent so much better than ourselves. All this mock exchange amuses and interests *them;* it only worries *us*.[71]

There is, however, a very striking difference between the world of the Dodds and the package tours of the 1960s. In 1854 the male worries had very little to do with the very rare sexual exchanges or intermarriages that actually took place between southern men and northern women. In the new south of the package tour the sexual division of labor changed in some ways. The Latin lover ceased to be a fantasy and became a vacation experience for many single women. The tables had turned. No longer was it a question of northern morals being threatened by the imagined laxities of the Mediterranean. Now it was the emancipated northern women who were active in search of a vacation affair. They brought new tensions into coastal communities.

This role reversal was very provoking to northern European male observers, as we have seen in some of the reactions from the sixties. It bothered rural women too. But what about the consenting lovers? As Susan Buck-Morss points out, a situation of seemingly carefree sexual exchanges in these settings was not uncomplicated:

> it might appear that whatever the politics and power balance, this is one of the utopian situations, where everybody wins. But the sides are playing different games, and their goals are incompatible. Separated by a cultural divide despite the physical intimacy, there is no mutuality in regard to the meaning of the sex act.[72]

For local women these female tourists were a threat, even if they never met face to face. In many villages the married men migrated to nearby tourist centers to work as waiters and cabdrivers, and their wives often had good reason to believe that they took advantage of the free sexual scenery available there.[73] The institutionalized prostitution that male tourists exploited had rigidly defined roles. Now the situation was more ambivalent. In the eyes of the locals, tourist women in search of local men were not an example of female emancipation; the only local category open for them was whores. The young men too operated within a secure double standard. Local girls had to be chaperoned, tourist girls were fair game. And because their own social and economic status was lower than these northern European outsiders', most of them weren't likely to think of going back with these women to northern Europe. It would mean accepting the inferior and dependent status of immigrant men. It would reverse the situation that brought a warning a century earlier to British men contemplating marriage with a lovely Italian girl: "What would you do with that at home?"[74]

In the two centuries of Mediterranean sexual politics in tourism we see old stereotypes and also hierarchies reproduced, even as new practices evolve, but there is also a complex power play involving various combinations of gender, class, age, and ethnicity. It is interesting to contrast the more established male sex tourism, especially in the third world, with the affairs of female tourists, which set off heated debates. One element that seems to make them so provoking is the age reversal: older women courting younger men.

HIBERNATING IN THE OLD AND NEW SOUTH

Cosmopolitan life is no longer an insignificant fact, an eccentricity of a few elegant women, who while they live in Paris, have their linen washed in London or betake themselves periodically from Spain or Germany to Biarritz or to Spa. Nowadays the whole aristocracy of Europe leads a comparable life. It scales the mountains of Switzerland or of Tyrol, makes yachting trips to the fjords of Norway, shoots grouse in the highlands of Scotland, goes to Bayreuth to hear Wagner's operas and to Monte Carlo to lose its money; it spends the Holy Week in Seville and the Carnival in Nice, ascends on the Nile in a *dahabeah*, and coasts down on the frozen slopes of St-Moritz on toboggans in winter. . . . The first thing that strikes me is that all these people who mingle do not really see one another. Each leads in his environment the life of his own country, remaining the slave of his own petty habits. An English company—the same one which owns the Hotel Metropole in London—has built very near Cannes an enormous hotel which is filled with English people. Why do they go there instead of to other hotels equally well, or even better, situated? Because the wallpaper, the furniture, the staff, even the fenders, all come from London; because they give bacon for breakfast in the morning and toast and muffins at afternoon tea; because in short, they provide themselves with the illusion of being on the shores of the Mediterranean without having left England.

Swedes abroad do not want to be abroad. They would rather be at home. This is seen in the way they often travel in groups, book into dreadful, fenced Swedish tour company ghettoes (with Swedish radio stations), and immediately seek out other Swedes, hunt for Swedish food, Swedish coffee, Swedish newspapers, anything at all so long as it is Swedish.

"Why do they travel?" one may wonder.

The main reason is that Sweden is rarely sunny and Swedes love the sun. There we have the basic problem. Swedes do not really go to Spain, Greece, or Florida. They go to the sun, where it shines does not matter. They are not interested in any local population, a new language, or new dishes. They just want to sit and get drunk on duty-free alcohol, their skins peeling from excess sun, grinning nervously along with their usually narrow-minded, unintelligent neighbors in the next condo.

There is over a century between these two complaints. The first one was made in 1898 by the baron de Coubertin, the internationalist and founder of the Olympic Games, while the other is from a 1994 issue of a Swedish magazine, but their frustration seems timeless.[75] What about those tourists? Why do they go abroad in order to keep themselves to themselves, enslaved by their petty habits?

This complaint is still alive in the ongoing battles between different categories of tourism. The first mistake they make is to measure *les hivernants* along the Mediterranean coasts against the exemplars of classic tourism. The participants in this vacation world I explore have totally different aims. *Les hivernants* of the French Riviera in the baron de Coubertin's times came from quite another social segment than the senior citizens spending the winter in a bungalow or hotel room today, but they share certain characteristics. They are not the Foggs but the Robinsons of the tourist world. They are here on the Mediterranean shores to get away, to relax and unwind, to enjoy themselves.

Today the old elite still visits the Mediterranean but has created its own sheltered spaces, like the Costa Smeralda on Sardinia, developed by the Aga Khan in the 1950s.

From the early start of mass tourism in the 1950s the image of the typical package tour traveler has had a more or less hidden class element and focuses on the shallow, prepackaged, and leveling experiences of such tourism, as well as its collective nature. The new travelers came from the lower middle class and later the working class. In 1958 a Swedish medical journal issued this warning:

> Qualified professionals, for whom it is important to obtain effective holiday rest and good relaxation, should avoid group tours and charter trips with their mixed clientele, collective service, and fixed timetables. Harried and tired persons in these categories along with their wives, such as architects, dentists, doctors, pharmacists, solicitors, veterinarians, managers, officials of various kinds, and of course grammar-school teachers and university lecturers, should allow themselves the somewhat more expensive form with normal scheduled trips by plane, train, and boat, and should use first-class hotels even if they are sometimes called luxury hotels.[76]

The critique of package tours was based on the traditional ideals of what tourism ought to be about. Those new tourists chose security before adventure and could not tell the inauthentic from the authentic.

The critique that a week in Turkey, Spain, or Morocco looks pretty much the same to these undiscerning consumers misses the point that the new package tour travelers had other priorities than the classic sightseers. A week in the Mediterranean had first of all to be available at affordable prices, and this meant mass travel. Second, it had to deliver certain basic elements: sun, sea, sand, and preferably also some local color. It had to supply freedom from regulated work and supervision, and freedom to do what you want, for example, nothing. The sense of liberation was very marked for the pioneers in this new mass exodus to the south. The hedonistic principle was central: "We are going to have fun!" The vacation began even in the airport lounge. You'd checked your baggage and left your worries behind you, and the first tax-free drink on the plane often became the magic rite de passage.

The whole construction of the new south fit the needs of not-so-travel-savvy tourists who wanted to go abroad. Its certainty and predictability made the package tour a mass phenomenon. It opened up international travel for the vast majority of working-class families for whom a trip abroad had previously been a utopia. Middle-class travelers with cosmopolitan competence and a command of international languages failed to understand that without the safety net of tour guides, excursion programs, and familiar restaurant menus, the northern European working class would never have gotten south. As a Swedish lorry driver put it, "It is absolutely fantastic to think that you can sit on a balcony in Spain and eat T-bone steak and drink rosé wine and meet people you would not otherwise have dared to speak to—even people from other countries." In many northern European settings the Mediterranean simply became "the South" and this south stretched easily to include other sun destinations like Gambia and Thailand. "South" became the territorialization of a certain kind of holiday, rather than a fixed geographical region.[77]

The south meant a number of freedoms, which included the freedom from being policed (or observed) by those other sophisticated tourists. You could choose if you wanted to be part of the easy-going gemeinschaft of the tour group. The new south provided easy routines for socializing. You could join others for a night out, with the help of the tour guides, and you could develop temporary friendships. You could also choose to keep yourself to yourself. The structure of the new package tour was also meant to eliminate much of the anxiety-ridden skills of mastering foreign cultures, such as language proficiency, or the etiquette of public behavior in hotels and restaurants.

If you felt intimidated by restaurant etiquette and headwaiters hovering over you as you tried to find out how the menu worked, you could choose restaurants where they served informal buffet meals or had menus with all the food in color photos, or you could cook your own meals back home in the kitchenette of the condo. Package tours started out with hotel accommodation, but operators soon found out that most travelers preferred the freedom of the condo.

The whole public sphere of vacation life in the new south used a simple sign and symbol language, much of it in pictures, which did not call for great language skills. You could also choose how much exoticism you wanted. Some guests decided to stay by the hotel pool the whole week, others went outside, on sightseeing tours or on their own.

When some tourists accuse those other tourists of not being good enough tourists, not open enough, not interested in adventures and new challenges, they fall back on the normative ideal developed from the days of the Grand Tour and onwards. They forget that behind the tourist label there are very different kinds of explorers. Some are out to discover exotic worlds or meet new people, for others a vacation is a chance to explore the body, their senses, or sexuality or just develop the difficult art of doing nothing.

In sketching the south's institutionalization, I used the past tense because the new south is not a static concept. During the 1980s and 1990s it grew more and more differentiated. The last four decades of package tours made visitors more demanding, more experienced in knowing what they want and what they are ready to pay for it.

In retrospect the first generation of package tourists seems naive—tourists fell for marketing tricks that never would work today. As mass tourism expanded, everyday life was invaded by the exotic. Northern Europeans savored the taste of newfangled words: playa, pommes frites, pizza, paella, charter, bodega, sangría, cappuccino, bungalow, poolbar. They domesticated these Mediterranean features in Swedish dining rooms and souvenir collections, retold them in photo albums and super-eight reels, showed and discussed them at the family get-together or at work.

There is a constant learning process involved here, learning to handle a new form of vacationing and getting your money's worth. The changing tone of travel catalogs mirrors this transformation. There is less and less of vague, romantic descriptions of local destinations, and more detailed and prosaic consumer information: the exact distance to the beach, the noise level of the street, the hours of air conditioning, the water temperature in September. It's a process of commoditization, certainly, and of growing interest in how to get your money's worth and specify your demands. Past tours were more markedly a collectivity; today you may find a wide spectrum within the same group, ready to split up as soon as the plane lands. Some will have no contact with their fellow travelers until the group reassembles at the airport for the journey home, others will interact intensively, by the hotel pool and during the excursions. The sharply rising demand for rental cars—much more fun than a stodgy old sightseeing tour!—reflects this change. But there's also a kind of cultural lag, a nostalgic marketing of the charter tour as the good old gemeinschaft of the bus tour.

There are many snakes in this paradise. The scale and structure of mass tourism create very real problems of congestion, pollution, noise, crime, and various forms of rip-offs. In Los Santos the restaurant cook knows that most of his customers are only here for a week, so why worry about good cooking, they won't come back anyway. The structure of weekly invasion and exodus also produces bad service or indifference to visitors.

Paradoxically, the structure of the new south also protects the old south. Tourism's fads for certain areas and certain beaten tracks also limit its negative impacts. Still, as package tourists desert the sightseeing buses, they bring traffic congestion to coastal areas and small islands: too many rental cars on the road.

FLOWS AND MOVEMENTS

"The Mediterranean has no unity but that created by the movements of men, the relationships they imply, and the routes they follow."[78] Braudel's characterization still holds for the shaping and reshaping of the south as a tourist region. Tourist empires spring up and disappear, in constant market competition, as operators flourish, merge, or go under. New destinations open up and old ones fade away. In the same way, movements—of tourists and those who live by the tourist trade—hold together and standardize this vast region.

Braudel's Mediterranean history balanced between the polarities of the permanent structures and the ephemeral conjunctures—the slow-moving and the fast. We find the same polarities in the making of Mediterranean tourist life. If Mediterranean peasants subsisted on what Braudel calls the triangle of wheat bread, olive oil, and wine, the basic tourist's triangle is the week, the sun, and the sea.[79] They give the industry a stable structure. There is, however, no timelessness in this world. The Mediterranean becomes polluted or hit by the algae effect, but the tourist industry builds more pools and artificial lagoons to take care of the need for swimming. Now the skin cancer scare is slowly making new generations of tourists less interested in baking themselves down on the beach.

Just as wars constantly reshaped the Mediterranean of Philip II, when the Balkan peninsula broke apart or fundamentalists of different creeds used bombs to destabilize the tourist trade in Turkey, Egypt, or Rhodes—to take some examples from the 1990s—tourists rapidly deserted the beaches or canceled their flights. And yet the Mediterranean age of the package tourist has not ended; the industry shows great resilience and adaptability.

Mass travel has created a new Mediterranean world, an industry without which large parts of the region would not survive. In Cyprus, for example, it accounts for 65 percent of the gross domestic product. It has rearranged the map in many ways: turned peripheries into centers, made the unmarketable a scarce and much sought-after resource. It has created patterns of rapid expansion, development, and aging. Against the might of international developers, local authorities have had little power. Short-term gains have often resulted in long-term costs of pollution and overexploitation, while investors have moved away in search of new projects.

Despite these harsh realities, tourists continue to long for the south, searching for different forms of liberation, not only from rain and cold, but also from a regimented everyday life, from stifling conventions. If one S, as in Sights, dominated the Grand Tour, the early package tour's sea, sand, sun, sex, and spirits syndrome now takes on another alliterative set: many of the package tour travelers today are in search of seclusion, silence, simplicity. Mediterranean madness is still there but has new forms. Now the great R unites all these experiences—Romance—and the chance to explore and perhaps expose different aspects of yourself or your relations to others. The Robinsonian quest is also about transcendence.

part 3

Between the Local and the Global

The Global Beach

Once I found a postcard in a secondhand shop. It was manufactured in New York, probably in the fifties, and carried the simple text: "By the beautiful sea." It is a good example of the universalization of the beach experience, the making of a truly global iconography and choreography of beach life. It is one of those many postcards without any hint of the "local," just sand, sea, and carefully arranged groups of beach visitors. Pictures like these turn up in any card rack along the coasts of the world. No surprise that I found it in Sweden.

What is a beach, what can a beach be used for? In the 1990s the Lego toy producers developed a transnational holiday world called PARADISA in the Esperanto of the global toy industry. If you bought kit number

213

Figure 23. "By the beautiful sea": the photographer has choreographed his models' posture to demonstrate the properly relaxed beach body. (Postcard from the 1950s, printed in New York)

6410 (and were over the age of six) you would be able to construct your own beach, with the following basic ingredients: 1 palm tree, 2 bathing huts, 1 parasol, 2 deck chairs, 1 surfboard, 1 fishing rod, 1 speedboat, 1 portable cassette player, 1 beach bar (complete with waiter and exotic drinks), 1 male and 1 female vacationer in swimsuits. This bricolage of props and activities comes from different settings and epochs all around the world and now, integrated and globalized, becomes a familiar place to play at being a teenager, a grownup, a tourist.

The concept of beach covers a lot of territory and history, as we have seen in the previous chapters. The range of beach life is amply demonstrated along a coast like that of California. In northern California there is the constant search for a beach of your own, a small cove, protected by cliffs and rocks. As the tide moves out, strings of small beaches suddenly become available to couples or single families—*nota bene,* if public access is possible. The idea of this kind of beach is that it belongs to nobody but you. Intruders are a provocation, they should move on to find their own beach. This beach is yours, you can collect shells and driftwood, build a castle in the sand, knowing that in a few hours it will be gone, washed away. The other end of the scale would be a beach like the famous Los Angeles beach studied in the 1970s by the sociologist Robert Edgerton. This "Southland," as he labeled it, attracted 400,000 visitors on a fine summer day.[1]

Beaches come in all forms and fashions, finding their position along this continuum from the Robinson beach, where there is just you, sand, water, and maybe a couple of palm trees, to the lively holiday beach, à la Coney Island or Blackpool. But any of these beaches represents a sedimentation of cultural traditions, from the eighteenth-century history of seashore invalids to the 1990s cult of *Baywatch.* Earlier chapters explore some of the stages in this historical development from the sublime, romantic beach to the fun beach of Antibes. For the eighteenth- and early nineteenth-century pioneers the beach was mainly an access to the ordeal of sea bathing, getting a quick dose of the healthy sea breeze and saltwater. The beach served for quiet strolls or as a site for sunset watching, but the idea of the beach as a playground was still far away.

In this global history some beaches occupy a limited stretch of sand but take up a huge mental space. These are the famous beaches that less famous beaches often try to emulate. There is the early example of the Lido outside Rome, later on the Murphys' beach, La Garoupe, at Antibes. "Romantic Rio can be yours" is the headline of a 1946 ad from Pan Am, which shows two women leisurely resting in the sand. The text continues, "In Rio de Janeiro it is summer! And by clipper Rio's Copacabana beach is just a weekend away from the United States."[2] For Mediterranean package tourists the beach of Las Palmas on the Canary Islands had a strong image, just like Miami Beach in Florida or Malibu in California.

THE TROPICAL DREAM

The props of the *PARADISA* beach have their own history. Already in the making of the Riviera, palm trees became a must, and this tropical plant has steadily expanded north. The collapsible deck chair was borrowed from the decks of ocean cruisers, while the bathing hut has many national variations (the *PARADISA* ones look rather French).

But the whole concept of paradise relies above all on the romance of the South Pacific and the tropical beach. The global notion of the beach as paradise began in the cult of Hawaii and the Waikiki beach next to Honolulu. The site of Hawaii is special. For a very long period it continued to be a fantasyland. The first modern resort hotel was built in 1901, but as late as 1955 the yearly number of tourists barely reached one hundred thousand and it was only with the arrival of cheap jet flights that Hawaii became a mass destination. Until the 1950s Waikiki remained a beach experience for a small, mainly American elite. The power of the Hawaiian imagery above all had to do with the fact that this was the first really mass-mediated paradise: a landscape not only to experience through colored postcards and illustrated magazine features but also a landscape set to music. As early as 1915 the tune "At the Beach of Waikiki" was a great hit at the Panama-Pacific Exposition in San Francisco.[3] Tin Pan Alley versions of Hawaiian sheet music started spreading around the world and their colorful covers established the image of the tropical beach, hula girls with flowers in their hair and palm trees swaying gently in the breeze, or just a pair of lovers admiring the silvery moon and the mountain silhouette of Diamond Head. Tropical nights on the beach became a new romantic fantasy, and as Hawaiian music on gramophone records complemented sheet music, everybody could create their own Waikiki atmosphere at home in the living room or even down at the local beach. It was the ultimate romantic beach serenade, with mass-distributed landscape sound and images. During the 1930s Waikiki became the first radio beach; there were countless shows broadcast from "the beach at Waikiki," and mass-syndicated radio shows like "Hawaii Calls" at times were heard on 750 radio stations worldwide.[4]

During the Second World War tourists vanished from the Waikiki beach, which was taken over by the hundreds of thousands of soldiers stationed in Honolulu or passing through. Discussions of tourism rarely mention the fact that masses of working-class men got their first experience of the exotic during the war, albeit in rather strange circumstances. Most of the GIs in Honolulu never came closer to their Polynesian dream girls than the offer of "Two Pictures with Hula Girl" for 75 cents, and then the hula girls usually weren't local Hawaiians but Puerto Ricans or Mainlander girls. The local women did not live up to the fantasy images of slender hula bodies that the men brought with them from back home.[5]

Many of the GIs came back later to Hawaii and the South Pacific with their families as tourists. During the 1950s active mass-media marketing furthered the fantasyland of the Pacific beach as an appetizingly exotic Eden of sensual women with inviting smiles. "Every man's vision of delight," as the *National Geographic* aptly called a 1962 feature on Tahiti. During the postwar period this influential magazine consistently pictured the Pacific as a friendly and secure paradise.[6]

On Waikiki the Hollywood presence had been strong since the 1920s. Movie moguls and stars simply had to spend a vacation in one of the fashionable resort hotels, and the result was a strong Hollywood interest in Hawaiian settings, which culminated in the 1950s with movies like *From Here to Eternity* and Elvis's *Blue Hawaii*. In those years the favorite prize on an American quiz show was often a romantic trip to Hawaii for two.[7]

By the time the mass tourists started flying in with the firmly established romance of Waikiki beach among their baggage, the actual beach

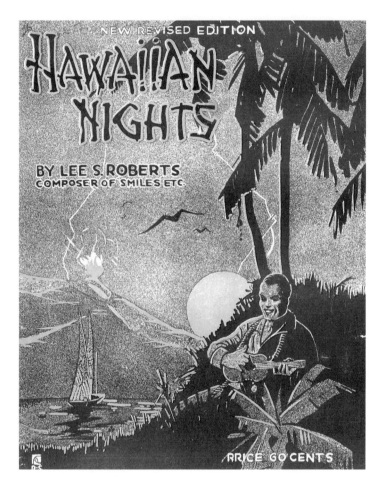

Figure 24. Sheet music created both visual and aural images of
Hawaii. (Culver Pictures, Inc.)

experience with its jungle of high-rise hotels, overcrowded beaches, and traffic congestions had difficulties in living up to these images.

Over in Europe there was a similar craze, which the French sociologist Jean-Didier Urbain labels "the polynesification" of European beach life; in the 1950s there was for example a Club Polynésie turning European destinations into images of Pacific romance.[8]

After Waikiki with its groves of coconut palms any serious beach had to have palm trees, like the PARADISA version. Another element on the PARADISA beach also had a Waikiki past: the surfboard, but it made the global beach through a detour to California.

When the tourists started visiting Waikiki beach, surfing was almost gone as local tradition, and mainland Americans helped revitalize it. Local surfers became one of the great sights at the beach. They produced all kinds of stunts, from surfing dogs to night surfing with torches, but they also brought the experience to the tourists. Visiting Hawaiian teams took the sport to California in the early twentieth century, but since few tourist seashores have good surf, the sport's diffusion was slow. Until the 1950s surfers made up a relatively small subculture, mainly confined to southern California.[9] Wearing swimming shorts, T-shirts, and sandals, they spent most of their summer on the beach and out in the surf, often staying overnight in the car and having improvised beach parties in the evenings. They also went on "surfing safaris" to distant beaches with great surf.

Surfing went global through the media, but in rather unorthodox ways. In the late fifties and early sixties low-cost surfing films were made and shown in high-school auditoriums and similar places. Surfing attracted attention in novels and later Hollywood movies, but the big breakthrough came when "surfing music" was transformed into an international success by some southern California musicians. When the Beach Boys (named after the famous surfers on Waikiki beach) had several surfing songs in the top ten during 1962 and 1963 the craze was already a fact. The number of surfers grew and, more important, a new image of teenage beach life spread around the world to the tunes of "Surfing Safari" and "California Girls": blond and tanned youth, jumping into their open cars to drive down to the beach for a summer of endless parties. Surfboards no longer had to be part of the surf scene, other than as a suitable backdrop, and the surf scene was no longer seen as a Hawaiian but a Californian innovation.[10] In the 1960s it also produced another global export: why not arrange a real California beach party down at the local beach or in your own backyard? It became an avant-garde form of informal socializing.

BEACH BASICS

Three basic elements make up the global beach: sand, sun, and sea. What are their characteristics? How did these three ordinary elements turn beaches into a global phenomenon?

Sand is usually not a popular terrain for human activity. It is hard to walk in, it gets into your clothes, eyes, and food. It moves too easily in the wind. The early seashore visitors who used the beach mainly as a vista or for a slow walk avoided the sandy dunes and made only quick expeditions over the banks when going into the water. People who went for a serious swim preferred other kinds of beaches. Sand was a strange and alien material, difficult to shape and control.

It was only when the swimming and sunning beach developed that sand acquired its new qualities. It became an extremely sensual element, caressing the body. From now on a real beach should have sand, and preferably either white or golden yellow, it should also look clean, virginal. The sand combined the fluidity of water and the warmth of the sun.

Once vacationers started to make contact with this new element, they found that it had all sorts of uses. Already during the early twentieth century sand and children were well linked. In northern Europe the sandbox was developed for children. Children needed sand, sand was good for them. It turned into a medium for play, and in suburban gardens and urban playgrounds small sand dunes, fenced in by planks, materialized. At the beach the sand brought out the child in the adult. Grown-ups joined the kids in fooling around with sand, building sand castles, canals, sculptures, covering each other in sand. Digging became a favorite pastime and in some cases led to stranger activities.

The craze for sandy beaches had some far-reaching consequences. Above all it began a burgeoning export of sand, not any sand, but the kind of perfect beach sand that does not occur just anywhere. All over the tourist world beaches have been constructed with the help of truck-loads of sand. One of the first experiments was made in Monaco, where Elsa Maxwell was hired to promote tourism and came up with the idea of a rubber beach to be spread with sand. It didn't turn out to be such a good idea.[11] Cannes and other resorts along the Riviera imported sand from the French west coast, where it had the right quality.

As we have seen earlier, the discovery of water as a hedonistic element was also slow. Body motions changed from slowly lowering yourself into the water to "taking a plunge," from controlled restraint to childish euphoria. People started to run rather than walk into the sea. All new kinds of water movements developed. In the water you could float, glide, stroke, paddle, dive, crawl. Again it was a chance of returning to the simple pleasures of childhood. Exploring water was like entering a different universe:

> there is the wonder of buoyancy, of being suspended in this thick, trans-parent medium that supports and embraces us. One can move in water, play with it, in a way that has no analogue in the air. . . . One can become a little hydroplane or submarine, investigating the physics of flow with one's body.[12]

You could also enjoy water from land. Water made you mellow, as the visitors to Southland beach put it. The languid movements, the rhythm of the surf had a calming, soothing effect, and the endless horizon proved to be a perfect medium for daydreaming. Its vastness opened up a wide space for wandering thoughts and fantasies. Out there, past a distant ship on its way to an exotic destination, are other worlds. The philosopher Bachelard sees a connection between the immensity of the seashore landscape and the depth of "inner space." Staring at the horizon, your eyes glaze—you are looking at nothing and at a hidden world at the same time.[13] Contemplating the ocean and trying to represent its magic also calls for a new language, as in the description of Waikiki beach from 1929: "Far out to the opalescent horizon stretches the ocean in broad bands of jeweled color—turquoise, sapphire, emerald, amethyst; and curving around it like a tawny topaz girdle presses the hard, firm sand of the shore."[14] At midday, as at sunset and in moonlight, Waikiki offered the perfect tropical beach: new combinations of light and colors, in the meeting of sky and ocean.

After learning to handle the water in new ways, tourists took the next step. They cultivated the art of sunbathing. A tanned body was previously a sign of manual labor and vulgarity: only bodies exposed to the sun in outdoor labor were tanned. As late as the 1920s Swedish magazines carried ads for lotions that would help you to get rid of a tan and regain the white, fashionable complexion, but a few years later the new fashion of sunbathing had spread to most of the Western world. (In some cases the same lotions that once promised to whiten the skin now offered a safe way of getting "the brown, beautiful summer tan.")[15]

Sunbathing as a hedonist project originated in Germany, already in the late nineteenth century, but the great expansion came when a new generation of war-weary youth craved a new life after 1918. The Englishman Stephen Spender was attracted to this movement and described the sun as "a primary social force in Germany": "Thousands of people went to the open-air swimming baths or lay down on the shores of rivers and lakes, almost nude, and sometimes quite nude, and the boys who had turned the deepest mahogany walked among those people with paler skins, like kings among their courtiers."[16]

Nudism and sunbathing were often linked in this pioneer period, as a utopia of modern and natural living. In Germany "Free Body Culture" (*Freikörperkultur*) camps started up, and from his experience in such a camp Kurt Barthel was one of those who brought nudism to the United States. Here the emphasis was to be more on tanning and informality than on athletics. Sunlight was seen as the cure for everything. Nudist camps developed all over the United States, often viewed with great suspicion (and curiosity) by the surrounding society. A promotional movie was made in 1933, called *Elysia Valley of the Nude*. "The Sunshine Park" in New Jersey became the headquarters of the American Sunbathing Association, where there were hopes for developing a whole "Nude City," but nudism never really caught on. "Nudists bodies are free, but their souls are in corsets," as one critic of the movement put it, and nudists spent as much time fighting one another as battling the ignorance of the public.[17]

The cult of sunshine did catch on, though, transforming vacations and beach life. Sometimes it made tanning rather than swimming the most important pastime on the beach. "Sunshine is healthy" was the new advice, but the British writer Evelyn Waugh, as usual, was critical. In 1930 he wrote for the *London Daily Mail:* "I hate the whole business. . . . All this is supposed to be good for you. Nowadays people believe anything they are told by 'scientists,' just as they used to believe anything they were told by clergymen."[18]

The health arguments soon faded as the sun became a liberating force, a highly sensual communion with nature. The sun warmed both your body and your senses, you should be drenched in it. It made you both beautiful and sexy. A new color scheme was developed, a cult of *bronzage,* to use the French term. The romance of Polynesia was part of the picture. Natives like hula girls or surfing beach boys were not black, they were just perfectly tanned.

The skills of acquiring the perfect bronze tan developed into a more and more complex art, comprising ointments, tanning hints, and the rituals of rubbing down. As an Australian newspaper advised its readers, "It turns out to be all too easy to obtain the uneven coloration deprecatingly termed a 'farmer's tan.' It takes time and commitment to get the all-over allure of deep and enduring brownness."[19] The term "sunbaking" replaced "sunbathing" in Australia, to mark this commitment (still quite serious in 1982; and in the United States the comic strip *Doonesbury* mocked and immortalized Zonker's quest for the perfect tan). At the beach you learned to massage yourself and your partner with all kinds of lotions, developing new forms of body consciousness as well as redefining acceptable and unacceptable forms of nudity.

No sooner was the art of tanning safely institutionalized than the first warnings appeared. In the 1980s cancer patrols started to patrol beaches over the world, offering to protect you from the dangers of the sun. In some sunny parts of the world tanning was no longer the thing, but on the whole pale Northern tourists kept working on their *bronzage.*

BEACH BODIES

The beach is very much the site of the making of the modern body. Wherever you look there are bodies, all kinds of bodies, old and young bodies, fat and thin, swimming or sleeping bodies, running bodies, bodies doing somersaults or rolling in the sand. Life at the modern beach becomes body work: exposing the body to sun, water, winds, and sand—as well as the critical eyes of others. On the beach you learn a lot about bodies, your own and others'. After three-quarters of a century of bodies in scant swimwear and various degrees of exposure we may have become so blasé that we don't realize what a revolutionary experience this has been.

One genre may help us recapture some of this early impact. It is what George Orwell called, in an essay from 1942, "the penny or twopenny postcards with their endless succession of fat women in tight bathing-dresses."[20] He was thinking of a specific comic postcard tradition that developed in Britain and elsewhere with the focus on beach bodies and beach situations. Orwell had an eye for popular culture but found it hard to repress his middle-class reactions to these images:

> Your first impression is of an overwhelming vulgarity. This is quite apart from the ever-present obscenity, and also apart from the hideousness of the colours. They have an utter lowness of mental atmosphere, which comes out not only in the nature of the jokes but, even more, in the grotesque, staring, blatant quality of the drawings . . . every gesture and attitude, are deliberately ugly, the faces grinning and vacuous, the women monstrously parodied, with bottoms like Hottentots.[21]

Of course Orwell is able to see these postcards as a cultural phenomenon that represents a different kind of humor and lifestyle from his own. The cards tell us something of the making of a new body-oriented beach culture, which certainly isn't one of middle-class constraint and decorum. First, there are all kinds of bodies parading here, fat, ugly bodies and broad backsides, as well as vulgar forms of bodily contact: the slapping of backs, the pinching of bottoms, unrestrained public kissing and hugging. Second, they draw attention to other bodily functions, such as gluttonous overeating, getting blind drunk, or frantically searching for the

Figure 25. Beach bottoms, backsides, buttocks, behinds, and bums—such is the dominating obsession in the British comic postcard tradition of George Orwell's day. (1930s postcard, author's collection)

rest rooms. So many activities that should occur in privacy go on here in the wrong place, at the wrong time. These are bodies lacking any form of moderation: loud laughs, large gestures, swelling forms. In some ways they represent a guerrilla warfare against middle-class taste and self-control, and they do this in a liberating, shameless way. These voluptuous ladies bending down to expose their enormous backsides and the men floating on their big bellies in the water are not hiding their "vulgar" bodies. They are on the beach to enjoy themselves: "Having a great time, wish you were here!" In this world backsides, buttocks, behinds, bums, and bottoms are always good for a laugh, as is any form of nudity. (The nudist camp jokes were among its basic ingredients.)

The point I want to make about the symbolism of this world is that it celebrates bodies enjoying themselves, bodies that definitely do not live up to the rigorous standards that later came to dominate beach culture.

Some bodies are there on the beach to enjoy themselves—other bodies are there to be judged. In the 1920s the concept of bathing beauties appeared, with an endless string of beauty pageants that chose the beach as their stage.[22] Starlets and models posed for photographers against the blue sea, and women's magazines started running advice on getting bodies ready for the beach season. Stern dieting programs later became part of this regime, creating the terror of pre-beach flab. And ads for men urged them to start building bodies during the winter to make sure some hunk on the beach didn't try to steal their girlfriend or trip them up in the sand. "Hey skinny—yer ribs are showing!" was the catching start of the 1950s ads about beach humiliations, in which Charles Atlas promised to make you into a new man for next summer, in only fifteen minutes a day.

In some settings the monitoring of the perfect body became so strong that some people stayed away or found other, less demanding beaches. But beach body work was not only about exposing your body or being judged, it was also about exploring the body in relation to the physicalities of sand, sea, and sun as well as different forms of motion. The languidness of swimming also influenced body movements on land. People learned to walk and move very differently on the beach. There was some kind of magic and liberating transformation occurring the moment your feet hit the sand.

The new beach bodies also demanded beachwear, a term that first appeared in 1928 on the Riviera beaches together with the two novelties of beach pajamas and beach gown, while items like beach bags and beach sandals appeared a few years later.[23]

BEACH ETIQUETTE

JIM: Wenn man an einem fremden Strand kommt, ist man immer zuerst etwas verlegen.

JAKOB: Man weiss nicht recht, wohin man gehen soll . . .

JIM: When a person lands at a strange shore, he is always a bit embarrassed at first.

JAKE: He doesn't rightly know, where he is to go to . . .

Brecht's lines from *Mahagonny* on the awkwardness of coming to an unknown beach would hold very true for most large beaches of the world. They hold an astonishing mix of people. Southland beach is a good example. Here groups of different ages and classes and cultural and ethnic identities mingle. Inner-city people and tourists who are new to the city, strangers, sit close together on the same strip of flat sand, in full exposure, with very little protective clothing. It is a mass confrontation that in many other settings would be volatile. But still the beach works. Even strangers soon make themselves at home.

The beach is supposed to be an arena of relaxation, of minding your own business, of doing what you want. But behind such notions of anarchy or individualism is heavily regimented behavior. The French sociologist Jean-Claude Kaufmann's study of topless bathing on French beaches illustrates this very clearly. Many of his beach informants stated strongly, "Here on the beach everybody does what they want," but a world of unwritten rules and regulations allowed them to do so. People knew exactly where the borders were, how to look, how to dress and undress, how to move their bodies.[24]

The rules were especially clear in the sensitive field of topless bathing, where women turned out to have very precise ideas about the propriety of this French tradition: when, where, and how to let go of the top piece. Kaufmann's choice of topic may sound esoteric, but it unearthed a whole universe of ideas about privacy, individualism, social relations, and gender.

One of his main arguments is that the beach is a laboratory for the sophistication of the gaze. People he interviewed often said, "I don't spend any time looking around, I am in my own world." There is, of course, no way you cannot look. People on the beach are constantly testing different ocular techniques, consciously or unconsciously switching between different ways of seeing: watching, staring, glancing, scanning, looking from the corner of your eye, pretending not to look, making brief eye contact, looking away.

There was constant observation of how other people handled these techniques and very quick registration of those who broke the rules. Topless women in particular monitored the male gaze as well as that of other females. "When bodies are naked glances are clothed," as the sociologist Erving Goffman once put it.[25]

All this doesn't come naturally. The ways in which people observe at the beach have changed over time.[26] The colonizing gaze of the Victorians would today be considered most provoking and unsophisticated. The degree of learning ocular competence also becomes obvious when kids constantly have to be told, "Don't stare." You have to learn to discipline the ways you look at others in a suitably disinterested way: observing but never staring.

The beach was also the place for another important innovation: sunglasses, which developed new forms of hiding yourself and at the same time offered new opportunities for unobtrusive observation.

A beach is, as we have seen, a very special arena, often with clear boundaries. The kind of behavior that is OK down by the water is not OK in the parking lot or on the other side of the beach road. Beach life may seem banal, but these banalities express very basic conceptions about private and public, decent and indecent, individuality and collectivity. Most of the rules regulating beach behavior have never been written down, many of them can hardly be verbalized, and yet—down at the beach—people know.

Unlike many other arenas, beaches bring classes together, sometimes in an uneasy coexistence, sometimes in strikingly unproblematic ways.

They offer the chance to observe, very close at hand, "those other people" at play. The history of British tourism emphasizes this role of the beach as one of the few "neutral grounds" that allowed the working class to enter the vacation scene much earlier than in many other nations. As the historian John K. Walton describes the situation in the late nineteenth century, "At the seaside rich and poor, respectable and ungodly, staid and rowdy, quiet and noisy not only rubbed shoulders . . . they also had to compete for access to, and use of, recreational space."[27] He overstates the classlessness of the beach, but a striking theme in early twentieth-century beach life is the idea of make-believe. Music-hall songs talked about "Beach Sultans"[28] and on the comic postcards you could see working-class girls exclaiming: "At home I might be nothing, but here I am at least something!" The seaside visit was that special place, "a geography of hope," which stood out as a highlight in the British working-class year.[29]

In a similar manner a place like Coney Island became an arena of social confrontations. In the middle of the nineteenth century it was still a desolate beach, visited by a few wealthy families in search of fresh air and solitude. By the 1870s it had developed into New York's leading resort. By 1900 up to a half million New Yorkers visited the beach and its amusement parks on summer weekend days. By then it offered what has been called a "linear visual study in American class structure" with different social groups distributed along the shore. While certain areas kept a middle-class focus, others catered for the working class. Some spots had a reputation as a hangout for underworld figures or attracted a socially mixed male audience of the "sporting" subculture.[30]

Beaches like Coney Island and Blackpool fostered endless debates about beach morals and beach rules as different lifestyles overlapped or clashed. On some global beaches debates take new, multicultural, forms.

BEACH BLANKETS

I grow up bathing in sea water
But nowadays that is bare horror
If I only venture down by the shore
Police is only telling me I can't bathe anymore.[31]

This Calypso text from Barbados is one of many comments on the conflicts about beach access in the Caribbean. Here, as in most other tourist regions of the world, beaches are public, but in reality local access has been constrained. Seaside resorts may try all sorts of tactics to monitor visitors. Tourists' complaints of being hassled by vendors or "beach boys" cruising for single female tourists led to an increased policing of beaches, as in the Barbados case, which opened up a discussion of who and what belongs on the beach. On many Caribbean islands, the natives feel that they have been forced out of the best beaches, or as a local paper put it, "The day could come when the ordinary Jamaican doesn't know what a good beach looks like."[32]

So who owns the beach? A Canadian travel ad from 1958 says: "Want to own an ocean?" There is a picture of a family on a beach blanket in the middle of vast empty space, an image of perfect order and relaxation, but most tourist beaches tend to be crowded, which has led to all sorts of tactics for creating private space. When Robert Edgerton interviewed Los Angeles beachgoers, the vast majority argued that the first thing they did was to carve out space on arrival by rolling out their towel and arranging their private belongings: "I pick out my little plot of sand and set down my towel. For the next few hours that is my own little world; it belongs to me."[33] To cross over this private territory or to sit down next to it was considered a provocation and rarely happened. Beach etiquette thus starts with the microrituals of installation, of making yourself at home, and at the same time marking a physical and mental distance from others.

Another common ritual of signaling privacy is to immerse yourself in some activity as soon as you have arranged your belongings, to bury yourself in a book or lie down in the sand. The strong sense of privacy even on a crowded beach also has to do with the techniques of daydreaming. By closing your eyes you are signaling that you are in your own private dream world, far away.

After such initial moves you can become more active later on. Some complain of beach life being too private, with people going to great lengths not to communicate with those close by. "It's like being in an elevator where nobody talks," one woman complained to David Edgerton. Those who consistently break these rules of privacy and noncommunication are small kids and dogs.

Against this complex regimentation of the private sphere the clash with beach vendors or beach boys on distant vacation beaches becomes more understandable. These are locals who don't know the rules the tourists have brought with them from back home. In Los Angeles many white middle-class visitors also complained about Chicano families: they did not understand the need to keep your distance.

On the whole, Southland visitors stressed how easy it was to be on the beach. "I feel so safe here, people are mellow, the environment makes people behave. . . . It may be one of the places a woman can go alone and yet feel safe," were some of the comments.

The ability of the beach to produce this mellowness is a statement that turns up again and again:

> Waikiki at that time was a very, very healing place. You would come there because you instinctively knew that's where you needed to be if you wanted a rest, if you needed to get well. The waters were beneficent, the breezes were soothing, the whole vibration of the place was something that just drew you in.[34]

MY HOME IS MY SAND CASTLE

On some German beaches you may spot a sign telling you that it is absolutely forbidden to build sand castles. This may, to an outside visitor, seem like a harsh attitude to a harmless occupation, but then you have probably not seen what a German sand castle may look like. We are not talking about miniatures here but the old tradition of building a secluded, circular wall around your beach territory, to protect yourself from the wind and the regards of others. These structures are nothing like the improvised shelters you might make out of a ring of stones, which appear on beaches all over the world. On a real German sand castle beach you may have to maneuver your way past castle after castle, and then it might also feel like walking through an art show, because the German tradition puts great emphasis on decoration, as Harald Kimpel and Johanna Werckmeister point out in their history of the phenomenon.[35]

The tradition of placing yourself inside a sand castle was well established in the nineteenth century. It probably started as a way of claiming space on the beach and also as a protection against the often chilly winds of German beaches. The tradition soon triggered off competition and the idea of building a more perfect and more beautiful structure around yourself. Some of the structures had elegant patterns accomplished with shells or wreckage, and many had sand sculptures.

Subtexts underlined the ways in which sand castles became personalized statements: "Young ladies welcome," "The unfinished," "Kalifornien," or "Castle Sansoucie." Less poetically they could be called "Düsseldorf," announcing your home town, or just presenting the occupants "Irmgard und Egon." The changing aesthetics and namings mirror different periods of beach life. The nastier ones are some of the sand castles from the 1930s, as the one with Hitler's portrait in sand and the title "Unser Führer." This sand castle is photographed surrounded with happy beachgoers in swimwear doing the Heil Hitler salute.

As I pointed out earlier, German tourists have often had a bad press, and the sand castle-building habit contributed to it. When German tourists after the Second World War started traveling abroad they brought along their building tradition, not always aware of the kind of signals they were sending. In countries like Holland and Denmark, where the same beaches had been occupied by Nazi troops, surprised Germans found their castles trampled down when they returned to the beach next morning. Local youths had demolished them during the night.

An earlier source of conflicts was the tradition of putting up flags on the beach. This was a late nineteenth-century tradition, found not only in Germany, but travelers from this young nation often took along flags when they went abroad. The tradition led to international conflicts, as locals saw it as a symbol of aggressive Germanness, the quest for *Lebensraum*. On one of the beaches in Denmark where there were many German castles and flags, local Danes went out and removed the flags. German tourists protested, and in the end the two governments had to exchange stern notes.

Figure 26. This German beach is littered with sand fortifications and flags, staking out individual territory. (Photo from 1935, Archiv für Kunst und Geschichte, Berlin)

Apart from its place in the stereotype of "typical German tourist," the sand-castle tradition had quite another aspect. One castle from 1913 bears the inscription in small shells: The Club of Work-Shy. This imposing artwork must have taken many hours of hard work to build, but the whole idea of the sand castle is that of non-work, it is work for pleasure, where you work off a lot of childish energy and creativity. You invest hours in building something that the wind and the tide will wash away. As the German authors point out, the investment may have to do with the fact that relaxation at the beach often produces boredom and restlessness: let's do something!

SEASIDES AND POOLSIDES

> Time isn't the great healer.
> Poolside seats are.

This 1997 slogan of an American resort chain is part of a move away from the beach.[36] In many coastal settings, sand and seawater have become less important. An appetizing destination must advertise its beach, but when you get there you often find out that there are very few people in the water: it is too cold, too windy, too polluted. The sand is sticky or full of cigarette butts. The tourists have withdrawn to the safer territory of the hotel pool, but they have brought with them all the necessary skills developed at the beach.

If you look up "swimming pool" in the *Encyclopedia Americana* you get "a tank constructed of cement, wood, steel, plastic, fiberglass or other material and used for swimming, or pleasure bathing." Behind this minimalistic definition lies a gradual development that has made the pool rather than the beach a focus of much vacation life. Pools have an impressive history, but in the Western world there is a long void from the Roman era to their reintroduction in the nineteenth century.[37]

Down at the old boardwalk of Santa Cruz you may view the ruins of the old giant swimming pool building from 1907, but the first tank was built next to the beach in the 1860s, as I mentioned in the introduction. In nearby San Francisco the even bigger Sutro Baths were developed in the 1890s. They covered three acres on the western headlands of San Francisco, with saltwater and freshwater pools, palm trees, a tropical beach, restaurants, galleries, and an amphitheater. The baths could accommodate ten thousand swimmers a day and were in use until 1966, when they were dismantled.[38]

In other big cities like Chicago and New York public swim baths were often introduced to encourage working-class cleanliness, but the public pools soon became popular playgrounds. By 1911 Chicago's outdoor pools were so popular that groups were marched in by the hour, supplied with swimsuits and towels, and then ordered out of the water one hour later, to make room for the next group in line.[39]

The waning popularity of these giant baths during the twentieth century had to do with the scale on which different groups and classes mixed. The future of the seaside pools turned out to be the more private hotel pools, often developed as alternatives to overcrowded beaches or polluted coastal waters. In the early 1950s a hotel developer at Waikiki surprised the world by developing a complex away from the high-cost beach locations but with its own hotel pool.[40] A new concept was born. Most hotel pools developed out of the Californian model, the testing ground not only for pool styles but also for pool etiquette. In southern California's roaring 1920s private pools became part of Hollywood stardom, but the real expansion came in the 1950s and 1960s, with new and cheaper techniques.[41]

During the 1980s hotel pools became more and more elaborate, as designers developed veritable water lands, with artificial sand beaches, waterfalls, slides, and lagoons. Water spectacles have become an increasingly important part of hotel aesthetics and entertainment.

The vacation pool culture shows an immense degree of standardization. The same azure blue nuance, imitating tropical beaches, similar pool shapes, springboards, chairs. We move our bodies according to a well-established choreography, pull our stomachs in before climbing onto the diving board, or nonchalantly rest one of our arms on the side of the pool as we make poolside conversation from the water, just the way we have seen in countless advertisements for Martini.

Today the pool is a condensation of the playa: a much better-managed version of the beach, nice water temperature, no sand between the toes, close to the hotel bar. The restricted space makes for new kinds of conflicts. All over the world people sneak down to the pool in the early morning to wrap a towel around a chair in a good position for basking in the sun. During the day they move their chairs around, group and re-group them, and then leave them for dinner in a frozen sociogram of the day's interaction.

LIFE'S A BEACH

Maybe it is the mix of activities and possibilities with an aura of luxurious living that has made beach and poolside life such a vacation success. Here you oscillate between very different vacation modes. Frolic in the water, daydream with the help of the horizon or a Walkman, float on your back in sand or water, drink cold beer or cappuccino, fool around with the sand, massage your own body or that of your partner with suntan lotion, and not least important: who could have guessed that the beach or pool chair would become one of the most cherished reading places in the world? Everywhere people are buried in their books, magazines, mysteries, thick paperback novels with sunscreen smudges. The beach has become a great read.

The fact that this is a territory for the pursuit of hedonism also means that it often becomes a place of boredom. Modes of awareness drift in and out: dozing, daydreaming, sitting up to take in the scenery, registering activities around you, reflecting on the behavior of others, becoming self-conscious when moving through the beach landscape or diving into the pool.

You learn so much at the beach without ever noticing that you're a vacationer in constant training. The global beach has an ability to detach itself from its immediate surroundings, which means that you can travel the world and usually feel quite at home on any beach. Changing beach aesthetics make the landscape more and more minimalistic, as two ads in the *New Yorker* from 1996 illustrate. The first for Australia shows a couple walking along a sandbank completely surrounded by water, a small island of sand, and nothing else. Apart from a small parked airplane, there is total stillness. Another ad for the Bahamas shows just a deck chair in the sunset, vast areas of sand, and a few palm trees in the distance. Nothingness, emptiness, seclusion, not a single soul, getting away from it all.

In his analysis of an Australian beach John Fiske focuses on the structuralist notion of the beach being in-between, an anomalous zone between nature and culture.[42] But the old slogan from the 1968 Paris student revolt is more telling: "The beach is under the street!" Just start breaking up the tarmac and you'll find the world of sand. However great its distance from city life, the holiday beach keeps its polarity to city life and work. Urban culture's competence of handling privacy and communication in crowds of strangers makes the beach as a global project possible.

The global beach is a fact, but there are still the fine distinctions of class and ethnicity. People on Southland beach complain of outsiders not sticking to the local rules and feel affronted at Chicanos who bathe with their clothes on, as well as at the Swedish woman who performs the classic Scandinavian tradition (and feat) of changing into swimwear with the help of a scanty beach towel. And in many settings the locals are still not very happy about the ways in which tourists expose their bodies on the beach. The tradition of going into the water fully clothed is still strong in many parts of the world.

There is a constant tension between the beach as an individual experience and the beach as a cultural arena, impregnated with rules, routines, rituals. When Jean-Claude Kaufmann tries to sum up his beach observations he finds himself saying things like: the beach does this or that, the beach thinks, the beach prefers . . . There was an unconscious cultural collectivity of beach life to set against the fact that individuals often experience the beach as a liberating space, a space to break habits, not make them. This ambiguity catches rather nicely the cultural complexities of beach life.

The beach may seem to standardize vacation life, and yet the closer you look at beach experiences, the more personal they seem. Let me end

Figure 27. The happy beach family has been a popular marketing theme since the 1920s—lacking only a back projection and gallons of sand in the photographer's studio. This 1966 version of the global beach appeared in a department store's summer campaign. (Photo Epa-Revyn)

the chapter with a quote from the Swedish novel *The Beach Man,* which
travels between distant beaches:

> First down the stairs is as usual the old couple from Rotterdam . . . they
> unfold their piece of Balinese cloth, seventeen years old. *Got,* how time
> passes, and arrange sandals, clothes, water bottle, books, towels, bags,
> lighters, a pack of Salem, according to a choreography, which has been
> perfected and made permanent after—I don't dare to think—how many
> vacations at the beach together. . . .
>
> They bring out a tube of Piz Buin from a plastic bag and rub it on
> each other's backs, in silence and without gestures, as if they were tak-
> ing turns to wipe the kitchen table, that's all. They look out toward the
> sea. He makes a short comment and gets a surprised smile back. They
> make themselves comfortable, getting the right angle to the sun. He puts
> two fingers on her hip and she gives his hand a brief pat: their parting
> ritual, because from now on they will be alone, each with their own
> sun.[43]

Resort Ruins

The 1920s and 1930s saw a new kind of summer resort emerging, based on the invigorating beach. The modernist cult of simplicity and functionalism found the outdoors an important terrain for human improvement and experiments with new aesthetics and lifestyles. The beach itself was so modern. On the clean white sand with the blue ocean as a backdrop the new modern man flexed his muscles, while the modern woman exposed her beautifully tanned body. On this classless terrain of new and healthy democratic mass tourism, the tanned body in overalls and sandals or just a swimsuit represented modernity, not class. All over Europe and America new kinds of resorts based on mass participation of workers and clerks developed, often inspired by different ideologies,

240

from the socialist holiday camps in Britain, the workers' own travel organizations in Scandinavia, and the leisure activities of the Popular Front in France, to the fascist experiments in Italy.[1]

By far the most ambitious or grandiose of these experiments opened at the 1937 World Exhibition in Paris, where it received a Grand Prix. It planned to house 20,000 tourists simultaneously, in hotel rooms with a simple, but modern, functionalist style in light colors, and best of all: every room had a guaranteed seaside view. This meant that the hotel buildings had to be narrow and stretched out for several miles along the beach. The enormous hotel complex would contain all kinds of facilities: cinema, cafés, and restaurants behind vast picture windows, a marina, a gigantic indoor swim-bath for bad weather spells, reading and writing rooms, billiard halls, and so on. Along the beach rows of deck chairs were waiting for the visitors, who could arrive by train or car. A small minirail was planned to ease communication within the resort.[2]

It was to be the most modern and the grandest resort in the world, and while it was under construction there were plans to develop a replica in Argentina. The style could be called "classical modern," with clear influences from architects like Le Corbusier. It was a modernist utopia, a veritable leisure city in glass and concrete, using the latest innovations such as central heating for all rooms and a number of state-of-the-art amenities. Words like "the most modern imaginable" kept reappearing in the presentations.

The foundation stone had already been laid in 1936 and an army of workers were busy turning the model of the exhibition into reality. The project was called KdF-Seebad Rügen and was part of Adolf Hitler's scheme for monitoring the leisure of the German working class. KdF stood for the organization Kraft durch Freude (strength through joy), which was founded in 1933. It was an organization for social and cultural politics, with a mixed ideological background. Some of it came from the radical or antibourgeois strands in early national socialist ideology, celebrating a new and modern mass culture, but the organization rapidly developed into a tool for controlling leisure and creating a classless *Volksgemeinschaft* of hobbyists, tourists, and pleasure-seekers. Emphasis was put on the idea of working for "the common man." The very

Figure 28. Modern bodies belong on the beach. This couple stands in front of the clock at the entrance of a newly opened municipal beach in Stockholm, 1935. (Photo Karl Sandels, IBL)

successful travel programs produced around seven million vacation package tours between 1934 and 1939, which made it the biggest travel organizer in the world. KdF cruise ships toured the Mediterranean as well as the Norwegian fjords. Our Workers On Madeira! was a typical slogan, showing how ordinary German workers now could discover the world at very reasonable rates.[3] As an excellent way of recreating the German workforce, the offer of KdF tourism was open to all, not only party members, which meant that Gestapo agents often mingled in the tourist crowds to observe and report on antisocial behavior.

The old bourgeois summer resorts did not qualify as proper settings for this new mass travel. Apart from the fleet of cruise ships, Hitler sanctioned plans for the construction of several gigantic seaside resorts, intended specifically for workers. KdF-Seebad Rügen was to be the first of these and planned to serve 350,000 tourists a year.[4]

Behind all these investments was a popular idea of the seaside resort as a remedy for urban ills. An advertisement for a German beach resort from 1929 promises that it will turn stressed urbanites into happy and healthy people, as it energizes their overworked nerves and puts pleasure back into work.[5] This notion of overworked nervous systems became a pet idea of Hitler, who believed that Germany lost the First World War because the soldiers lost their nerve. By offering healthy and fun-packed seaside vacations at low rates, the new vacation camps would invigorate the entire German nation. In their happy and healthy surroundings a new strength would prepare workers for coming challenges. "Only with a people who can keep their nerve is great politics possible," as the Führer put it.

But when the Second World War broke out this modernist megacomplex was only partially finished. Work continued with enforced Russian labor. After the fall of the Third Reich the complex was taken over by the Russian Red Army and later the DDR Volksarmee. Some parts of the unfinished buildings were demolished, others finished and transformed into army barracks and later into a holiday camp for army officers of the DDR. The whole area remained out of bounds for ordinary citizens.

Today it is possible to walk along these gigantic structures, which have been shaped by two different totalitarian regimes—that of German national socialism and that of East German communism—and there have been heated debates about the future of these remains.

What makes this gigantic project interesting is that when you look at the detailed plans, from the spartan and rational simplicity of the hotel rooms to the well planned beach area, you could be anywhere in the modernist world of leisure, were it not for the swastika emblems of the KdF waving from the flagstaffs. Reading the plans for this resort life, you almost see the project of modern mass tourism carried to its extreme: from the Taylorist calculations that even with full occupancy each guest would have a space of 5 square meters of beach at his or her disposal to the careful planning of the package. For two Reichsmarks a day the visitor would get not only food and lodging, but also bathing suit, towel, and the specially designed beach chairs, as well as "all the pleasures of life at his disposal." In some ways this anticipates the global grammar of the perfect package deal: a week with everything included at Club Med, Sandals, or Blue Village.

On the surface, then, such a project looked progressive and modern: giving workers access to fun-filled vacations. But the mass scale was not simply an effort to keep prices down, or follow Hitler's megalomania. It also had to do with the Nazi strategies of crowd psychology. The gatherings on the beach or in the movie theaters had a pedagogical function. KdF-Seebad Rügen included an arena for the staging of mass rallies.

BUTLINISM

As a student in London in the early sixties I used to walk past a travel agency for Butlin's Holiday Camps. In the window was a model in bright colors of a camp, a strange, fenced-in community on the seashore with rows of small cabins, swimming pools, cafeterias, bars, and a dance hall. The whole idea was exotic to me. A holiday camp for adults? I had never heard about that kind of institution in Scandinavia, where a summer camp was something for children.

The same year that the foundation was laid for Hitler's dream resort on Rügen, Billy Butlin opened his first holiday camp in Britain. He could build on a strong British tradition for improvised holiday camps, often with the idea of providing affordable vacations for the working class, as Colin Ward and Dennis Hardy show in their history of the British holiday camp.[6] The inspiration originally came from the United States, but the social and political context of those summer camps belonged to the left-wing politics of Europe—a wish both to democratize vacations and to create modern citizens.

In the early 1930s it was still the old seaside resorts and their boardinghouses that attracted most vacationers in Britain. During the 1920s Butlin had experienced the tyranny of boardinghouse proprietors, who would not permit their guests to stay indoors between meals, and he had seen families huddling in the rain out at the amusement arcades on the beach walk, waiting to be allowed to return to their rooms. As a boy he had spent some years in Canada and there he had experienced something quite different, a summer camp for kids. So let us look briefly at his source of inspiration.

As summer approaches, one section in the Sunday edition of the *New York Times* grows thicker and thicker. To a European the items under the heading of "summer camps" look exotic. There are the classic camps, often with names out of the wilderness movement, like Eagle Hill, Camp Redwood, Indian Lake Camp, or Camp Shane, promising action, excitement, fun, friends, and adventure. But over the years the listings fluctuate, reflecting the popularity of newer camps. Back in the 1980s the number of computer camps was growing, in the 1990s the expansion was in weight loss for kids. Have fun and lose weight at the same time!

The American summer camp came out of the back-to-nature movements, originally with the idea of offering a healthy rural experience for underprivileged inner-city children. Already in the 1870s the *New York Times* had started to arrange one-day trips to the countryside for slum children, and similar programs developed in other cities. A classic story, recounted by the historian Peter J. Schmitt, who analyzes the summer camp in its back-to-nature context, runs like this: a rich benefactor, impressed with the attempts to get working-class children out into the fresh air, chartered a steamboat and sent several hundred kids from the New York slums up the river for a day in the woods. Once in the Catskills the children were sent ashore to have a glorious nature experience. A short time later he found them scattered about in the bushes, smoking cigarettes, shooting dice, playing cards, and waiting to get home to civilization. Such an experience made one observer state: "It is not enough to take men out of doors, we must also teach them to enjoy it."[7]

American summer camps found their present form at the beginning of the twentieth century. By 1915 there were hundreds of them.[8] In the United States the summer camp became a middle-class institution, mainly on the East Coast. As school vacation continued to be long and parents' vacation time short, there was a steady market for sending the kids on a long stay out in the country for those who could afford it. Camp management turned into an American art, and it was often argued that the character building during the summer was a way of compensating for lack of firmness in parental supervision. The idea was that kids should have fun *and* return back home better prepared for future career building.

I remember listening a few years ago with awe to a college student who told me of her summer job taking care of rich kids from Los Angeles. They arrived with trunks of designer clothes at a wilderness camp where sleeping outdoors in hammocks was part of the educational experience. A procession of BMWs arrived at the end of the camp to bring them back to civilization, dirty but excited about this well organized primitive life.

The British tradition developed in other directions. Using his short but memorable summer camp experience Billy Butlin organized his first British holiday camp. It attracted a thousand visitors. Butlin had decided to keep the scale large, and everything seemed to work fine. The visitors were happy with the new chalets and all the amenities of the campground, but there was something missing. Observing the guests in the large cafeteria, around the pool, and down at the beach, Butlin recognized that they were bored stiff. The large scale made for anonymity, and one evening Butlin's associate Norman Bradford grabbed the microphone and started to make jokes. The atmosphere changed, and by next morning Billy Butlin had invented one of the key elements of his future success: the redcoats, in red blazers and white flannels. Their job was to act as holiday angels, warming up audiences, organizing games, improvising on the stage, being generally helpful, and, above all, jolly.

Next Bradford instituted the ritual of "Now I want everyone to turn to the person on your right, introduce yourself and shake hands," a ritual that is now a staple item for group integration all over the world. Addressing the campers from the stage, he also invented the Butlin rallying cry: "Hi-di-Hi," to which the guests spontaneously answered "Ho-di-Ho." A new tradition was born.

The Butlin concept was to provide not only a holiday package, with everything included, but a holiday program as well. The morning started with the wake-up call from the Butlin camp radio: "Wakey, wakey!" He organized children's programs to give the parents time for themselves and, even more important, had girls stationed in the chalets at night to act as baby-sitters and make it possible for Mum and Dad to dance every night in the camp's ballroom, where Henry Mancini might be playing. "Every night is party night!" There were all kinds of silly games and competitions, amateur nights, and then the brilliant idea of how to get people out of the bars at the end of the evening, making the Salvation Army song "Come and join us" into a follow-the-leader routine, with a redcoat leading a wriggling row of guests out into the night.

Butlin and his competitors created a holiday package whose golden days were the 1950s, the days when even the working class could afford a vacation and before the south had become the new magnet. The scale of these camps called for a very tight organization. In Butlin's Bognor camp 6,000 guests arrived every Saturday, as 6,000 left. They were served by a staff of 1,300, of which 1,150 lived in. For the women this structure was fantastic, it gave them a chance of a real vacation. When the pattern reverted to an emphasis on self-catering in the 1960s and 1970s, they found themselves back in the kitchen again.

Butlin became an icon of popular British culture but also a target for the critics of the mass-produced and regimented holiday. Little did it help to point out that the barbed wire and the security guards existed not to prevent guests from escaping but to keep out free-riders, who broke into empty chalets. In the 1960s the slogan Butlin Land Is Freedom

Land launched an attempt to tone down the regimentation of vacationing, which had worked so well for the early generations but now seemed less attractive. After the experiences of the Second World War, camp became an uneasy word, with many unpleasant connotations. Butlin tried to rename his establishments "holiday villages," but the old camp label was hard to stamp out.

Both Butlin and his competitors tried to export their idea of the holiday to sunnier destinations, when the mass exodus from the rainy English shores started, but with varying success. It was the Club Med concept, started already in 1950, with its rhetoric of primitivism, carefree pleasures, and sexy tropical freedom, that came to be the 1960s new alternative.[9]

THE PINK PALACE

As we have seen, the imagery of the tropical beach spread from Waikiki, and it was also the site of a new kind of total resort concept, a camp for the very rich.

In the 1920s as the numbers of American millionaires grew, Hawaii tried to compete with the French Riviera to attract the big spenders among American vacationers. The boat trip to both destinations took roughly the same time, but Hawaii could not compete with Europe when it came to luxurious travel or resort life. The Matson Navigation Company, which ran the San Francisco-Honolulu line, wanted to promote a new kind of elite tourism and decided to invest in a new luxury liner and a fashionable resort on Waikiki beach. The hotel was planned to become something new and exciting, and the management toured famous resorts all over North America to develop an avant-garde approach to vacationing. In 1927 the Royal Hawaiian Hotel opened with a grand historic pageant recreating the arrival of King Kamehameha the Great to the island. One thousand two hundred specially invited guests witnessed the show that a local paper called "colorful and semibarbaric" (in a 1915 version of this pageant all the warriors sweated in skin-colored long underwear to satisfy the Honolulu morality laws, which declared that "showing of unclad skin on the beach is immoral").[10]

The Royal Hawaiian was a truly cosmopolitan hybrid. It was built in "Spanish style." The ballroom was decorated with landscapes from the Nile, the outdoor restaurant was in "Persian style," and the lobby boys were dressed in Chinese costumes. Twelve acres of hotel grounds were developed into a tropical paradise, where three men held the full-time job of trimming the eight hundred palm trees to make sure that coconuts did not fall on the guests. In the large gardens there were tennis, badminton, archery, lawn bowling, as well as golf at the nearby hotel course. The intense daily program included ukulele lessons as well as hula dancing, and there were daily shows of the Hawaiian serenaders, the Royal Hawaiian Girls' Glee Club, coconut-tree climbing by natives, and dancing to the Royal Hawaiian Band. Another innovation was an array of hotel shops.

The beach was roped off and serviced by the Royal Hawaiian beach patrol, recruited from the ranks of another Waikiki innovation: the beach boys. When the Hawaiian swimmer "Bronze" Duke Kahanomoku took the gold medal in swimming at the Stockholm Olympics in 1912 he declared to the impressed journalists that he was just "a beach boy from Waikiki."[11] What *were* these beach boys? On Waikiki they developed as local guides, entertainers, lifeguards. Beach boys lived on the beach and off the beach, surfing and canoeing, partying and making music, getting gifts from the tourists but also living from fish they caught and fruit they picked, coconuts, bananas, mangoes, and dates. They formed the perfect paradise myth, forever adolescents, constantly on vacation, and thus a perfect source of inspiration for the stressed tourists stepping down from the gangways of the steamship or the clipper.

The Royal Hawaiian institutionalized the beach boy concept into something of an equivalent to the Butlin redcoats. Beach boys made sure the guests had a great time, offering them outrigger canoe trips and surfing lessons, as well as improvised partying. The beach boys' status was ambivalent: were they just fun-loving locals who enjoyed giving tourists a great time, inviting them into their own carefree world, or were they hustlers, trying to milk rich tourists for as much as possible, or seducing

Figure 29. View of the Royal Hawaiian and Moana hotels, from a menu card, 1929.

divorcées? The concept of the beach boy spread around the world, but the institution developed more or less independently as mass tourism descended on beaches everywhere. We met some aspects of it along the Mediterranean, with its specific tradition of the Latin lover. Beach boys became an institution on the beaches of the Caribbean as well as Gambia and Morocco.

The Royal Hawaiian was the idea of the total resort, a kingdom, where guests should not have to leave the hotel grounds in search of entertainment. Here was a vacation package for the very rich, which started with the luxury cruise across the Pacific and an elaborately staged Hawaiian welcome with ukulele music and leis—the local term for wreaths of highly scented tropical flowers.

Hawaiian tourism skyrocketed after the arrival of cheap jet flights, at the same time as the Mediterranean expansion in the late fifties and sixties, from a hundred thousand tourists in 1955 to two millions in 1970 and six and a half million in 1990.[12] Jumbo jets called for jumbo high-rise hotels encircling the Royal Hawaiian, which suddenly looked very small.

REGIMENTED RESORTS?

The formula of Butlin's Holiday Camps and the Royal Hawaiian catered for rather different clienteles but developed the same concept, which would turn out to be a global success.

I first experienced the Butlin heritage staying with my family at a Swedish resort complex on Cyprus in the 1980s. There was a resort radio channel, and instead of redcoats there were guides in mauve uniforms who took care of problems, excursions, and the kids' club and then jumped onto the stage every night to provide entertainment. Just like the Butlin redcoats many of them had taken the (rather low-paid) job as a starting point for a career in entertainment.

Our resort had a fixed program of daily events, making up the basic unit of the week, all kinds of buffet dinners and shows. Down at the beach there was the Poseidon Taverna. It too echoed this global formula. Its faded poster advertised:

Tuesday: Tropical Night (with a 12-member dance show) or Asian Night (with an Oriental dance show)

Wednesday: Cyprus Night or Greek Night (with a Folklore dance show)

Thursday: Italian Night

Saturday: B.B.Q. Night (with a Magic show)

In a similar manner the legacy of the Royal Hawaiian remains at most beach resorts in Hawaii. Down at the pool the listing of today's activities is found: 7.30 Fish feeding. 10.00 Ukulele lessons. 1.00 Intro to Lei making. 3.00 Beach volleyball. 6.00 Torches are lit. Tomorrow is Luau night, there'll be traditional Hawaiian dancing, unlimited supply of Hawaiian punch and as much you can eat of the traditional local dish: roast pork. The village fiesta today is truly global.

The success of Club Med and other attempts at creating tropical fantasylands all over the world owe quite a lot to the Pink Palace of Waikiki as well as to Billy Butlin. During the interwar years the idea of the total resort acquired embellishments and many local variations. New Yorkers going to the resorts of the Catskills in the interwar years would encounter a typical and very familiar structure. In his study of Jewish resorts like the famous Grossinger's Hotel—"the epicenter of the Borscht Belt"—Stefan Kanfer outlines the standard program. Sunday was Introduction Night, introducing new guests and pointed toward girl-meets-boy. If there was a shortage of boys the staff had to dress up: "ordered into their Sunday-go-to-meeting clothes and stationed around the dining hall. The girls never knew who was a rich guest and who was a peasant," as one of the organizers recalled it.

Monday was campfire night, Tuesday Costume or Dress-Up Night with changing themes like "Hillbilly Time, a Night in Old Japan, and a Night in Old Montmartre." Wednesday was Amateur Night and Thursday Nightclub Night, Friday was Basketball Night, Saturday a revue by the staff, and so on.[13] Many of the Catskill mountain resorts functioned as a New York marriage market. People were constantly appraised, judged, and ranked. There were also the uneasy social boundaries between the guests and the servants, who in the 1960s ranged from college students earning a bit of summer money to African Americans and Hispanics washing the dishes and cleaning. The constant shortages of young men at the resorts led many owners to replace the old professional waiters with young college boys, preferably studying law and medicine. They turned out to be the employer's ideal: attractive to girls, well mannered, ready to work for minuscule salaries. Kanfer gives an example:

> David Katz, owner of the Totem Lodge, made a policy of hiring future doctors, dentists, and lawyers for his dining room staff. Each week he called a meeting to remind the male employers that they were not on a salary for their abilities to balance plates: "I hire you to socialize with the guests. You're all clean-looking boys. You're all eligible for marriage. . . . We want you to romance the girls, but be discreet."[14]

There was a definite parallel to the world of the redcoats at Butlin's across the Atlantic, as well as to the fun-loving beach boys on the private beach of the Pink Palace. Although Butlin always denied it, his camps were a haven for sexual experiments, especially among the many teenagers brought along, experiments that often crossed the boundaries between staff and guests. The similar atmosphere of the Catskill resorts was to be immortalized in the movie *Dirty Dancing*.

LOOKING FOR THE PIANO BAR

In 1968 Grossinger's was blown up to make room for a more modern concept of vacation resorts, and by that time the golden days of British holiday camps were well over. At the Rügen beach Hitler's ruins are still standing. The Pink Palace is only a nostalgic centerpiece in a giant highrise hotel complex. All these holiday concepts developed in the 1930s are long outdated or have been transformed into new kinds of resorts.

Beaches possess eternal youth. They may look tired in the late afternoon but next morning, when the tide or the local sanitation crews have rejuvenated them, beaches start from zero again. For hotels and resorts it is not so easy. All around the world tourism steadily produces new vacation ruins, deserted or barely surviving resorts and hotels, reminding us of the fickleness of the industry and its ever-changing trends. It is the fate of resorts to go out of fashion, and hotels are especially vulnerable.

Once the process starts it may be hard to revert. Vacation guests immediately notice the smell of failure, sense the downward spiral of canceled reservations. It shows in all kinds of details, the depressed waiters, the dirty rind along the side of the pool, the deserted cocktail bar.

Many hotels seem to live under the law of cultural lags, invented by the Chicago sociologist William Ogburn. He did not draw his ideas about the ways in which cultural forms tend to lag behind social changes from research into the resort business, but they are always at work here. During a long tourist life I have witnessed many hotels that seem like hopeless utopias and ruins in the making. Once, when they were constructed, there were grand plans of keeping the guests happy within the resort complex. And once, this matrix *did* exist, in the pioneering hotels of Switzerland and then on the Riviera—where the elite arrived at their favorite hotels with twenty-seven trunks and the ambition to transform their suites into a home-away-from-home for weeks and weeks, and enjoy an intensive social life within the confines of the hotel—thus the grand plans run through the dreams of all resort developers. Nobody should need to venture outside, hotel managers believe. In the evenings they should flock to the cocktail bar, play minigolf behind the pool or sit down at the bridge tables in the lobby. The hotel dining room should be an exciting place with nightly entertainment, to attract visitors from the outside as well. But today we sit at the buffet breakfast and wonder if we should say good morning to the other guests or not. The cocktail bar is as deserted as the dilapidated minigolf course, and who wants to eat in the hotel dining room, even if it's renamed El Toro, when the whole town is bursting with interesting restaurants?

Old resort veterans can bear witness to this development from utopia to decline. After a few weeks the pianist disappears from the piano bar, later the piano is taken away, and all that is left is a deserted space to which the sign "To the piano bar" lures unsuspecting newcomers. And yet the dreams of the total resort remain and constantly ignite new projects.

Resort histories tell us something about the wear and tear of vacationing, the flipside of the craving for novelty. Places that seem on the cutting edge of modernity all of a sudden slide back into decay and oblivion. How do things go out of fashion, become tacky, tired? A man brought back his children to the Catskills thirty years later to show them his old summer resort:

> The building was still standing, even though it was abandoned. They couldn't get over the smallness of it. The entire bungalow wouldn't fit into a normal-size living room. The bedrooms were just big enough to accommodate two double beds with a space for one person to stand between them. The living room—there was no living room. There was just a very tiny kitchen, a three-burner stove, a wooden icebox, cold water. No shower.[15]

The famous Mountain House in the Catskills also ended up as a ruin. It catered to a wealthy clientele from 1824 into the 1930s, when the depression and changing times forced it out of business. Between 1942 and 1963 it survived as a slowly decaying ruin, a sightseeing destination for those who wanted to "recharge their nostalgic batteries," as a journalist put it in 1950.[16] Roofs caved in, the Greek pillars of this classic complex tumbled, and in 1963 it burned down.

Other hotels get a new lease on life by revitalizing themselves. They become rather like theme parks celebrating their earlier selves. Raffle's in Singapore, the Hua Hin Railway Hotel in Thailand, or the Negresco in Nice are examples of this, as is the Royal Hawaiian. Others survive only as nostalgia in mediascapes, like the *Dirty Dancing* film version of Grossinger life or the immensely popular BBC series on Butlinism, *Hi-di-hi,* trying to evoke the grand old times of the late 1950s.

Then there are those places that drift into kitsch or nostalgia without any conscious effort. The aging hotel district encircling the original Disneyland at Anaheim today looks a bit like a theme park of the 1950s and 1960s tourist world.

In Ralph Rugoff's loving description of "theme park slums," like Santa's Village, Tiki World, or Alpine Village, he notes how relaxing it is to be away from the perpetual freshness and the mandatory friendliness of the perfect resorts. Here, in a world of peeling paint and makeshift repairs, the employees are free to look as depressed as they feel, and you don't have to worry about any systematic demystification by Jean Baudrillard, Umberto Eco, or all those other tourist researchers who rush impatiently through the gates of Disneyworld—you can just enjoy the place.[17]

CAMP EXPERIENCES

It is tempting to name the twentieth century the era of camps: summer camps, auto camps, nudist camps, wilderness camps, fitness camps, trailer camps, baseball camps, holiday camps all proliferated. And other, more menacing, kinds of camps appeared: correction camps, military camps, POW camps, refugee camps . . . Although these two categories of camp belong to very different spheres, they have elements of a common structure—the idea of large scale, detailed planning and control, self-sufficient communities with clear boundaries. Management experiences, as well as blueprints of Tayloristic planning, are in constant circulation between the different kinds of camps. Sometimes one and the same setting can hold either one. During the Second World War the army took over most of the British holiday camps, and at Butlin's right after the war you could find holiday makers in one half, and recruits drilling in the other. In Sweden in the 1980s, when the flow of refugees mounted, many resort complexes were converted into refugee camps, only to be emptied when the summer season arrived and the tourists moved into the cabins previously occupied by Iranians or Bosnians.

The Mountain House, the KdF-Seebad Rügen, the Royal Hawaiian, Grossinger's, and Butlin's were all examples of the idea of the total resort, catering to all the needs of their visitors, but with very different clienteles. Their versions of this project went out of fashion, only to be reinvented in new forms by later resorts. Not far from the Rügen ruins you'll find a new resort that promises "summer all year round," a huge indoor water land with grottoes, slides, waterfalls, and Jacuzzis along with a mix of shops and eating places.

The idea of the total resort will always be attractive to investors, because it makes for much better control of tourist spending. For many visitors this concept holds an attraction too because it is a safe and manageable vacation world. For some a lot of people is a crowd, for others it's just a lot of interesting people. And at times the total resort works as a training ground for beginners. After this experience you might be ready for more independent travel.

During the last few decades many new examples of total resorts have appeared, aiming at keeping the guests happy within the confines of the hotel grounds. For several reasons America leads this development of hotels into destinations, which started already with the Mountain House. As early as in 1887 a French traveler observed: "in Europe the hotel is a means to an end. In America it is the end. . . . Hotels are for [the Americans] what cathedrals, monuments and the beauties of nature are for us."[18] He may be overstating it, but the shorter vacations of Americans obviously favor the concept of the hotel vacation. Thus Hyatt assures us that it is no longer just a hotel, but a place to experience.

If the charter week gave the basic structure to European vacationing, the American hotel weekend, together with the mass scale of the American market, produced a tourist landscape of total resorts, where everything is within easy reach and aimed at fun for all the family.

Las Vegas is a good example of the most recent phase of this development. When Robert Venturi published his famous study *Learning from Las Vegas* in 1972, the era of the megahotels had just started, but the focus was still on the adult world of casinos and nightclubs. Twenty years later Las Vegas had more hotel rooms (and a higher occupancy rate) than London, and the city was becoming a vacation destination for the whole family. In the roaring 1990s it also became evident how much Las Vegas had learned from the history of global tourism. A drive through this pleasure-zone architecture became a compressed postmodern journey through the history of tourist destinations, or rather Hollywood versions of them. Las Vegas teaches you which kinds of destinations lend themselves to export and recycling, in the tourist mode of production called "theming": the Kon Tiki village at the Hotel Tropicana,

Figure 30. The New York-New York is one of the Las Vegas mega-hotels of the 1990s, with a rollercoaster ride taking you through Manhattan, "recreating the very best of the Big Apple." (Photo courtesy of New York-New York Hotel & Casino)

the Excalibur Castle, the Luxor, Caesar's Roman Palace, the Mirage with its erupting volcano, Bellagio, and Treasure Island with its battles between huge pirate ships. But yesterday's hotel may be gone tomorrow. During the 1990s old hotels have been razed to make room for new megaresorts at an amazing pace to cater to close to 30 million visitors per year. The latest projects include scaled-down versions or collages of Manhattan, Paris, and Venice, including many of their famous sights.

Las Vegas has been said to perfect the art of the real fake. But the resorts of the 1990s do not copy; they combine the burlesque and the baroque in a totally uninhibited mix of styles, images, and effects. These resorts blur the boundary between theme parks, shopping malls, multimedia shows, and megahotels. They compress tourist destinations, tightening and heightening events in a constant sensual bombardment, through elements like sound, light, and—not least important—water. Small ponds, reflecting pools, babbling brooks, rain forests, waterfalls, and water lands are everywhere. At Caesar's the Roman sun rises and sets at rapid speed. Here, and elsewhere, the actual process and timing of taking in the landscape change as one moves from a cruise along the Strip to a walk around the different stages and arenas of the megahotel.[19] The reinvention of the walk is very evident in the work of the 1990s master of tourist architecture, Jon Jerde, who roofed the classic Las Vegas drive-by Freemont Street to make it into "the Freemont Street Experience" and also created "CityWalk," a cleaned up version of Los Angeles for Universal Studios. "We think of it as designing experiences rather than buildings," he states,[20] but this miniaturization and compression of sights and attractions have a long history. Jerde is carrying on the tradition not only from the grand resorts but also from the eighteenth-century romantic garden and what Walter Benjamin called the dream spaces of nineteenth-century architecture: arcades, the grand exhibitions, department stores, panoramas, winter gardens, wax-figure cabinets, railroad stations, and public spas.[21]

Another form that the constant revival of total resorts takes is the cruise ship industry, which has learned a lot from earlier total holiday institutions like Butlin's and the Royal Hawaiian. Never a dull moment!

Looking for Tourists

In the 1990s the Royal Caribbean Cruise Line built the perfect tropical island, as a stopover for cruise ships. There snorkelers can enjoy a replica of a three-hundred-year-old ship, which is sunk next to the harbor and cleaned up every other month. There are imported native shops next to the beach, rustic buildings, and a hidden garbage dump on the other side of the island. The project is a great success. Tourists love this model island, where nothing can go wrong, a company spokesman tells the journalist from the upscale travel magazine *Condé Nast Traveler*.[1] The article presents this fake island and other newly constructed tourist settings, from Disney towns to a Japanese indoor ocean beach, under the heading "Manufactured vacations: The brave new world of synthetic travel." The text has an indignant tone: "now, this is really going too far, where will it all end!" But when you leaf through the other pages of the magazine you see an ongoing battle against vulgar tourism. In the same issue you find "The 1996 Gold List: Best places to stay in the whole world." Unwittingly or not, the *Condé Nast* joins the fight against those other, undiscerning tourists who cannot afford or, even worse, cannot understand the benefits of real, high-quality travel. The dividing line is between the authentic and the in-authentic. The obsession about defining and locating the authentic is one of the characteristics of the modern world, and its struggle constantly redraws the battle lines for different ideological or economic purposes. Some argue that it is *the* driving force in modern tourism, but that is a far too sweeping statement.[2] In certain situations and for certain tourists, the search for the authentic may be the focus; for others in other settings, a more relaxed attitude may be the goal, even an enjoyment of the "real fake," which is not a postmodern innovation.

Debates about the authentic never end. What about the fake island? The water must be real, all right, but then on the other hand the beaches may be made of imported sand. What about the vendors? They are natives, but not locals, and they work under contract. The Spanish galleon is a fake, but the nearby wreck of an airplane is not, although it was transported here to be sunk for the benefit of the snorkelers. As tourists we get drawn into this battle, and some more than others. What nags at me is the thought that the new Disney towns have cicada sounds, which can be turned off at bedtime, through the loudspeakers outside the hotel, hidden in the lawn. Why is this thought so provocative?

Debates about the authentic remind us that tourism, like all forms of consumption, always involves moral distinctions of too much, too little, good or bad, wrong or right. And often the debates center on the ways we relate to other tourists, ignore them, mock them, admire them, emulate them, distance ourselves from them.

In the long history of modern tourism one element is striking. The main tourist attraction tends to be those other tourists. We devote a lot of time and energy to observing and commenting on fellow travelers. At the beach or the café on the piazza we turn into amateur vacation sociologists. In the evening we will share our observations with our companion(s): "Did you see that German couple? Those Canadians were really . . . " This habit seems especially strong among the middle classes, which in the history of tourism form a vague and changing social category.

Some travelers have always needed to set themselves apart from others—from tourists. And almost as soon as the word tourist appeared at the start of the nineteenth century, it began to carry derogatory overtones, but the democratization of travel has charged the word with greater irritation and scorn. As more and more tourists from different social backgrounds crowd into the same cafés and hotels, tensions mount. The stereotyping of others reflects this social diversity. As we have seen, it may take different forms. The rising nineteenth-century bourgeoisie was anxious to distance itself from the common people and in some ways too from the old aristocracy. There were animosities between those with the cultural capital of education (from academia and the professions) and those with a lot more economic capital (from the world of commerce), as well as the petite bourgeoisie, whom everybody loved to ridicule. Many of these old tensions are still with us, albeit in new forms, represented in changing metaphors. They may take the form of a national stereotyping or generational conflicts, or be presented as opposing lifestyles, but the language of class is nearly always there, sometimes translated into, or combined with, ethnicity (the American view of Europeans as more class-ridden tells us more of an American tradition of translating class into other cultural categories than actual social differences).

In the tourist world the hierarchies shift endlessly. I talked earlier about the low prestige of bus tourists; in recent years cruise-ship passengers have often been stereotyped in a similar fashion. There is an old stock of folklore surrounding these various labels. The same jokes made about the stupid Britons in Florence of the 1820s easily describe those awful package tourists, swarming down from the gangways of the cruise ships, or transfix resort experiences as "petit-bourgeois utopias."

One classic way to organize these distinctions is to separate oneself as a "real traveler" from "those tourists" or use the stance of "the anti-tourist." This concept of tourists anxious not to be seen as tourists

Figure 31. "Those other tourists": a gray, uniform mass looking for trivial photo opportunities—and allowing us to assert our own individuality? (Chinese tour group in front of local temple, 1982 photo by the author)

appears in France of the 1970s,[3] but the tension has a much longer history, as Jean-Didier Urbain shows in his book with the suitable title *L'Idiot au voyage*.[4]

Unlike anti-tourists, elite tourists don't have to worry about those other tourists. They have always been able to pay for privacy and exclusivity. The anti-tourists have a more difficult position, because they belong to the category of tourists who crave a chance to experience the unspoiled, the unexploited, and for them it is crucial to be off the beaten tourist track. Thus their irritation at finding their favorite haunts swamped by other visitors is understandable. Then there is a third and new category, called the "post-tourists," who may be defined as reformed anti-tourists, who have resigned their project and decided to join in with those other tourists, but always with an ironic distance. Let's have fun at Disneyland, anyway, even though we know it's a total fake! But what about all those other tourists? They sometimes become specimens of *Turistus vulgaris*. As their function is that of Othering, they are a symbolic mass, constantly changing color, form and content.

As mass tourism develops, the middle-class stance of the anti-tourist becomes a more common strategy, and it continues to single out the symbol of the vulgar tourist:

> The sublime buildings of Pisa's religious center are placed on their emerald lawn like carved ivory pieces in a great game. Yet the tawdry flotsam of the tourist tide laps all about in waves of loathsome souvenir tat. The litter of the package tourists shifts around the wind as aimlessly as they themselves.[5]

This 1987 image could have been written a century earlier. *Turistus vulgaris* is an animal that is never alone: *T. vulgaris* appears in herds, flocks, droves, packs, or swarms.[6] In lumps and clumps, they follow the guides from sight to sight, and they descend on villages or swamp the art museums.

The cultural energy that goes into getting upset or provoked by those other tourists is striking. In the anti-tourist discourse there is very little "live and let live." One such symbol of indignation is the colorful jumpsuit favored by many northern European vacationers. There are endless comments about "those other tourists" slumming around in their bulging jumpsuits. The fact that a husband and wife often walk around in an identical set makes their appearance even more irritating. Why do people invest so much feeling in a reaction to a piece of clothing? Again, the collectivity of it all, anything that smacks of a uniform, is provoking. According to basic middle-class values, husband and wife should appear as individuals, complementing, not imitating, each other. The heat of such comments tells us about central issues of self-understanding.

The urge to classify and make distinctions is also a result of the ample material available. On vacations we come up against strangers from very different backgrounds, and not only as passengers on an urban commute or passersby in the street. We observe them having meals, dressing up, fooling around, enjoying themselves, waging family arguments. Tourists meet in situations where they often have plenty of time to observe those others at close hand, from the endless wait in airport lounges to lines outside the museums. Another reason for our social curiosity is the belief that vacationlands have always been territories of make-believe, where we meet people away from their home ground. Already in the resorts of the early nineteenth century there was a theme of social uncertainty: are those other tourists what they seem to be, or are they just posing, trying to be someone else?[7]

Our incessant commentary on others gives insights into the tourist or vacation mode of consumption. "Those other tourists" come to represent a commodified, fragmented tourism. Here we find a model of tourism as consumption, with vacationers moving along the shelves of the tourist supermarket, falling for today's special offers, the well-advertised, the cheap, the easily digested, and standardized items of tourist experiences. The commentator sees himself or herself in other terms, not as a consumer but as a producer of experiences, or as a Swedish inter-railer and archetypal anti-tourist puts it:

> For me it would feel fairly meaningless to travel with the intention of resting, sitting down and enjoying the fruits of a comfortable life in some overexploited tourist area. At most this could be called a dead experience . . . traveling must be given its own meaning, its own value, as free and untrammeled as possible. . . . For me traveling has become some-

thing extremely important. A way to really live and experience things for a while. The richest way I know.[8]

What is it that makes some people define some experiences as shallow or rich, meaningful or meaningless, sublime moments of personal bliss or just another prepackaged item from the tourist industry? And how do we project our own interpretations of what happens in others' lives? The anti-tourist rhetoric of consumption usually goes like this:

> *Your* holidays demonstrate a lack of sophistication. You indulge in cheap pleasures and buy tacky souvenirs. You show no restraint or moderation, you overeat, overdrink, overspend. You are far too passive, just dozing in the hammock, hanging around the pool, or letting yourself be transported from sight to sight. You live beyond your means, squandering your money on the wrong things . . . your vacation experiences are shallow.
>
> *We,* on the other hand, have higher ambitions for our vacations. We want to experience new things, expand our minds, understand history or other cultures. We search for the genuine and the authentic. Even during our vacations we live a richer life than you.

In this way the sophisticated tourist gourmets distance themselves from the common vacation gourmands, but today we are all tourists. Even many of those who used to be called "the locals" are tourists themselves. This general involvement also accounts for the fact that we can't talk about tourism without bringing in our judgments and values—even if we are doing research on the topic. There are scholars who believe they can distance themselves from their object of study, "those tourists," but the attempt often turns out to be naive or overambitious. Whereas many tourist writers and researchers formerly positioned themselves as anti-tourists, today they are likely to assume the role of post-tourist, bashing the naïveté of both anti-tourists and vulgar tourists.

The game of distinction also feeds on another tendency in the tourist industry: that of trying to categorize tourists, to label them. It is a common practice in marketing research, to identify and quantify different lifestyles for target marketing, but the craze for classification has had a strong impact on much tourism research. Here is one attempt to sort out tourists' sociopsychological motives for travel:

1. Escape from a perceived mundane environment;
2. Exploration and evaluation of self;
3. Relaxation;
4. Prestige;
5. Regression (less constrained behavior);
6. Enhancement of kinship relationships;
7. Facilitation of social interaction.

As typical acts to illustrate the fifth category, the list notes, "Lying on the warm sand, being buried in the sand, being practically nude are all examples of pleasures which in themselves represent manifestations of partial regression."[9] There are endless examples of such lists, and they represent a tradition of flat-footed sociology and unimaginative psychology. It could probably squeeze most of us into all seven categories above.

This obsession with taxonomies is the result of an unhappy marriage between marketing research and positivist ambitions of scientific labeling. Vacationers, however, continue to move in and out of such neat boxes and juggle or discard various mindsets and interests. A main attraction of being on holiday is that there is a possibility to choose among a great many activities or mental states, between sightseeing, shopping, dozing on the beach, going for a walk, reading a novel, or having too many Tequila Sunrises.

THE IMPORTANCE OF BEING MODERN

But what about the categories of Foggs and Robinsons I started out with? These ideal types illustrate the crucial role of tourism in developing the mentalities and dispositions of modernity. In the history of tourism they have lived parallel and intermingled lives, but the Foggs were first onstage.

In 1765 Diderot's famous *Encyclopédie* defines travel as something that enriches the mind and delivers it from national prejudice. It is a mode of studying that cannot be replaced with books or the stories of others. You have to create your own image of people, places, and objects. Travel thus becomes "one of the most important elements in the education of the young."[10]

This is the optimistic tone of the Enlightenment, which sets the stage for the classic, male focus of Phileas Fogg tourism: the energetic and curious travelers who depart with the ambition to learn something, to widen their horizons. But the didactic element may be present in all forms of vacationing, although not in the programmatic mode of self-improvement. The question is then, what do vacationers with different backgrounds learn, in changing situations and eras? To what extent are the ideal types of Fogg and Robinson male and middle-class projects?

Tourism has had a crucial role in making room(s) for modernity, and especially for new sensibilities. The early pioneers discovered and cultivated their own subjectivity, reflecting on new sensual and visual experiences, contemplated their emotional reactions to new environments, held a constant dialogue with themselves. The credo of modernity is "Life can always be improved." To be part of the modern project is to be on the move, advancing through unknown terrain, making new discoveries, getting rid of old habits and traditions, striding freely forward with an open, but also restless, mind. The Fogg tradition fits well into such an agenda, especially since the movement to free zones and new spaces often has the magic effect of opening up your mind, in the dialectics of motion and emotion—moving ahead and being moved by the experience.

The early tourists, traveling within the spirit of the French encyclopedia, had a rational attitude to travel, but as we have seen many of them encountered and took up the new sensibilities of the sublime, which preached a message of allowing oneself to be surprised, even to search out emotional upheavals, to let oneself be caught off guard. This interest mirrors the other face of modernity, a reaction against routines and rationality, a longing for the unplanned, the irrational, the emotional, and the nostalgic, for romance and adventure.

This is where the Robinsonian quest enters the drama, as a project to create a utopian alternative to the humdrum of everyday life—a laid-back modernity. In this quest of "getting away from it all" we have to look closer at what this "it all" is that people are escaping from. The longing to be elsewhere tells us something about new polarities of the modern world. First of all there is the new domesticity of the urban bourgeoisie emerging during the late eighteenth and nineteenth centuries. The concept of the home as a haven and safe territory requires comings and goings. The new intimacy and the familiarity of domestic routines and rituals may also produce feelings of confinement.[11] The longing for home and for adventure constitute each other. In the same way, the regimentation of work and wage labor balances the concept of "free" leisure time in the new industrial society.

Going on a vacation meant taking yourself, as a tourist, to another time and space, a transformation emphasizing being outside normal life, the routines of home and workplace. Such rituals of passage could produce the pleasant release of pressure from your back, easing the burden of everyday commitments, routines, and demands. Any activity, from repairing a roof to building a sand castle, became nonwork. Vacation life became territorialized hedonism.

But the ways of organizing this hedonism depended on the kind of everyday existence you were leaving. And experiences of domesticity and work differed by gender and by generation and by class during these two centuries. The Robinsonian quest depended on very different freedoms *from* and freedoms *to*. For those vacationers whose daily life was shaped by strict supervision in a low-paid, monotonous job, the freedom from control and from the need to economize became important. For the stressed executive in 1920 the good vacation involved few decisions. The overworked housewife of the 1950s may first of all have craved the freedom of being away from the demands of the rest of the family, or from the claustrophobic confinement of the home. As work and living conditions change, so do vacation priorities.

Vacationing carries an emancipatory potential, to try something different, or to keep the world as it is (was). Getting away from it all might be an attempt to get it all back together again. Cottage cultures idealize the times "when families were families," beaches become repair shops for career-stressed marriages, wilderness hikes offer a chance to reinvent masculinity. At times new forms of mass tourism hold out the hope of changing the world, turning locals into cosmopolitans, breaking down artificial boundaries between nations, localities, classes, or generations—creating global communities. But moving out can also be a way of staying the same. While the skills of becoming a cosmopolitan can be important cultural capital for some, they don't work for others.[12] Tourism can both open and close the mind.

For Foggs and Robinsons alike, the metaphor of vacationing as a cultural laboratory makes sense, but what kind of experiment is it to be? It can be a new awareness of the body, the luxury of regressing into playful childhood, the feeling of freedom of choice or the luxury of not having to chose. It may be the challenge of handling new social relations or re-defining old ones, allowing other sides of your personality to come forward or experimenting with different behavior, stretching old rules or even transgressing them. The fact that next week you'll be back in the old routines again may make such an experiment seem less dangerous. Or, as an old regular visitor to Waikiki put it:

> You see more people here, darling, than any other place in the world. And the best part of it is that, *here,* they are in a festive mood. At home they're different. It's a regular Jekyll and Hyde situation. I don't give people a chance on their home ground. I don't look them up.[13]

It is obvious that the beach blanket, the family trailer, the cabin by the lake, or the hike in the wild open up these possibilities of finding new sides of yourself, your relations to others or with nature. The fact that such experiments come with the safety net of a bus tour, a visit to a wilderness trailer camp, a regimented resort, instead of independent travel, or a glass-bottom boat rather than a snorkel dive, may seem provoking to some. It is "too safe" a way of being adventurous. But this critique of "safe vacationing," which turns up among certain tourists as well as researchers, reveals the danger of imposing your own standards on others.[14]

Perhaps the most important tourist experiments concern daydreaming and mindtraveling, skills of transcendence, which vacationers explore and practice. Here, you learn to move simultaneously through landscapes and mindscapes, in time travel and flights of the mind, as fantasy turns into social practice in constant interaction with the very concrete materiality of technologies and flows of media.

There are other basic themes of the modern world that vacationing elaborates. I have mentioned the constant, but often very subdued or metaphorically handled, question of class. Class is something you both learn about and reflect on in new ways on your vacation, not least because the leisure project in modern society often sets out to be a new arena of classlessness, but, as we have seen, so much of the normative discourse on tourism—what to do and how to do it—comes from the traveling middle classes, and their domination often blocks alternative understandings of what vacations can be about.

Another polarity has to do with the tourist as a future-oriented mover, always in search of newness, or as a nostalgic dreamer longing for times when life was more simple and natural. These tendencies often mingle, as the search for newness may mean recreating the past in novel ways.

WHY SHOULD THE STATE WORRY ABOUT VACATIONS?

One striking testimony to the importance of vacations in modernity is the fact that nation-states started to take a keen interest in them early on. Why should the state be interested in tourism, promote it, and even try to shape it? The making of the modern tourist is part of the making of the modern citizen. Campaigns for domestic tourism have been not only attempts to keep tourists from squandering their money abroad, but also ideas about national integration: a nation under canvas united around the campfires all over the country, a meeting of classes down at the beach, citizens on pilgrimages to national shrines, learning to share a common heritage. This integrative role of tourism was evident already in nineteenth-century nation building, but in the later era of welfare nationalism, circa 1930–1980, there was intensified attention to the world of leisure and vacationing.[15]

When the Social Democrats came into power in Sweden in the early 1930s leisure became a symbol of modernity. Biking through Sweden, camping in the woods, or mingling on the beach was supposed to foster a new and classless breed of modern citizens, in healthy tanned bodies, overalls, and sandals. For the new ideologues there was a focus on mobility in all kinds of forms: physical and mental. The new welfare state

Figure 32. A Swedish farm worker family returning from their first paid vacation in 1936, proudly wearing the symbol of modern vacationers: sunglasses. (Photo Gunnar Lundh, Nordic museum)

had to be a nation on the move, discarding antiquated routines and habits of the past, a nation forging a new unity by doing things together: community gymnastics, sports, singing, traveling. The tourist became a progressive symbol.

Similar ambitions took hold in other settings of the 1930s, from Roosevelt's New Deal and the French Popular Front to the totalitarian settings of Germany, Italy, and the Soviet Union, but although there are striking similarities in the rhetorics of this modern mass tourism, the ways in which different political regimes turned the campaigns for domestic tourism into practice point to important differences, as we have seen, for example, in Hitler's resort dreams. In the case of Sweden the programmatic ambitions of the Social Democrats seem to typify the plans of a meddling or controlling state, but a less hegemonic picture emerges from the uses people actually made of their leisure. Tourists experienced a new liberation, exploring novel aspects of themselves and their relations both to the landscape and to other vacationers. Mass tourism was part of the making of welfare state citizens, but it was also a democratizing and emancipatory movement, which was very difficult to monitor.[16]

The postwar years saw an increased interest in the didactic importance of tourism and leisure, which seems to have culminated in the 1960s. In both Sweden and the United States the government tried different approaches to promote outdoor life. Not only was it good for the nation, a number of American studies in the 1960s and 1970s declared, wasn't there a correlation between family cohesion and camping? (The answer turned out to be Yes and No.)

This was the era when state and market increasingly cooperated to develop common strategies for domestic tourism. In some national settings the strategies resulted in attempts to develop "a science of tourism" that would provide tools for government planning and development and would make sure that vacations were "good for you," their consumer, as well as for the GNP. But there has been a constant ambivalence during the twentieth-century history of the regulations of vacations: leisure time was a creative resource and an asset that would produce a happier and more effective nation; even so, too much unstructured free time could be dysfunctional. The question of meaningful vacations appeared on government agendas with varying intensity in different periods and ideological climates.[17] On the one hand the state moved in and out of the scene, and, on the other, the market has always been there, as tourism turned into *the* global industry.

PRICING THE PRICELESS

> The Caribbean holiday, after all, is a mass-marketed product as well as a place. Like a tin of fruit cocktail, the promise of a holiday experience has been manufactured out of the material and ideological resources available to contemporary culture. The "destination," as they say in the business, is an integral part of the identity of the Caribbean holiday product at the same time as it's strangely irrelevant: basically anything with sun and palm trees will do.[18]

If the making of mass tourism is an important part of the modern project—an avant-garde scene of experiments with new forms of desires and sensibilities—it is also a field where new forms of production are a consistent feature. It has been argued that the mass tourism of the twentieth century is an example of applying Fordist methods of standardized mass production to travel, but the history of tourism rather illustrates the ways in which such evolutionary schemes do not fit very well.[19] Even before the classic Fordist era, the tourist world exhibited the characteristics of "post-Fordist" production, which uses mobile, "flat," organizations as well as manufacturing systems that rely heavily on a cultural production of symbols, moods, events, and spectacles, often with a very rapid turnover (a shift from consumer durables to new forms of nondurables).[20] In many ways the tourist industry has been a training ground for avant-garde capitalism. In the Catskills, at Niagara Falls, in Florence, or at the seaside spas of the early nineteenth century the market was already busy finding forms to package, distribute, and promote vistas, moods, and events.[21] The tourist industry has always tried to get away with the paradox of selling "the things money can't buy," from campfire memories to freedom from all worries. The hedonist urge of spoiling yourself, indulging your desires, giving yourself a treat, which is seen as so typical of hypermodern consumption, has been part of the industry for the last two centuries.

We met this long history of standardization and mass production of goods and services in the making of the Mediterranean experience, which also illustrates the strange mix between conservatism and innovation in the industry. Both Mr. Cook and the charter industry learned to produce (in large quantities and at competitive prices) not only tangible commodities like hotel beds, excursion seats, charter flights, souvenirs, meals, and guides, but also "eye candy," local atmosphere, and exotic adventure. In this process the industry learned to standardize and differentiate, to produce endless cultural variations within a rather stable structure: more of the same, but different.[22] It exploited the restlessness, the desire for new and different experiences and sensual impressions that drive many generations of modern tourists.

Behind this expansion is an accumulated knowledge about how to identify and produce tourist items that can be assembled into packages or commodities on a large scale. The first step in this commodification is itemization: the selection and framing of possible ingredients in a vacation package. This process starts very early with the globalization of the picturesque and the sublime into various scenic regimes. In locating and fixing attractive sceneries, the process helps turn landscapes into commodities, not only as pictorial representations but also as forms that the market can package, sell, and copy.[23]

There are also early jokes about this process. In 1880 the German professor Ernst Rudorff describes the economy of the tourist sunset in this manner:

> The waiter asks: "What do you prefer? Soup or sunset first, or the other way round? We can take care of both wishes." The sunset ranges after the lobster salad and the champagne, the billiard game and the conversation, as one of the elements provided to kill people's time in a pleasant way.[24]

In the same ways the standardization of local culture diffuses blueprints for "what a real culture should look like" and what kinds of cultural forms it can easily package or stage—folklore events, arts and crafts, heritage buildings—and what elements it can market across national borders.

The process of commodification develops further as the industry tries to put together specific holiday offers: a romantic getaway, a family adventure, a week in paradise. It can be an overwhelming experience to leaf through the best-selling magazine *Honeymoon: The Romantic Travel Magazine*. In the spring 1997 issue the attempts to outsell the competitors in designing "Escape to Romance Packages" result in overkill: they itemize romance into free champagne at sunset or your own champagne-glass-shaped bubble bath, scented candles, breathtaking golf, perfect solitude, and the ultimate in sybaritic seclusion. We have seen the history of selection and framing behind such offers of escape to romance. When sunsets become romantic they become a must, when champagne turns into a lover's potion it transforms sunsets or bubble baths into what the industry can market as an even stronger romantic package.

The strange conglomerate called the tourist industry is strikingly Janus-faced. It is an industry often trying hard not to look like one. In its world the romance for the south may result in a gigantic sex industry, or the quest for the exotic may wipe out local cultures, turning them into "desti-nations," all dressed up for outside cultural consumption. We have already met these locals, who desperately need the tourist money but often wish they could do without the visitors. They welcome the first tourists but, as the invasion of visitors and investors mounts, the locals realize that their community is now a vacationland. Be friendly to these often arrogant and demanding visitors, who come just for a great weekend of fun and hard play! (A good desti-nation has smiling natives.) Local authorities stress the need to make their wishes a priority: casinos, golf courses, gift shops, marinas, theme parks, and parking lots. Money floats in and out, together with crime, pollution, and endless numbers of seasonal service jobs. As the region becomes overexploited and gets out of control, tourists start moving elsewhere in search of clean beaches, roads without traffic jams, and more authentic culture. The mobile investors with their slash-and-burn strategy also hasten elsewhere, taking most of the profits with them. The locals are left in the resort ruins. Over the last few decades this pace of development and decay has been accelerating, especially in those third-world settings in which the local control of the tourist industry is weak.

A cultural industry manufacturing symbolic capital, fashions, and trends secures a rapid turnover but also produces unfashionable destinations as well as tourist slums. The industry makes itself vulnerable to sudden changes in tourist preferences and tastes. Where will they want to go next?

VACATION GENERATIONS

The standardization and homogenization of sightseeing spots, the charter week, souvenir shops, or the language of marketing does not mean that tourist experiences are standardized. They are, of course, intensely personal.

Two centuries of vacationing illustrate the tensions between continuity and discontinuity, between standardization on some levels and diversification on others. In some respects tourism reproduces itself with a marked stability: those of us who enjoy a swim at the beach, a hike in the mountains, a sunset evening from the porch or who like to pick a nice view from the postcard rack, operate within a rather stable cultural framework molded mainly in the nineteenth century. And yet its innovations never stop.

The campsite developed from a temporary glade in the wilderness into a well organized trailer community. In the same manner, the wilderness that the early nineteenth-century traveler saw as chaotic and inharmonious acquired a titillating fascination for the next generation. Later it subsided into images of harmony and calm and then came to signify functionalist simplicity and a fitting backdrop for the naturalness of modern life. But the institutionalization of vistas, sceneries, and tourist sights also runs the risk of becoming routinized and trivialized: an old idyll can lose its power to arouse strong emotions in the observer.

Such transformations tell us not only how certain forms of tourism endure a process of cultural wear and tear, becoming unmodern or boring, but also how each new generation finds its new utopias and arenas in the vacation landscape. In this process people often react to the practices of previous generations. The wilderness tourists ironized about those early Yosemite visitors, who never got out of their carriages. The sunburned sporty tourists of the 1930s chortled at the way the muffled-up Victorians cautiously interacted with nature, the sea, and the local population. In the 1960s many tourists found the Butlin's holiday concept tacky and comical compared to the sexy week at Club Med.

Finding a picturesque view or visiting a waterfall was an unforgettable experience in 1790. Going for a swim in 1890 was a way to explore a new, sensual medium; pitching a tent in the forest in 1920 brought a sense of exhilarating freedom; getting the family into the new car for the first trip to the countryside was an event never forgotten. Over time adventure can turn into routine, only later to shift into nostalgia or perhaps adventure again.

These transformations of wear and tear must not trap us into an evolutionary interpretation of tourism. Different groups mess up the narrative as they develop different vacation worlds, although they may use the same institutions or gather at the same sights. The "trickle-down thesis" still remains in some tourism research, but the idea that "mass follows class" and that new tourist groups emulate the patterns of the old elite does not work. It doesn't work in the history of working-class tourism and it doesn't work in the discussions of how new groups in the third world enter the tourist arenas. Such notions generalize the experiences of one, dominant, and verbal group of tourists, as I pointed out earlier.

The middle-class utopia of cottage cultures does not recreate the holiday habits of the elite in their fashionable resorts, it reacts against them. The trailer camp is not just a low-budget copy of the cottage community, it carries other priorities and social patterns. When certain forms of vacationing are said to go out of fashion, we always need to ask for whom, but also at what stage in life?

Tourism is a process of learning, and most people see themselves as becoming more competent and more sophisticated consumers over the years. In retrospect they might describe the first generation of package tourists as naive, falling for marketing tricks that never would work today.

Learning to be a tourist also includes growing tired of some attractions, experiences, or props: they become too trivial, too common, or too predictable: "There is nothing to see in Nuoro, which to tell the truth is always a relief. Sights are an irritating bore," wrote D. H. Lawrence in his travel book from Sardinia in the 1920s,[25] and we find the same jadedness in the contemporary tourist industry.

The yearning for new experiences, for adventure, improvisation, and surprise is always there as a disturbing factor in rational tour planning. The security of the charter holiday must not go so far as to become dull— and travel experience should never grow predictable! A century of promoting Hawaii as a paradise has meant a constant devaluation of the term. In a Hawaiian telephone directory you will find column after column of paradise outfits: their subjects range from Paradise Safaris and Paradise Weddings to Paradise Taxi and Paradise Plumbing.[26] Prolonged exposure to vacation marketing campaigns makes you feel that concepts like adventure, romance, and paradise are in dire need of reinvention (and doubtless tourists and tour operators alike are at work on the job right now).

Tour operators scramble to change their acts, as more and more package tourists venture beyond the safety of the hotel area and the sightseeing coach. As the number of cruise ship passengers grows rapidly, so does the number of independent travelers, in search of more individualized vacation experiences. The tourist industry never goes in a simple unilinear direction precisely because it can't predict what the next generation of tourists may search for.

This unpredictability makes it important to avoid a devolutionary or evolutionary analysis of tourist life, whether "from individual adventure to pre-packaged experiences" or "from naive Victorians to reflexive postmodern tourists." Behind many of the devolutionary scenarios of the lost golden days lurks the really strong cultural lag of the tourist debate that measures all kinds of tourist experiences against the classic ideal type of the Fogg tourist, traveling for education, for elevating sights, for new knowledge about exotic landscapes, peoples, and

Figure 33. Learning to be auto campers. On this cover of *The Motor Camper and Tourist* from 1925, the husband patrols the territory while his wife kneels at the stove and the child looks on from a sheltered position inside the tent. (Library of Congress)

customs. When observers accuse cruise ship passengers of staying on-
board or just doing a quick tour of the local port of call, the critics don't
realize what people might get out of a cruise. The ship's often the main
attraction, not the route. It is in fact a totally different kind of holiday,
much more like the Robinsonian total resort tradition, a deluxe version
of the summer camp or Billy Butlin's, but still it gets judged according to
the Fogg matrix.

LONGING FOR ELSEWHERELAND

"It seems so easy to fall in love here," an early twentieth-century visitor
to a Swedish seaside resort remarked, and if there is a basic structure in
the vacation mode of consumption it deals with the organization of appetizing otherness.

Vacationing has served as a laboratory for trying out new lifestyles or
forms of consumption: discovering the body, improving the art of daydreaming, exploring the possibilities of hedonism, defining the modern
family, living naturally, or perfecting the art of self-reflexivity. In this light
the history of holiday-making includes a constant process of learning and
relearning, and a growing amount of help in getting wherever tourists
want to go: travel guides and tour operators, handbooks and hints for
travelers, advice on what to pack, what to wear, how to behave toward
the locals or other tourists, how to select sights and understand the tourist
etiquette of train compartments, hotel lobbies, and charter flights. Somehow, those observers who predict that future tourists will be content with
a virtual reality trip back home in the living room do not understand the
magic of bodily movement on the road to elsewhere. Going there in person will continue to be the most important medium of learning to be a
tourist. Even participation in the most overexploited and trivialized
event, like the sunset down at the beach, still works for most of us, when
we line up along the dunes. In the mind of each participant in this ritual
today's evening sun results in very special and personal mind travel.

Vacationing is not just a schooling within a given curriculum or a hidden agenda. It is also a history of emancipation, of exploring new possi-

bilities and challenges. If today's tourists are no longer satisfied with sun and tour guides, history teaches us that many tourists never seem to be satisfied, whether in 1799 or 1999. Restlessness, frustration, and boredom are part of the search for that great personal experience. A strange and often insatiable longing for transcendence gives tourism an element of secular religion, a quest for that fulfillment waiting out there somewhere—in the elsewherelands. As soon as our vacation is over we start to fantasize about the next one: the perfect holiday.

Notes

INTRODUCTION

1. The statistics from the World Travel and Tourism Council were presented by Barbara Crosette in "Surprises in the Global Tourism Boom," *New York Times,* Sunday, 12 April 1998. See also the statistics in Yiorgos Apostolopoulos, Stella Leivade, and Andrew Yiannakis, eds., *The Sociology of Tourism: Theoretical and Empirical Investigations* (London: Routledge, 1996).

2. Examples of such works with a broader scope that I have found inspiring are the classic studies by Hans Magnus Enzensberger, "Eine Theorie des Tourismus," in *Einzelheiten: Bewusstseins-Industrie* (Frankfurt am Main: Rowohlt, 1971), 1:179–205; Paul Shepard, *Man in the Landscape: A Historical View of the Esthetics of Nature* (New York: Alfred A. Knopf, 1967); as well as later books like Jean-Didier Urbain, *L'Idiot du voyage: Histoires de touristes* (Paris: Plon, 1991); Eric J. Leed, *The Mind of the Traveller: From Gilgamesh to Global Tourism* (New York: Basic Books, 1991); Georges Van Den Abbeele, *Travel as Metaphor: From Montaigne to Rousseau*

(Minneapolis: University of Minneapolis Press, 1992); and James Clifford, *Routes: Travel and Translation in the Late Twentieth Century* (Cambridge, Mass.: Harvard University Press, 1997).

3.   See the discussion in Arjun Appadurai, *Modernity at Large: Cultural Dimensions of Globalization* (Minneapolis: University of Minnesota Press, 1996).

4.   My Swedish material is based upon observations, interviews, and a wide range of archival sources and media products presented mainly in my earlier studies published in Swedish; see for example "Turism som kultur- och klassmöte," in *Turisme og reiseliv,* ed. Lars Henrik Schmidt and Jens Kristian Jacobsen (Aalborg: Arbejdspapir fra NSU, 20, 1984); "Längtan till landet Annorlunda," in *Längtan till landet Annorlunda: Om turism i historia och nutid,* Orvar Löfgren, Göran Andolf, Thomas Lundén, et al. (Stockholm: Gidlunds, 1989), 9–49; and "Landskabet," in *Den nordiske verden,* ed. Kirsten Hastrup (Copenhagen: Gyldendal, 1992), 1:109–192. For some studies in English see "Wish you were here! Holiday images and picture postcards," *Ethnologia Scandinavica* 15 (1985): 90–107; "Mindscapes and landscapes," *Folk* 31 (1990): 183–208; and "Learning to Be a Tourist," *Ethnologia Scandinavica* 24 (1994): 102–125.

In using the international literature I have been struck by a systematic tendency of national academic communities to ignore works published beyond their physical borders. The lively and innovative research carried out in countries like France and Germany rarely travels across the English Channel or the Atlantic. Academic divisions also still isolate historians from sociologists and anthropologists, although the boundaries are slowly eroding.

5.   See the discussion in Soile Veijola and Eeva Jokinen, "The Body in Tourism," *Theory, Culture and Society* 11 (1994): 125–151.

6.   See Jean-Didier Urbain, *Sur la plage: Moeurs et coutumes balnéaires* (Paris: Payot, 1994), 9–36.

LOOKING FOR SIGHTS

1.   Advertisement for Inter-Continental Hotels in *New York Times,* 1 June 1997.

2.   Advertisement in *New York Times,* 1 June 1997.

3.   Jeffrey A. Kottler, *Travel That Can Change Your Life: How to Create a Transformative Experience* (San Francisco: Jossey-Bass, 1997).

4.   See Gerhard Schulze, *Die Erlebnisgesellschaft: Kultursoziologie der Gegenwart* (Frankfurt am Main: Campus, 1995). *Erlebnis* has the same root as the Swedish *upplevelse* and translates roughly into "living through something," an event that turns experience into *an experience,* something uplifting and out of the ordinary—something with an end and a beginning and thus also articulated and transformed into expression. The following discussion keeps the less pregnant En-

glish term, "an experience": see Victor Turner and Edward M. Bruner, *The Anthropology of Experience* (Chicago: University of Illinois Press, 1986).

5.   The result is what Schulze calls *Erlebnisrationalität*—a systematization and routinization of an orientation toward searching for experiences.

6.   See Carl von Linné, *Lappländska resa* (Stockholm: Natur Kultur, 1961).

7.   See Carl Jonas Linnerhielm, *Bref under resor i Sverige* (Stockholm, 1797).

8.   Ibid., 7. All translations from Swedish, Danish, German, or French are mine, unless otherwise noted.

9.   See Malcolm Andrews, *The Search for the Picturesque: Landscape Aesthetics and Tourism in Britain, 1760–1800* (Stanford: Stanford University Press, 1989), 67.

10.   See Shepard, *Man in the Landscape*, 130.

11.   See ibid., 19.

12.   Quoted in David E. Nye, *American Technological Sublime* (Cambridge, Mass.: MIT Press, 1996), 20.

13.   There is a rich literature on the making of the picturesque, see for example Andrews, *Search for the Picturesque*.

14.   Quoted in Olausson, *Den engelska parken i Sverige under gustaviansk tid* (Stockholm: Piper Press, 1993), 265.

15.   Quoted in John Dixon Hunt, *Gardens and the Picturesque: Studies in the History of Landscape Architecture* (Cambridge, Mass: MIT Press, 1992), 105.

16.   Quoted in Anne D. Wallace, *Walking, Literature, and English Culture: The Origins and Uses of peripatetic in the Nineteenth Century* (Oxford: Oxford University Press, 1993), 47.

17.   See the discussion in Andrews, *Search for the Picturesque*, 67 ff.

18.   Quoted in Karin Johannisson, "Det sköna i det vilda," in *Paradiset och vildmarken: Studier kring synen på naturen och naturresurserna*, ed. Tore Frängsmyr (Stockholm: Liber, 1984), 62.

19.   See Carl Jonas Linnerhielm, *Bref under senare resor i Sverige* (Stockholm, 1816), 140.

20.   See Shepard, *Man in the Landscape*, 124.

21.   See Povl Schmidt and Jørgen Gleerup, *Livsrum og oplevelseformer: Kulturhistorisk billedrække, 1700–1900* (Odense: Odense universitetsforlag, 1982), 43.

22.   In Olausson, *Den engelska parken*, 316.

23.   See the discussion in Dona Brown, *Inventing New England: Regional Tourism in the Nineteenth Century* (Washington, D.C.: Smithsonian Institution Press, 1995), 47.

24.   See the discussion in Jonas Frykman and Orvar Löfgren, *Culture Builders: A Historical Anthropology of Middle-Class Life*, trans. Alan Crozier (New Brunswick: Rutgers University Press, 1987), 42 ff.

25.   Quoted in Andrews, *Search for the Picturesque*, 76.

26.   Quoted in D. G. Charlton, *New Images of the Natural in France* (Cambridge: Cambridge University Press, 1984), 57.

27.   Quoted in Anders Hedvall, *Bohuslän i konsten: Från Allaert van Everdingen till Carl Wilhelmsson*, Sveriges Allmänna Konstförenings publication 64 (Stockholm: Nordstedt, 1956), 41.

28.   Linnerhielm, *Bref under resor*, 16.

29.   In Olausson, *Den engelska parken*, 266.

30.   See Patricia Jasen, *Wild Things: Nature, Culture, and Tourism in Ontario, 1790–1914* (Toronto: University of Toronto Press, 1995), 31.

31.   See Pehr Kalm, *Resejournal över resan till Norra Amerika*, ed. John E. Roos and Harry Krogerus (Helsingfors: Skrifter utgivna av Svenska litteratursällskapet, 1988), 4:223–234.

32.   For two recent studies of the tourist history of Niagara, see Jasen, *Wild Things*; and William Irwin, *The New Niagara: Tourism, Technology, and the Landscape of Niagara Falls, 1776–1917* (University Park: University of Pennsylvania Press, 1996).

33.   Quoted in Jasen, *Wild Things*, 31.

34.   See the discussion in Nye, *American Sublime*, 29–32.

35.   The examples are quoted in Shepard, *Man in the Landscape*, 178.

36.   Quoted in Irwin, *New Niagara*, 19.

37.   See Jasen, *Wild Things*, 53.

38.   For a discussion of the Niagara honeymoon, see Rob Shields, *Places on the Margin: Alternative Geographies of Modernity* (London: Routledge, 1991), 137 ff. On billiard rooms and other attractions, see Shepard, *Man in the Landscape*, 149.

39.   Quoted in Bertil Gullander, *Linné i Lappland: Utdrag ur Carl Linneaus' dagbok från resan till Lappland 1732, ur hans lapska flora och reseberättelsen till Vetenskaps-societeten i Uppsala, ur anteckningar och brev m.m.* (Stockholm: Forum, 1969), 144.

40.   Quoted in John Rennie Short, *Imagined Country: Environment, Culture and Society* (London: Routledge, 1991), 16.

41.   See ibid., 16 ff.

42.   Quoted in Axel Bolvig, *Det kultiverede landskab* (Copenhagen: Landsbrugsraadet,1988), 13.

43.   See Matthias Eberle, *Individuum und Landschaft: Zur Entstehung und Entwicklung der Landschaftsmalerei* (Giessen: Anabas, 1986), 211.

44.   See Götz Grossklaus and Ernst Oldemeyer, *Natur als Gegenwelt: Beiträge zur Kulturgeschichte der Natur* (Karlsruhe: von Loeper Verlag, 1983).

45.   See for example Brown, *Inventing New England*, 66.

46.   See the discussion in Löfgren, "Landskabet."

47.   See Rudolf Zeitler, "Några drag ur det europeiska landskapsmåleriets historia under 1800-talets första hälft," in *Romantik—svenskt landskapsmåleri*

1780–1870, catalog 354 (Malmö: Malmö museer, 1985), 5–28; and the discussion in Brit Berggreen, *Da kulturen kom til Norge* (Oslo: Aschehoug, 1989).

48.   Quoted in Linnerhielm, *Bref under resor*, 126.

49.   Quoted in Johannisson, "Det sköna i det vilda," 57.

50.   See John F. Sears, *Sacred Places: American Tourist Attractions in the Nineteenth Century* (New York: Oxford University Press, 1989).

51.   Richard Hofstadter, *Anti-Intellectualism in American Life* (New York: Vintage Books, 1963), 405.

52.   Quoted in Shepard, *Man in the Landscape*, 186.

53.   See the discussion in Roderick Nash, *Wilderness and the American Mind*, 3d ed. (New Haven: Yale University Press, 1982), 67 ff.

54.   See Robert Hughes, *American Visions: The Epic History of Art in America* (New York: Alfred A. Knopf, 1997), 142–147.

55.   George Curtis, quoted in Shepard, *Man in the Landscape*, 149.

56.   See Stephen F. Mills, *The American Landscape* (Edinburgh: Keele University Press, 1997), 57 ff.; on the production of wilderness prints, see Martha A. Sandweiss, "The Public Life of Western Art," in *Discovered Lands, Invented Pasts: Transforming Visions of the American West*, ed. Jules David Prown, Nancy K. Anderson, et al. (New Haven: Yale University Press, 1992), 117–134. On the proliferation of guidebooks see Brown, *Inventing New England*, 28–32.

57.   Samuel Bowles, *Across the Continent* (1866), quoted in Sears, *Sacred Places*, 122.

58.   See the discussion in Short, *Imagined Country*, 95; and Hughes, *American Visions*, 137–146.

59.   See the discussion in Rebecca Solnit, *Savage Dreams: A Journey into the Hidden Wars of the American West* (San Francisco: Sierra Club Books, 1994).

60.   Quoted in Sears, *Sacred Places*, 141.

61.   In Thomas Cole's essay, "The Painter of American Scenery" (1835), quoted in Hughes, *American Visions*, 142.

ON THE MOVE

1.   See Carlton Jackson, *Hounds of the Road: A History of the Greyhound Bus Company* (Bowling Green: Bowling Green University Popular Press, 1984), 69 ff.; and Kip S. Farrington, *Railroading the Modern Way* (New York: Coward-McCann, 1951), 241.

2.   See Jasen, *Wild Things*, 57–58.

3.   Quoted in Gustaf Näsström, "Linnerhielm—naturens känslofulle vän," *Bygd och Natur* 42 (1961): 54.

4.   See William Hauptman, "Philippe de Loutherbourg," in *The Dictionary of Art*, ed. Jane Turner (New York: Grove, 1996), vol. 19.

5. See Stefan Oetterman, *Das Panorama: Die Geschichte eines Massenmediums* (Frankfurt am Main, 1980).

6. Nicholas Green, *The Spectacle of Nature: Landscape and Bourgeois Culture in Nineteenth-Century France* (Manchester: Manchester University Press, 1990), 2.

7. Quoted in Sears, *Sacred Places*, 51.

8. Göran Rosander, ed., *Turisternas Leksand* (Malung: Leksands sockenbeskrivning IX, 1987), 51 ff.

9. Quoted in Sears, *Sacred Places*, 71.

10. Quoted in Löfgren, "Landskabet," where the new genre of railway guides is also discussed.

11. Quoted in Martin Kylhammar, *Teknik och pastorala ideal hos Strindberg och Heidenstam* (Stockholm: Liber, 1985), 96.

12. Quoted in John R. Stilgoe, *Metropolitan Corridor: Railroads and the American Scene* (New Haven: Yale University Press, 1983), 250.

13. See Hans Christian Andersen, *En Digters Bazar* (Copenhagen, 1854), 21.

14. See the discussion in Stilgoe, *Metropolitan Corridor*, 249 ff.

15. See Wolfgang Schivelbusch, *The Railway Journey: The Industrialisation of Time and Space in the Nineteenth Century* (Leamington Spa: Berg, 1977).

16. Quoted in Bo Grandien, "Landskap och människa: Om den litterära och konstnärliga fotvandringen under 1800-talet," in *Historiens vingslag: Konst, historia och ornitologi,* ed. Hedvig Brander Jonsson, Gunnar Broberg, and Lena Johannesson (Stockholm: Atlantis, 1988), 47.

17. See Tony Davies, "Transport as Pleasure. Fiction and Its Audience in the Later Nineteenth Century," in *Formations of Pleasure,* ed. Fredric Jameson (London: Routledge and Kegan Paul, 1983), 46–58.

18. See the discussion in Orvar Löfgren, "Mellanrum: Vita fläckar och svarta hål i storstadens utkant," in *Moderna landskap: Identifikation och tradition i vardagen,* ed. Katarina Saltzman and Birgitta Svensson (Stockholm: Natur och Kultur, 1997), 45–69; and Gudrun König, *Eine Kulturgeschichte des Spazierganges: Spuren einer bürgerlichen Praktik, 1780–1850* (Vienna: Böhlau, 1996).

19. Wallace, *Walking, Literature, and English Culture.*

20. Quoted in James Buzard, *The Beaten Track: European Tourism, Literature and the Ways to Culture, 1800–1918* (Oxford: Clarendon Press, 1993), 34.

21. See Andrew, *Search for the Picturesque*, 67 ff.

22. Quoted in Grandien, "Landskap och människa," 38.

23. See the discussion in Kent C. Ryden, *Mapping the Invisible Landscape: Folklore, Writing, and the Sense of Place* (Iowa City: University of Iowa Press, 1993), 221–231.

24. Quoted in John Towner, *An Historical Geography of Recreation and Tourism in the Western World* (Chichester: John Wiley and Sons, 1996), 115.

25.   See the discussion in Green, *Spectacle of Nature*, 171 ff.; and Simon Schama, *Landscape and Memory* (London: Harper Collins, 1995), 546 ff.

26.   See Zeitler, "Några drag," 6.

27.   See Stanford E. Demars, *The Tourist in Yosemite, 1855–1985* (Salt Lake City: University of Utah Press, 1991), 58.

28.   Quoted in Carl-Julius Anrick, *En krönika om Svenska Turistföreningen vid 50-årsjubileet 1935* (Stockholm: STF, 1935).

29.   Louis Améen, "Om bergsklättring," *STF's årsskrift* (1889): 54.

30.   In Ella Ödmann, Eivor Bucht, and Maria Nordström, *Vildmarken och välfärden: Om naturskyddslagstiftningens tillkomst* (Malmö: Liber, 1982), 130.

31.   In John O'Grady, *Pilgrims to the Wild: Everett Hughes, Henry David Thoreau, John Muir, Clarence King, Mary Austin* (Salt Lake City: University of Utah Press, 1993), 67.

32.   C. L. Rawlins, "The Meadow at the Corner of your Eye," in *Discovered Country: Tourism and Survival in the American West*, ed. Scott Norris (Albuquerque: Stone Ladder Press, 1994), 89.

33.   See the discussion in Nye, *American Sublime*, 31 ff.

34.   Quoted in Nash, *Wilderness and the American Mind*, 56.

35.   Quoted in Heidi Richardson, "Kraftanstrengelse og ensomhet" (master's thesis in ethnology, University of Bergen, 1994), 75.

36.   See the discussion in Jonas Frykman, "On the Hardening of Men," in *Identities in Pain*, ed. Jonas Frykman, Nadia Seremetakis, and Susanne Ewert (Lund: Nordic Academic Press, 1998), 126–150.

37.   Quoted in Louis Améen, "Turistväsendet, folket och naturen," *Svenska Turistförenings årsskrift* (1913): 1–13.

38.   Quoted in Richard Reinhardt, "Careless Love: An Unfinished Report on the De-development of Yosemite National Park," in *Discovered Country: Tourism and Survival in the American West*, ed. Scott Norris (Albuquerque: Stone Ladder Press, 1994), 55.

39.   See Demars, *Tourist in Yosemite*, 48.

40.   John Muir, letters 1866–79, quoted in Earl Pomeroy, *In Search of the Golden West: The Tourist in Western America* (New York: Alfred A. Knopf, 1957), 51.

41.   Quoted in Demars, *Tourist in Yosemite*, 104.

42.   Quoted in Peter J. Schmitt, *Back to Nature: The Arcadian Myth in Urban America* (Baltimore: Johns Hopkins University Press, 1990), 171.

43.   See Roland Van Zandt, *The Catskill Mountain House* (New Brunswick: Rutgers University Press, 1966), 295.

44.   Robert Lynd and Helen Merrel Lynd, *Middletown: A Study in American Culture* (New York: Harcourt, Brace, 1929), 258–259.

45.   See the discussion in James Hillman, *A Blue Fire: Selected Writings* (New York: Harper, 1991), 177.

46.   See Fredrik Böök, *Resa i Sverige* (Stockholm: Bonniers, 1928).

47.   See G. B. Bett, "The Rediscovery of America by the Automobile," *Outing* 42 (May 1903): 437.

48.   Norman S. Hayner, "Auto Camping in the Evergreen Playground," *Social Forces* 9 (December 1930): 257.

49.   See Brown, *Inventing New England*, 206.

50.   See Löfgren, "Landskabet," 143.

51.   See the discussion in Paul Virilio, *The Art of the Motor* (Minneapolis: University of Minnesota Press, 1995).

52.   Halvar Sehlin, ed., *Svenska Turistföreningen 100 år* (Stockholm: STF, 1985), 162.

53.   John Steinbeck, *Travels with Charley: In Search of America* (New York: Penguin Books, 1986), 94.

54.   Quoted in John Baeder, *Gas, Food, and Lodging: A Postcard Odyssey Through the Great American Roadside* (New York: Abbeville Press, 1982), 107.

55.   Demars, *Tourist in Yosemite*, 84 ff.

56.   Hamlin Garland, *Daughter of the Middle Border* (New York: Macmillan, 1929), 237.

57.   "Tin-can tourism," *New York Times*, 21 March 1996.

58.   Foster Rhea Dulles, *America Learns to Play: A History of Popular Recreation, 1607–1940* (Gloucester, Mass.: Peter Smith, 1959), 317.

59.   See the discussion in Brown, *Inventing New England*, 205 ff.

60.   Lynd and Lynd, *Middletown*, 261.

61.   In 1951 24 percent of the French used a car for vacation travel, in 1957 40 percent; see Joffre Dumazedier, *Toward a Society of Leisure*, trans. Stewart E. McClure (New York: Free Press, 1966), 127.

62.   Lynd and Lynd, *Middletown*, 257.

63.   Billy Ehn, "Hem till bilen," in *Trafik*, ed. Carl Heideken (Stockholm: Stockholms stadsmuseum, 1989), 49.

64.   Julian Barnes, "Gnossienne," *Granta* 50 (1995): 151–164.

65.   Quoted from Göran Rosander, *Dette å ferieri . . .* (Oslo: Meddelelser fra Norsk Etnologisk Gransking, 1988), 10.

66.   Quoted in John A. Jakle, *The Tourist: Travel in Twentieth-Century North America* (Lincoln: University of Nebraska Press, 1985), 162.

67.   See Robert L. Janiskee, "Resort Camping in America," *Journal of Leisure Research* (1989): 385–398.

68.   The quotes from the manual are in Joseph L. Sax, *Mountains Without Handrails: Reflections on the National Parks* (Ann Arbor: University of Michigan Press, 1989), 99 ff.

69.   Nash, *Wilderness and the American Mind*, 5.

70.   Jakle, *The Tourist*, 155.

71.   Ellen Meloy, "Communiqué from the Vortex of Gravity Sports," in *Discovered Country: Tourism and Survival in the American West*, ed. Scott Norris (Albuquerque: Stone Ladder Press, 1994), 95–96.

72.   Leaflet for "Whitewater Voyages," El Sobrante, Calif., 1995.

73.   Sax, *Mountains*, 97 ff.

74.   Quoted in Pomeroy, *In Search of the Golden West*, 211.

75.   Torsten Orre, "Med sportstugan på släp," *Svenska Turistföreningens årsskrift* (1949): 335.

76.   See Colin Ward and Dennis Hardy, *Goodnight Campers! The History of the British Holiday Camp* (London: Mansell Publishing, 1986), 1ff.

77.   Advertisement in the *New Yorker*, 22 December 1997.

78.   Cyril Connolly, *The Selected Essays of Cyril Connolly*, ed. Peter Quennell (New York: Persea Books, 1984), 26.

TELLING STORIES

1.   See Germaine Greer, "Shanghai Express," *Granta* 50 (1995): 225–248.

2.   Roland Barthes, *Mythologies* (London: Penguin Books, 1973), 74.

3.   See the discussion in Nye, *American Sublime*.

4.   See Enzensberger, "Eine Theorie."

5.   For a general discussion of the history of the picture postcard, see Löfgren, "Wish you were here!"

6.   See Manda Cesara, *Reflections of a Woman Anthropologist: No Hiding Place* (New York: Columbia University Press, 1982), 55.

7.   For comparative material on the panoramic view and the sunset, see Grossklaus and Oldemeyer, eds., *Natur als Gegenwelt*.

8.   Martin Stannard, "Debunking the Jungle: The Context of Evelyn Waugh's Travel Books, 1930–39," in *The Art of Travel Writing: Essays on Travel Writing*, ed. Philip Dodd (London: Frank Cass, 1982), 111.

9.   Rita Ariyoshi, "Wailea—Sun and Sunsets," *Spirit of Aloha*, June 1997, 8–9.

10.   See the discussion in Alexander Wilson, *The Culture of Nature: North American Landscape from Disney to the Exxon Valdez* (Oxford: Blackwell, 1992), 46 ff.

11.   See Willy D. Wenger, Jr., and Richard Videbeck, "Eye Pupillary Measurement of Aesthetic Response to Forest Scenes," *Journal of Leisure Research* 1, no. 2 (1969): 149–162; and George L. Peterson and Edward S. Neumann, "Modeling and Predicting Human Response to the Visual Recreation Environment," *Journal of Leisure Research* 1, no. 3 (1969): 219–237.

12.   Elwood L. Shafer, John F. Hamilton, and Elizabeth Schmidt, "Natural Landscape Preferences: A Predictive Model," *Journal of Leisure Research* 1, no. 1 (1969): 19.

13. Se Peterson and Neumann, "Modeling and Predicting."

14. See N. Koch and F. Søndergaard Jensen, *Skovernes friluftsfunktion i Danmark: Befolkningens ønsker til skovenes og det åbne lands udformning* (Copenhagen: Statens forstlige forsøgsvæsen, 1988), vol. 4.

15. Robert Graves, *The Crane Bag and Other Disputed Subjects* (London: Cassell, 1969), 16.

16. In John Pemble, *The Mediterranean Passion: Victorians and Edwardians in the South* (Oxford: Oxford University Press, 1987), 5.

17. See Towner, *Recreation and Tourism*, 137.

18. See Jasen, *Wild Things*, 40, 50.

19. Susan Stewart, *On Longing: Narratives of the Miniature, the Gigantic, the Souvenir, the Collection* (Baltimore: Johns Hopkins University Press, 1984).

20. See Gaston Bachelard, *The Poetics of Space*, trans. Maria Jolas (Boston: Beacon Press, 1994), 148 ff.

21. See the discussion in Orvar Löfgren, "My Life as Consumer," in *Narrative and Genre*, ed. Mary Chamberlain and Paul Thompson (London: Routledge, 1998), 114–125.

22. See Henry Glassie, *Passing the Time in Ballymenone: Culture and History of an Ulster Community* (Philadelphia: University of Pennsylvania Press, 1982), 369 ff.

23. Quoted in Demars, *Tourist in Yosemite*, 14.

24. See for example Ali Behdad, *Belated Travels: Orientalism in the Age of Colonial Dissolution* (Durham: Duke University Press, 1994); Philip Dodd, ed., *The Art of Travel Writing: Essays on Travel Writing* (London: Frank Cass, 1982); Sabine Gorsemann, *Bildungsgut und touristische Gebrauchsanweisung: Produktion, Aufbau und Funktion von Reiseführern* (Münster:Waxmann, 1992); and Van Den Abbeele, *Travel as Metaphor*.

25. See Pemble, *Mediterranean Passion*, 7.

26. See Louise Purwin Zobel, *The Travel Writer's Handbook: How to Write and Sell Your Own Travel Experiences* (Chicago: Surrey Books, 1992).

27. In Lennart Sjögren, "Landskapets estetik," *Bygd och Natur* 3 (1961): 207.

28. Quoted in Nye, *American Sublime*, 21.

29. Anna Nordlund, "Fiktionen är en del av verkligheten," *Dagens Nyheter* (Stockholm), 15 August 1996.

30. Appadurai, *Modernity at Large*, 27ff.

31. Thomas Cole, "Essay on American Scenery" (1836), quoted in Shepard, *Man in the Landscape*, 186.

32. See Roger Abrahams, "Ordinary and Extraordinary Experiences," in *The Anthropology of Experience*, ed. Victor Turner and Edward M. Bruner (Chicago: University of Illinois Press, 1986), 45–72.

33.   Allen Feldman, *Formations of Violence: The Narrative of the Body and Political Terror in Northern Ireland* (Chicago: University of Chicago Press, 1991), 14.

34.   See Connolly, *Selected Essays*, 25.

35.   George William Curtis, *Lotus Eating* (1856), quoted in Shepard, *Man in the Landscape*, 147.

36.   Quoted in Shepard, *Man in the Landscape*, 146.

37.   Quoted in Demars, *Tourist in Yosemite*, 31.

38.   Buzard, *Beaten Track*, 177.

39.   See the discussion in Ryden, *Mapping the Invisible Landscape*, 223–225.

40.   See the discussion in Janet Wolff, "On the Road Again: Metaphors of Travel in Cultural Criticism," *Cultural Studies* 7 (May 1993): 224–239; Leed, *Mind of the Traveller*; Ron Eyerman and Orvar Löfgren, "Romancing the Road: Road Movies and Images of Mobility," *Theory, Culture and Society* 12 (February 1995): 53–79; as well as the contributions in Chris Rojek and John Urry, eds., *Touring Cultures: Transformations of Travel and Theory* (London: Routledge, 1997).

41.   See Marilyn Ivy, *Discourses of the Vanishing: Modernity, Phantasm, Japan* (Chicago: University of Chicago Press, 1995).

42.   In Peter Bailey, *Leisure and Class in Victorian England: Rational Recreation and the Contest for Control* (London: Routledge and Kegan Paul, 1978), 104.

43.   See the quote in Kathy Peiss, *Cheap Amusements: Working Women and Leisure in Turn-of-the-Century New York* (Philadelphia: Temple University Press, 1986), 115.

44.   Yosemite was taken to mean "Grizzly Bear," but what the soldiers did not know was that it also meant "some of them are murderers"; see the discussion in Solnit, *Savage Dreams*.

45.   Lafayette Bunnell, *Discovery of the Yosemite, and the Indian War of 1851* (1880), quoted in Sears, *Sacred Places*, 152.

46.   See Solnit, *Savage Dreams*.

47.   See Pomeroy, *In Search of the Golden West*, 153.

48.   See Anders Linde-Laursen, "Solvang: An Historical Anthropological Illumination of an Ethnicized Space," paper presented at the annual meeting of the Society of Architectural Historians, Los Angeles, 15–19 April 1998.

49.   Cleveland Amory, *The Last Resorts* (New York: Harper and Brothers, 1948), 370.

50.   See Stefan Kanfer, *A Summer World: The Attempt to Build a Jewish Eden in the Catskills from the Days of the Ghetto to the Rise and Decline of the Borscht Belt* (New York: Farrar Straus Giroux, 1989), 26 ff.

51.   Amory, *Last Resorts*, 367.

52.   Chester Himes, *The Quality of Hurt* (New York: Paragon, 1978).

53.   Judith Okely, "Picturing and Placing Constable Country," in *Siting Culture: The Shifting Anthropological Object*, ed. Karen Fog Olwig and Kirsten Hastrup (London: Routledge, 1997), 193–222.

COTTAGE CULTURES

1.   From H. Hendricks, *Guide to the Catskills Mountains* (1903), quoted in van Zandt, *Catskill Mountain House*, 249.

2.   For the history of Medevi, see Gustaf Näsström, *Det gamla Medevi: Kulturhistoriska anteckningar* (Stockholm: Nordiska museet, 1978). The following historical examples come from his text; for a discussion of the sources, see Löfgren, "Landskabet."

3.   See Näsström, *Det gamla Medevi*, 178.

4.   See the discussion in Towner, *Recreation and Tourism*, 53 ff.

5.   Alain Corbin, *The Lure of the Sea: The Discovery of the Seaside, 1750–1840,* trans. Jocelyn Phelps (Cambridge: Polity Press, 1994).

6.   See the discussion in Löfgren, "Learning to Be a Tourist," 105 ff.

7.   See Corbin, *Lure of the Sea;* and John R. Stilgoe, *Alongshore* (New Haven: Yale University Press, 1994).

8.   See Stilgoe, *Alongshore.*

9.   Quoted in Löfgren, "Learning to Be a Tourist," 105.

10.   See Niels Kayser Nielsen, "Fare, frihed og sundhed—om vandforestillinger i moderne tid," *Den jydske historiker* 65 (1993): 7–24.

11.   Quoted in Jørn Hansen, "Havets modernisering—Lystsejladsens og kaproningens etablering i Danmark og 'opdagelsen' af havet," *Den jyske historiker* 65 (1993): 116.

12.   See Corbin, *Lure of the Sea,* 89.

13.   See Jørn Hansen, "Kroppen på rejse: Fra kurrejse til La Santa Sport," *Den jyske historiker* 48 (1988): 112.

14.   See the discussion in Corbin, *Lure of the Sea,* 73–86; and John K. Walton, *The English Seaside Resort: A Social History, 1750–1914* (New York: St. Martin's Press, 1983), 10 ff.

15.   See the discussion in Stilgoe, *Alongshore,* 345–353.

16.   Quoted from Kjell Regfeldt, "Och alla badgäster!" *Svenska Turistföreningens årsskrift* (1976): 118.

17.   See Ann Katrin Pihl Atmer, *Sommarnöjet i skärgården: Sommarbebyggelse i Stockholms inre skärgård 1860–1915* (Stockholm: Stockholms stadsmuseum, 1987), 577 ff.

18.   Quoted in Hansen, "Havets modernisering," 112.

19.   Quoted in Lena A:son Palmqvist and Kristina Edfeldt, "Badortsliv i Onsala," *Varbergs museum årsbok* (1981): 17.

20.   Quoted in Löfgren, "Landskabet," 163.

21.   Lennart Nyblom, "Att vara badgäst," *Svenska Turistföreningens årsskrift* (1949): 196.

22.   See Charlotte Bøgh, "Badehoteller—borgerskabets borge," *Arv og Eje* (1985): 149–198.

23.   See the discussion of this modernist lifestyle in Jonas Frykman, "In motion," *Ethnologia Scandianavica* 22 (1992): 36–51.

24.   See Löfgren, "Learning to Be a Tourist."

25.   Quoted in Kristina Dahllöf, "Badtraditioner i Varberg," *Varbergs museum årsbok* (1974): 19.

26.   See the discussion in Anders Gustavsson, *Sommargäster och bofasta: Kulturmöte och motsättningar vid bohuskusten* (Lund: Liber, 1981).

27.   L. Lindroth, "Kortfattade badresor för turister," *Svenska Turistföreningens årsskrift* (1903): 135.

28.   Quoted in Torbjörn Holmgren, "På upptäcktsfärd i bohuslänska skärgården," *Kattegat-Skagerrak projektet, Meddelelser* 3 (1983): 79.

29.   See Bøgh, "Badehoteller," 62.

30.   Quoted from Rosander, *Dette å feriere*, 5.

31.   Quoted in Löfgren, "Learning to Be a Tourist," 113.

32.   See the discussion in Magnus Wikdahl, *Varvets tid: Arbetarliv och kulturell förändring i en skeppsbyggarstad* (Stockholm: Gidlunds, 1992).

33.   Bengt Finnveden, "Semesterstranden," *Svenska Turistförenings årsskrift* (1958): 209.

34.   Quoted from Jonas Frykman, *Dansbaneeländet: Ungdomen, populärkulturen och opinionen* (Stockholm: Natur och Kultur, 1988), 17.

35.   Quoted from Martin S. Allwood and Inga-Britt Ranemark, *Medelby: En sociologisk studie* (Stockholm: Bonniers, 1943), 238.

36.   See Amory, *Last Resorts*, 14.

37.   See the overview in J. T. Coppock, ed., *Second Homes: Curse or Blessing?* (Oxford: Pergamon Press, 1977); and Douglas G. Pearce, *Tourist Development* (New York: Longman, 1989), 82 ff. For New England, see Brown, *Inventing New England;* and Towner, *Recreation and Tourism,* 260 ff.

38.   "Changes in Summer Migration" (1891), quoted in Pomeroy, *In Search of the Golden West,* 116.

39.   See Brown, *Inventing New England,* 75 ff.; Jason, *Wild Things,* 124 ff.; Pomeroy, *In Search of the Golden West,* 117.

40.   Pomeroy, In *Search of the Golden West,* 117.

41.   Ursula K. Le Guin, *Searoad: Chronicles of Klatsand* (London: Harper Collins, 1995), 16.

42.   Quoted in Jakle, *The Tourist,* 63.

43.   Quoted in Kanfer, *Summer World,* 67.

44.   R. I. Wolfe, "Summer cottages in Ontario: Purpose-built for an inessential purpose," in *Second Homes: Curse or Blessing?,* ed. J. T. Coppock (Oxford: Pergamon Press, 1977), 23.

45.   See Bachelard, *Poetics of Space,* 7.

46.   Randy Johnson, "Summer Places," *Hemispheres,* July 1997, 81.

47. See Green, *Spectacle of Nature*, 87.

48. Bertha H. Smith, "Sandyland! They Who Go down to the Sea in Summer" (1914), quoted in Pomeroy, *In Search of the Golden West*, 118.

49. See the discussion in Frykman and Löfgren, *Culture Builders*, 64 ff.

50. Eliot Porter, *Summer Island: Penobscot Country* (New York: Ballantine Books, 1968), 42.

51. Åsa Lundegård, "Kanske blir barnen hemma här," *Dagens Nyheter*, 20 July 1997.

52. E. Annie Proulx, *Heart Songs and Other Stories* (New York: Simon and Schuster, 1995), 161.

53. See Amory, *Last Resorts*, 322.

54. James William Jordan, "The Summer People and the Natives: Some Effects of Tourism in a Vermont Vacation Village," *Annals of Tourism Research* 7 (1980): 45.

55. See Amory, *Last Resorts*, 321.

56. Greg Halseth and Mark W. Rosenberg, "Cottagers in an Urban Field," *Professional Geographer* 47, no. 2 (1995): 150.

57. See Amory, *Last Resorts*, 23.

58. See the discussion in Peiss, *Cheap Amusements*, 117–121; and Brown, *Inventing New England*, 169 ff.

59. Quoted in Brown, *Inventing New England*, 175.

60. Quoted in Gustavsson, *Sommargäster och bofasta*, 86.

61. Quoted in Löfgren, "Learning to Be a Tourist," 120.

62. Jane Snow, "Long Island's Quiet Side," *National Geographic* 157, no. 5 (May 1980): 670.

63. B. K. Sandwell, "Us amphibious Canadians" (1946), quoted in Wolfe, *Summer Cottages in Ontario*, 23.

64. See Berit Charlotte Kaae, "Turisme og territorialitet," in *Territorialitet: Rumlige, historiske og kulturelle perspektiver*, ed. Jens Tonboe (Odense: Odense Universitetsforlag, 1994), 159–182.

65. Georgia Bockoven, *The Beach House* (New York: Harper Paperbacks, 1997), 3.

66. See John Gillis, *A World of Their Own Making: Myth, Ritual, and the Quest for Family Values* (New York: Basic Books, 1996).

67. See Appadurai, *Modernity at Large*, 77 ff.

68. Advertisement for Heat-N-Glo, in *Elle Decoration*, March 1998, 89.

69. David Updike, "Summer," in *20 Under 30: Best Stories by America's New Young Writers*, ed. Debra Sparks (New York: Charles Scribner's Sons), 139.

70. See Porter, *Summer Island*, 92.

71. E. B. White, "Once More to the Lake," quoted in Ryden, *Mapping the Invisible Landscape*, 278.

72.   Anne-Marie Berglund, "Om sommaren minns de bleka hur bleka de är," *Dagens Nyheter,* 10 June 1997.

73.   Margaret Atwood, "Bored," in *The Best American Poetry 1995,* ed. Richard Howard and David Lehman (New York: Simon and Schuster, 1955), 21.

74.   Stina Jofs, "Ständig vikarie i sommarlandet" *Dagens Nyheter,* 19 July 1997.

75.   Quouted in Bachelard, *Poetics of Space,* 63.

76.   See Reiner Jaakson, "Second-Home Domestic Tourism," *Annals of Tourism Research* 13 (1986): 367–391.

THE MEDITERRANEAN IN THE AGE OF THE PACKAGE TOUR

1.   Fernand Braudel, *The Mediterranean and the Mediterranean World in the Age of Philip II,* trans. Siân Reynolds (1949; London: Fontana, 1975), 1:277.

2.   Douglas G. Pearce, "Mediterranean charters—a comparative geographic perspective," *Tourism Management* (December 1987): 291–305.

3.   Quoted in James Boswell, *Life of Samuel Johnson,* ed. R. W. Chapman (Oxford: Oxford University Press, 1970), 742.

4.   See the presentation of this early genre in Gorsemann, *Bildungsgut,* 44.

5.   Henri Beyle Stendhal, *Rome, Naples and Florence,* trans. Richard N. Coe (1826; New York: George Braziller, 1959), 300 ff.

6.   Connolly, *Selected Essays,* 8.

7.   Quoted in Jeremy Black, *The British Abroad: The Grand Tour in the Eighteenth Century* (New York: St. Martin's Press, 1992), 5.

8.   See Pemble, *Mediterranean Passion,* 48 ff.

9.   See ibid., 18–27.

10.   Quoted in ibid., 47.

11.   W. J. Loftie, *Orient Line Guide: Chapters for Travellers by Sea and Land* (London: Sampson Low, Marston, 1896), 2.

12.   Ibid., 8.

13.   See the discussion in John Urry, *The Tourist Gaze: Leisure and Travel in Contemporary Societies* (London: Sage, 1990).

14.   Norman Douglas, *Siren Land* (1911), quoted in Pemble, *Mediterranean Passion,* 12.

15.   See ibid., 87.

16.   Quoted in Corbin, *Lure of the Sea,* 154.

17.   Quoted in Black, *British Abroad,* 31.

18.   Quoted in Mary Blume, *Côte d'Azur: Inventing the French Riviera* (London: Thames and Hudson, 1994), 35.

19.   See James C. Haug, *Leisure and Urbanism in Nineteenth-Century Nice* (Lawrence, Kans.: Regents Press, 1982), xiv ff.

20.   See Blume, *Côte d'Azur,* 60.

21.   See Urbain, *Sur la plage,* 62, on *rentiers* (who live on their income or securities) and the earlier population of invalids.

22.   See Blume, *Côte d'Azur,* 66; and Haug, *Leisure and Urbanism,* 58.

23.   Haug, *Leisure and Urbanism,* 57.

24.   Scott Fitzgerald, *Tender Is the Night* (rev. ed. 1951; London: Penguin Books, 1986), 26.

25.   See Pemble, *Mediterranean Passion,* 134.

26.   Gerald Murphy interviewed in Calvin Tomkins, *Living Well Is the Best Revenge* (New York: Viking Press, 1978), 34.

27.   See Tomkins, *Living Well,* 41.

28.   See Blume, *Côte d'Azur,* 90.

29.   Quoted in Paul Fussell, *Abroad: British Literary Travelling between the Wars* (New York: Oxford University Press, 1980), 138.

30.   In Blume, *Côte d'Azur,* 74.

31.   Cyril Connolly, *The Rock Pool* (1936; London: Hamish Hamilton, 1947), 31.

32.   Fitzgerald, *Tender Is the Night,* 302.

33.   Tomkins, *Living Well,* 3.

34.   Allan M. Williams and Gareth Shaw, *Tourism and Economic Development: Western European Experiences* (London: Belhaven Press, 1988), 12 ff.

35.   See the discussion in L. Turner and J. Ash, *The Golden Hordes* (London: Constable, 1975); and Scott Lash and John Urry, *Economies of Sign and Space* (London: Sage, 1994), 260 ff.

36.   In 1950, 585 Swedes braved the journey to Majorca; by 1962 its Swedish visitors numbered almost 40,000; in 1995 a total of 13 million tourists visited the island. For a discussion of this transformation see Jacqueline Waldren, *Insiders and Outsiders: Paradise and Reality in Mallorca* (Providence, R.I.: Berghahn Books, 1996).

37.   See Pearce, "Mediterranean charters," 299.

38.   See the discussion in Löfgren, "Längtan till landet," 32 ff.

39.   See Williams and Shaw, eds., *Tourism and Economic Development.*

40.   Kenneth Moore, "Modernization in a Canary Island Village," *Journal of the Steward Anthropological Society* (fall 1970).

41.   See Lila Leontidu, "Greece: Prospects and Contradictions of Tourism in the 1980s," in *Tourism and Economic Development: Western European Experiences,* ed. Allan M. Williams and Gareth Shaw (London: Belhaven Press, 1988), 80–100.

42.   Peter Weber, "Der Fremdenverkehr im Küstenbereich des Algarve (Portugal)," in *Beiträge zur Kulturgeographie der Mittelmeerländer,* ed. Carl Schott (Marburg: Geographisches Institut der Universität Marburg, 1970), 1:7–32.

43.   See Willams and Shaw, eds., *Tourism and Economic Development.*

44.   See the discussion in Michael Herzfeld, *Ours Once More: Folklore, Ideology and the Making of Modern Greece* (Austin: University of Texas Press, 1978).

45.   John Sallnow, "Yugoslavia: tourism in a socialist federal state," *Tourism Management* (June 1985): 113–124.

46.   See Michael V. Pearlman, "Conflicts and Constraints in Bulgaria's Tourism Sector," *Annals of Tourism Research* 16 (1989): 103–121.

47.   See Michael Morgan, "Dressing up to survive: Marketing Majorca anew," *Tourism Management* (March 1991): 15.

48.   Emilio Beceheri, "Rimini and Co.—the end of a legend: Dealing with the algae effect," *Tourism Management* (September 1991): 231.

49.   See for example the cases discussed in Morgan, "Dressing up"; Bruce Young, "Touristization of traditional Maltese fishing-farming villages," *Tourism Management* (March 1983): 35–41; and Stephen Witt, "Tourism in Cyprus: Balancing the benefits and costs," *Tourism Management* (March 1991): 37–46.

50.   D. H. Lawrence, *Sea and Sardinia* (London: Olive Press, 1989), 52–53.

51.   Henry Miller, *The Colossus of Maroussi* (London: Penguin Books, 1941), 117.

52.   See the discussion in Fussell, *Abroad;* and Stannard, "Debunking the Jungle."

53.   William Thackeray, *Notes of a Journey from Cornhill to Cairo* (1846), quoted in Pemble, *Mediterranean Passion,* 171.

54.   Henry Christmas, *The Shores and Islands of the Mediterranean: Including a Visit to the Seven Churches of Asia* (1851), quoted in Pemble, *Mediterranean Passion,* 171.

55.   Quoted in *Coping with Tourists: European Reactions to Mass Tourism,* ed. Jeremy Boissevain (Providence, R.I.: Berghahn Books, 1996), 58.

56.   It has been estimated that a tourist in Agadir uses 300 liters of water a day—thus in 26 days equaling a local inhabitant's standard yearly consumption. See Helmut Riedl, "Fremdenverkhrsgeographische Prozesse in Griechenland und ihre Beziehung zu Raumdisparitäten," in *Tourismus und Regionalkultur,* ed. Burkhard Pöttler (Vienna: Selbstverlag des Vereins für Volkskunde, 1994), 221–238.

57.   See Annabel Black, "Negotiating the Tourist Gaze: The Example of Malta," in *Coping with Tourists: European Reactions to Mass Tourism,* ed. Jeremy Boissevain (Providence, R.I.: Berghahn Books, 1996), 113.

58.   David Lodge, *Paradise News* (Harmondsworth: Penguin Books, 1992), 32.

59.   Annelies Tappe, *Cyprus* (Stuttgart: Belser, 1981), 109.

60.   Quoted in Pemble, *Mediterranean Passion,* 170.

61.   Quoted in ibid.

62.   Author's interview with middle-aged Swedish tourist.

63.   See for example the discussion in Oriol Pi-Sunyer, "Changing perceptions of tourism and tourists in a Catalan resort," in *Hosts and Guests: The Anthropology*

of Tourism, ed. Valene L. Smith, 2d ed. (Philadelphia: University of Pennsylvania Press, 1989), 187–202.

64. Susan Buck-Morss, "Semiotic Boundaries and the Politics of Meaning: Modernity on Tour—A Village in Transition," in *New Ways of Knowing: The Science, Society and Reconstructive Knowledge,* ed. Marcus G. Raskin et al. (Ottowa: Rowman and Littlefield, 1987).

65. See Boissevain, *Coping with Tourists.*

66. Connolly, *The Rock Pool,* 74.

67. Black, *British Abroad,* 190.

68. Haug, *Leisure and Urbanism,* 52 ff.

69. In Blume, *Côte d'Azur,* 62.

70. See the discussion in Pemble, *Mediterranean Passion,* 159 ff.; and Buzard, *Beaten Track,* 130 ff.

71. Quoted in Buzard, *Beaten Track,* 144 (from *The Novels of Charles Lever,* [1894–95]).

72. Buck-Morss, "Semiotic Boundaries," 216.

73. See Lila Leontidu, "Gender Dimensions of Tourism in Greece," in *Tourism: A Gender Analysis,* ed. Vivian Kinnaird and Derek Hall (Chichester: John Wiley and Sons, 1994), 74–105.

74. Buzard, *Beaten Track,* 132.

75. The baron's 1898 complaint is quoted in John L. MacAloon, *This Great Symbol: Pierre de Coubertin and the Origins of the Modern Olympic Games* (Chicago: University of Chicago Press, 1989), 263. Its 1994 Swedish counterpart is Calle Norlén, "Mitt sommarhat," *Veckojournalen,* 28, 25.

76. Quoted in Löfgren, "Längtan till landet," 43.

77. For a discussion of this perspective on "going to the south," see Runar Døving, "Syden—sted, moral og nytelse: Om det nytende individuelle objekt som turisten kan sies at være," *Tradisjon* 27, no. 2 (1997): 3–14.

78. Braudel, *Mediterranean,* 276.

79. See Fernand Braudel, *La Méditerranée, l'espace et l'histoire* (Paris: Flammarion, 1985).

THE GLOBAL BEACH

1. See Robert B. Edgerton, *Alone Together: Social Order on an Urban Beach* (Berkeley: University of California Press, 1979).

2. The text goes on to assure you that personnel speaking both Portuguese and English will meet you at the airport and take care of your needs; quoted in Roger E. Bilstein, *Flight in America: From the Wrights to the Astronauts,* 2d ed. (Baltimore: Johns Hopkins University Press, 1994), 117.

3. See Glen Grant, *Waikiki Yesteryear* (Honolulu: Mutual Publishing, 1996), 60.

4. See ibid., 68.

5. See Beth Bailey and David Farber, *The First Strange Place: Race and Sex in World War II Hawaii* (Baltimore: Johns Hopkins University Press, 1992), 212.

6. Catherine A. Lutz and Jane L. Collins, *Reading National Geographic* (Chicago: University of Chicago Press, 1993), 133 ff.

7. See Grant, *Waikiki Yesteryear*.

8. Urbain, *Sur la plage*, 151.

9. See the discussion in Ben Finney and James D. Houton, *Surfing: A History of the Ancient Hawaiian Sport* (San Francisco: Pomegranate Art Books, 1996); and Grady Timmons, *Waikiki Beachboy* (Honolulu: Editions Ltd., 1986), 42 ff.

10. See the discussion in John Irwin, *Scenes* (Beverely Hills: Sage, 1977), 84 ff.

11. See Blume, *Côte d'Azur*, 75.

12. Oliver Sacks, "Water Babies: The Boundless Possibilities of Being in the Water," *New Yorker*, 26 May 1997, 45.

13. See Bachelard, *Poetics of Space*, 205–209.

14. Frances Parkinson Keyes, "Hawaii gets under their skin" (1926), quoted in Timmons, *Waikiki Beachboy*, 43.

15. See Göran Andolf, "Turismen i historien," in *Längtan till landet Annorlunda: Om turism i historia och nutid*, ed. Orvar Löfgren et al. (Stockholm: Gidlunds, 1989), 79. See also Stilgoe, *Alongshore*, 355–358.

16. Quoted in Fussell, *Abroad*, 140.

17. For an overview of the nudism movement see Fred Ilfled, Jr., and Roger Lauer, *Social Nudism in America* (New Haven, Conn.: College and University Press, 1964).

18. Quoted in Fussell, *Abroad*, 141.

19. Quoted in John Fiske, *Reading the Popular* (London: Unwin, 1989), 47.

20. See George Orwell, "The Art of Donald McGill," in *The Collected Essays, Journalism and Letters of George Orwell* (1942; London: Penguin Books, 1968), 2:183–194.

21. Ibid., 183.

22. See Colleen Cohen Beallinero, Beverly Stoeltje, and Richard Wilk, *The Beauty Queen on the Global Stage: Gender, Contest and Power* (New York: Routledge, 1996).

23. See under "beach-" in the *Oxford English Dictionary*.

24. Jean-Claude Kaufmann, *Corps de femmes: Regards d'hommes* (Paris: Nathan, 1995).

25. Quoted in Edgerton, *Alone Together*, 152. See also Jack Douglas and Paul K. Rasmussen, with Carol Ann Flanagan, *The Nude Beach* (Beverly Hills: Sage, 1977), which discusses nudity and privacy on a southern California beach.

26.   See the discussion in Urbain, *Sur la plage*, 83 ff.

27.   See Walton, *English Seaside Resort*, 190–191.

28.   Charles Sprawson, *Haunts of the Black Masseur: The Swimmer as Hero* (London: Vintage, 1993), 19.

29.   See the discussion in Towner, *Recreation and Tourism*, 211 ff.

30.   See the discussion in Robert Snow and David Wright, "Coney Island: A Case Study in Popular Culture and Technical Change" *Journal of Popular Culture* 9 (spring 1976): 960–975; and in Peiss, *Cheap Amusements*, 115–138, where the gendering of the beach also is analyzed.

31.   Quoted in Polly Pattullo, *Last Resorts: The Cost of Tourism in the Caribbean* (London Cassell, 1996), 83.

32.   Ibid., 80 ff.

33.   See Edgerton, *Alone Together*, 150.

34.   Quoted in Timmons, *Waikiki Beachboy*, 34.

35.   Harald Kimpel and Johanna Werckmeister, *Die Strandburg: Ein versandetes Freizeitsvergnügen* (Marburg: Jonas Verlag,1995).

36.   Advertisement for Omni Hotels, *New York Times*, 15 June 1997.

37.   On the history of pools see Phyllis Elving, *Sunset Swimming Pools*, 4th ed. (Menlo Park, Calif., 1972); and Sprawson, *Haunts of the Black Masseur.*

38.   See Alex Lyle Croutier, *Taking the Waters: Spirit, Art, Sensuality* (New York: Abbeville Press, 1992), 159; and Sprawson, *Haunts of the Black Masseur*, 268.

39.   Galen Crantz, *The Politics of Park Design: A History of Urban Parks in America* (Cambridge, Mass.: MIT Press, 1982), 72.

40.   See Grant, *Waikiki Yesteryear*, 82.

41.   See Spawson, *Haunts of the Black Masseur*, 267 ff.; Elving, *Sunset Swimming Pools;* and Cleo Baldon and Ib Melchior, *Reflections on the Pool: California Designs for Swimming* (New York: Rizzoli, 1997).

42.   Fiske, *Reading the Popular.*

43.   Quoted from Peter Kihlgård, *Strandmannen* (Stockholm: Bonnier, 1992), 7.

RESORT RUINS

1.   For the French situation see Ellen Furlough, "Making Mass Vacations: Tourism and Consumer Culture in France, 1930s–1970s," *Comparative Studies in Society and History* 40, no. 2 (April 1998): 247–286; and for the Italian, Victoria De Grazia, *How Fascism Ruled Women, Italy 1922–1945* (Berkeley: University of California Press, 1992); for a general discussion see Ward and Hardy, *Goodnight Campers*, 17 ff.; and Orvar Löfgren, "Know Your Country: A Comparative Analysis of Tourism and Nation-building," in *Tourism, Commercial Leisure and National Identities in 19th- and 20th-Century Europe and North America*, ed. Shelley Baranowski and Ellen Furlough (forthcoming).

2.   The following description of the project is based on Jürgen Rostock and Franz Zadniček, *Paradiesruinen: Das KdF-Seebad der Zwanzigtausend auf Rügen* (Berlin: C. Links Verlag, 1995).

3.   See Peter Reichel, *Der Schönen Schein des Dritten Reiches: Faszination und Gewalt des Faschismus* (Munich: Hanser, 1992), 243 ff., who stresses the inspiration from Italian fascism.

4.   See ibid., 252.

5.   See Kimpel and Werckmeister, *Die Strandburg*, 43.

6.   See Ward and Hardy, *Goodnight Campers*, on which the following discussion of Butlinism is based.

7.   See Schmitt, *Back to Nature*, 106.

8.   See the discussion in ibid., 106 ff.

9.   See the discussion in Furlough, "Grandes Vacances."

10.   See Grant, *Waikiki Yesteryear*, 43.

11.   See ibid., 71.

12.   See ibid., 82.

13.   Kanfer, *Summer World*, 100 ff.

14.   Ibid., 139.

15.   Ibid., 288.

16.   Van Zandt, *Catskill Mountain House*, 315.

17.   Ralph Rugoff, *Circus Americanus* (New York: Verso, 1995), 15–19.

18.   Quoted in Demars, *Tourist in Yosemite*, 42.

19.   For a discussion of this transformation of Las Vegas, see Rugoff, *Circus Americanus*, 3–7; Mark Gottdiener, *The Theming of America: Dreams, Visions, and Commercial Spaces* (Boulder, Colo.: Westview Press 1997); Nye, *American Sublime*, 291–296; and Ada Louise Huxtable, *The Unreal America: Architecture and Illusion* (New York: New Press, 1998).

20.   Quoted in Sindre Kartvedt, "Take a Walk on the Mild Side," *Scanorama Magazine*, October 1997, 28.

21.   See Allan Pred's discussion of the grand exhibition and the production of spectacles in *Recognizing European Modernities: A Montage of the Present* (London: Routledge, 1995), 31 ff.; and Susan Buck-Morss's treatment of Benjamin's dream spaces in *The Dialectics of Seeing: Walter Benjamin and the Arcades Project* (Cambridge, Mass.: MIT Press, 1991), 271ff.

LOOKING FOR TOURISTS

1.   See Wendy Perry, "Manufactured vacations: The brave new world of synthetic travel," *Condé Nast Traveler*, January 1996, 42–44.

2.   This is the classic argument in Dean MacCannell, *The Tourist: A New Theory of the Leisure Class* (New York: Schocken, 1989).

3.   See Pascal Bruckner and Alain Finkielkraut, *Au coin de la rue, l'aventure* (Paris: Seuil, 1982).

4.   See Urbain, *L'Idiot au voyage.*

5.   David Gwyn Jones, "Tourism as Pandora's Box," *The Geographical Magazine* 59 (1987): 559.

6.   See the discussion in Jonathan Culler, "The Semiotics of Tourism," *American Journal of Semiotics* 1 (1981): 127–140.

7.   See the discussion in Brown, *Inventing New England,* 38.

8.   Löfgren, "Längtan till landet," 45.

9.   The discussion is taken from Pearce, *Tourist Development,* 114–115, a book very typical of this approach.

10.   See the discussion in Van Den Abbeele, *Travel as Metaphor,* xv.

11.   See the discussion in Gillis, *World of Their Own,* 109 ff.

12.   See the discussion in Ulf Hannerz, *Transnational Connections: Culture, People, Places* (London: Routledge, 1996).

13.   From an interview by Steve Wilcox in *The Honolulu Beacon* (1966), quoted in Timmons, *Waikiki Beachboy,* 106.

14.   For an example of this problematic and predictable genre see George Ritzer and Allan Liska, "McDisneyization and Post-Tourism," in *Touring Cultures: Transformations of Travel and Theory,* ed. Chris Rojek and John Urry (London: Routledge, 1997), 96–112.

15.   See Löfgren, "Know Your Country."

16.   See the discussion in Jonas Frykman, "Becoming the Perfect Swede: Modernity, Body Politics, and National Processes in 20th-Century Sweden," *Ethnos* 58, nos. 3–4 (1993): 259–274.

17.   See for example the discussion in Wilson, *The Culture of Nature,* 15.

18.   Ibid., 4.

19.   See for example John Urry's far too crude attempt at creating typologies of "Fordist" and "Post-Fordist" modes of production in *Consuming Places* (London: Routledge, 1995), 147 ff.

20.   See David Harvey, "Flexible Accumulation through Urbanization: Reflections on 'Post-Modernism' in the American City," in *Post-Fordism: A Reader,* ed. Ash Amin (Oxford: Blackwell, 1994), 361–386.

21.   See the discussion of this process in nineteenth-century New England, in Brown, *Inventing New England,* 5 ff.

22.   See the discussion in Richard Wilk, "Learning to be Local in Belize: Global Systems of Common Differences," in *Worlds Apart: Modernity Through the Prism of the Local,* ed. Daniel Miller (London: Routledge, 1995); and Sharon Zukin, *Landscapes of Power: From Detroit to Disneyland* (Berkely: University of California Press, 1991), 179 ff.

23. See the discussion in Andrews, *Search for the Picturesque,* 239 ff.; and Greene, *Spectacle of Nature,* 95–110.

24. Quoted in Silke Göttsch, "Frühe Tourismuskritik in der Heimatschutzbewegung" in *Tourismus und Regionalkultur,* ed. Burkhard Pöttler (Vienna: Vereins für Volkskunde, 1994), 28.

25. See Lawrence, *Sea and Sardinia,* 16.

26. For a discussion of American paradise dreams and local realities, see Jonathan Friedman, "Simplifying Complexity: Assimilating the Global in a Small Paradise," in *Siting Culture: The Shifting Anthropological Object,* ed. Karen Fog Olwig and Kirsten Hastrup (London: Routledge, 1997), 268–291.

Selected Bibliography

Andrews, Malcolm. *The Search for the Picturesque: Landscape Aesthetics and Tourism in Britain, 1760–1800*. Stanford: Stanford University Press, 1989.

Apostolopoulos, Yiorgos, Stella Leivade, and Andrew Yiannakis, eds. *The Sociology of Tourism: Theoretical and Empirical Investigations*. London: Routledge, 1996.

Appadurai, Arjun. *Modernity at Large: Cultural Dimensions of Globalization*. Minneapolis: University of Minnesota Press, 1996.

Behdad, Ali. *Belated Travels: Orientalism in the Age of Colonial Dissolution*. Durham: Duke University Press, 1994.

Black, Jeremy. *The British Abroad: The Grand Tour in the Eighteenth Century*. New York: St. Martin's Press, 1992.

Blume, Mary. *Côte d'Azur: Inventing the French Riviera*. London: Thames and Hudson, 1994.

Boissevain, Jeremy, ed. *Coping with Tourists: European Reactions to Mass Tourism*. Providence, R.I.: Berghahn Books, 1996.

307

Brown, Dona. *Inventing New England: Regional Tourism in the Nineteenth Century.* Washington, D.C.: Smithsonian Institution Press, 1995.

Buzard, James. *The Beaten Track: European Tourism, Literature and the Ways to Culture, 1800–1918.* Oxford: Clarendon Press, 1993.

Clifford, James. *Routes: Travel and Translation in the Late Twentieth Century.* Cambridge, Mass.: Harvard University Press, 1997.

Corbin, Alain. *The Lure of the Sea: The Discovery of the Seaside, 1750–1840.* Trans. Jocelyn Phelps. Cambridge: Polity Press, 1994.

Demars, Stanford E. *The Tourist in Yosemite, 1855–1985.* Salt Lake City: University of Utah Press, 1991.

Edgerton, Robert B. *Alone Together: Social Order on an Urban Beach.* Berkeley: University of California Press, 1979.

Enzensberger, Hans Magnus. "Eine Theorie des Tourismus." In *Einzelheiten: Bewusstseins-Industrie,* 1:179–205. Frankfurt am Main: Rowohlt, 1971.

Eyerman, Ron, and Orvar Löfgren. "Romancing the Road: Road Movies and Images of Mobility." *Theory, Culture and Society* 12 (February 1995): 53–79.

Frykman, Jonas. "Becoming the Perfect Swede: Modernity, Body Politics, and National Processes in 20th-Century Sweden." *Ethnos* 58, nos. 3–4 (1993): 259–274.

Frykman, Jonas, and Orvar Löfgren. *Culture Builders: A Historical Anthropology of Middle-Class Life.* Trans. Alan Crozier. New Brunswick: Rutgers University Press, 1987.

Furlough, Ellen. "Making Mass Vacations: Tourism and Consumer Culture in France, 1930s–1970s." *Comparative Studies in Society and History* 40, no. 2 (April 1998): 247–286.

Fussell, Paul. *Abroad: British Literary Travelling between the Wars.* New York: Oxford University Press, 1980.

Green, Nicholas. *The Spectacle of Nature: Landscape and Bourgeois Culture in Nineteenth-Century France.* Manchester: Manchester University Press, 1990.

Hannerz, Ulf. *Transnational Connections: Culture, People, Places.* London: Routledge, 1996.

Irwin, William. *The New Niagara: Tourism, Technology, and the Landscape of Niagara Falls, 1776–1917.* University Park: University of Pennsylvania Press, 1996.

Ivy, Marilyn. *Discourses of the Vanishing: Modernity, Phantasm, Japan.* Chicago: University of Chicago Press, 1995.

Jakle, John A. *The Tourist: Travel in Twentieth-Century North America.* Lincoln: University of Nebraska Press, 1985.

Jasen, Patricia. *Wild Things: Nature, Culture, and Tourism in Ontario, 1790–1914.* Toronto: University of Toronto Press, 1995.

Kanfer, Stefan. *A Summer World: The Attempt to Build a Jewish Eden in the Catskills—From the Days of the Ghetto to the Rise and Decline of the Borscht Belt.* New York: Farrar Straus Giroux, 1989.

Kaufmann, Jean-Claude. *Corps de femmes: Regards d'hommes*. Paris: Nathan, 1995.

Kinnaird, Vivian, and Derek Hall. *Tourism: A Gender Analysis*. Chichester: John Wiley and Sons, 1994.

Leed, Eric J. *The Mind of the Traveller: From Gilgamesh to Global Tourism*. New York: Basic Books, 1991.

Löfgren, Orvar. "Learning to Be a Tourist." *Ethnologia Scandinavica* 24 (1994): 102–125.

———. "Wish you were here! Holiday images and picture postcards." *Ethnologia Scandinavica* (1985): 96–108.

MacCannell, Dean. *The Tourist: A New Theory of the Leisure Class*. New York: Schocken Books, 1989.

Nash, Roderick. *Wilderness and the American Mind*. 3d ed. New Haven: Yale University Press, 1982.

Norris, Scott, ed. *Discovered Country: Tourism and Survival in the American West*. Albuquerque: Stone Ladder Press, 1994.

Nye, David E. *American Technological Sublime*. Cambridge, Mass.: MIT Press, 1996.

Pattullo, Polly. *Last Resorts: The Cost of Tourism in the Caribbean*. London: Cassell, 1996.

Pearce, Douglas G. *Tourist Development*. New York: Longman, 1989.

Peiss, Kathy. *Cheap Amusements: Working Women and Leisure in Turn-of-the-Century New York*. Philadelphia: Temple University Press, 1986.

Pemble, John. *The Mediterranean Passion: Victorians and Edwardians in the South*. Oxford: Oxford University Press, 1987.

Pomeroy, Earl. *In Search of the Golden West: The Tourist in Western America*. New York: Alfred A. Knopf, 1957.

Pred, Allan. *Recognizing European Modernities: A Montage of the Present*. London: Routledge, 1995.

Rojek, Chris, and John Urry, eds. *Touring Cultures: Transformations of Travel and Theory*. London: Routledge, 1997.

Schmitt, Peter J. *Back to Nature: The Arcadian Myth in Urban America*. With a foreword by John R. Stilgoe. Baltimore: Johns Hopkins University Press, 1990.

Sears, John F. *Sacred Places: American Tourist Attractions in the Nineteenth Century*. New York: Oxford University Press, 1989.

Shepard, Paul. *Man in the Landscape: A Historical View of the Esthetics of Nature*. New York: Alfred A. Knopf, 1967.

Shields, Rob. *Places on the Margin: Alternative Geographies of Modernity*. London: Routledge, 1991.

Short, John Rennie. *Imagined Country: Environment, Culture and Society*. London: Routledge, 1991.

Solnit, Rebecca. *Savage Dreams: A Journey into the Hidden Wars of the American West*. San Francisco: Sierra Club Books, 1994.

Sprawson, Charles. *Haunts of the Black Masseur: The Swimmer as Hero.* London: Vintage, 1993.

Stewart, Susan. *On Longing: Narratives of the Miniature, the Gigantic, the Souvenir, the Collection.* Baltimore: Johns Hopkins University Press, 1984.

Stilgoe, John R. *Alongshore.* New Haven: Yale University Press, 1994.

Towner, John. *An Historical Geography of Recreation and Tourism in the Western World.* Chichester: John Wiley and Sons, 1996.

Turner, L., and J. Ash. *The Golden Hordes.* London: Constable, 1975.

Urbain, Jean-Didier. *L'Idiot du voyage: Histoires de touristes.* Paris: Payot, 1991.

———. *Sur la plage: Moeurs et coutumes balnéaires.* Paris: Payot, 1994.

Urry, John. *Consuming Places.* London: Routledge, 1995.

———. *The Tourist Gaze: Leisure and Travel in Contemporary Societies.* London: Sage, 1990.

Van Den Abbeele, Georges. *Travel as Metaphor: From Montaigne to Rousseau.* Minneapolis: University of Minneapolis Press, 1992.

Van Zandt, Roland. *The Catskill Mountain House.* New Brunswick: Rutgers University Press, 1966.

Veijola, Soile, and Eeva Jokinen. "The Body in Tourism." *Theory, Culture and Society* 11 (1994): 125–131.

Waldren, Jacqueline. *Insiders and Outsiders: Paradise and Reality in Mallorca.* London: Berghahn Books, 1996.

Wallace, Anne D. *Walking, Literature, and English Culture: The Origins and Uses of peripatetic in the Nineteenth Century.* Oxford: Oxford University Press, 1993.

Walton, John K. *The English Seaside Resort: A Social History, 1750–1914.* New York: St. Martin's Press, 1983.

Ward, Colin, and Dennis Hardy. *Goodnight Campers! The History of the British Holiday Camp.* London: Mansell Publishing, 1986.

Wilson, Alexander. *The Culture of Nature: North American Landscape from Disney to the Exxon Valdez.* Oxford: Blackwell, 1992.

Wolff, Janet. "On the Road Again: Metaphors of Travel in Cultural Criticism." *Cultural Studies* 7 (May 1993): 224–239.

Zukin, Sharon. *Landscapes of Power: From Detroit to Disneyworld.* Berkeley: University of California Press, 1991.

Index

Design: Nola Burger
Text: 10/14 Palatino
Display: Matrix Script
Composition: Impressions Book and Journal Services, Inc.
Printing and binding: Edwards Brothers, Inc.
Index: Carol Roberts